A Monster
with a Thousand Hands

A MONSTER
with a
THOUSAND HANDS

The Discursive Spectator
in Early Modern England

Amy J. Rodgers

PENN

UNIVERSITY OF PENNSYLVANIA PRESS

PHILADELPHIA

Published by
University of Pennsylvania Press
Philadelphia, Pennsylvania 19104-4112
www.upenn.edu/pennpress

Printed in the United States of America on acid-free paper
1 3 5 7 9 10 8 6 4 2

Library of Congress Cataloging-in-Publication Data

Names: Rodgers, Amy J., author.
Title: A monster with a thousand hands: the discursive
    spectator in early modern England / Amy J. Rodgers.
Description: 1st edition. | Philadelphia: University of
    Pennsylvania Press, [2018] | Includes bibliographical
    references and index.
Identifiers: LCCN 2017059429 | ISBN 9780812250329
    (hardcover: alk. paper)
Subjects: LCSH: Theater audiences—England—
    History—16th century. | Theater audiences—England—
    History—17th century. | English drama—Early modern
    and Elizabethan, 1500–1600—History and criticism.
Classification: LCC PR658.A88 R63 2018 | DDC 792.0942/
    09031—dc23 LC record available at https://lccn.loc.gov/
    2017059429

For Kentston

CONTENTS

Discursive Iterations/Fearful Symmetries

For if . . . our youth seriously listen to such unworthy representations of the gods . . . hardly will any of them deem that he himself, being but a man, can be dishonored by similar actions; neither will he rebuke any inclination which may arise in his mind to say and do the like.

—Plato, *The Republic*, c. 386 B.C.E.

As soon as he saw the [gladiator's] blood, he at once drank in savagery and did not turn away. His eyes were riveted. He imbibed madness. He found delight in the murderous contest and was inebriated by bloodthirsty pleasure. He was not now the person who had come in, but just one of the crowd which he had joined . . . He looked, he yelled, he was on fire, he took the madness home with him.

—Augustine, *Confessions*, c. 400

Also, sithen [miraclis pleyinge] makith to see veyne sightis of desgyse, aray of men and wymmen by yvil continaunse, eyther stiryng other to leccherie and debatis, as aftir most bodily myrthe comen moste debatis, as siche myrthe more undisposith a man to paciencie and ablith to glotonye and to othere vicis, wherefore it suffrith not a man to beholden enterly the werde of God over his heued, but makith to thenken on alle siche thingis that Crist by the dedis of his passion badde us to forgeten.

—Anonymous Wycliffite author, *Miracle Plays*, c. 1360

As the style and subject matter of stage-plays is scurrilous and obscene, so likewise it is bloody and tyrannical, breathing out malice, fury, anger, murder, cruelty, tyranny, treachery, frenzy, treason, and revenge . . . which efferate and enrage the hearts and minds of actors and spectators; yea, oft times animate and excite them to anger, malice, duels, murders, revenge, and more than barbarous cruelty, to the great disturbance of the public peace.

—William Prynne, *Histrio-mastix*, 1633

The spectator at the play experiences too little; he feels like a "Misero, to whom nothing worth while can happen"; he has long since had to moderate, been obliged to damp down, or better direct elsewhere, his ambition to occupy a central place in the stream of world events; he wants to feel, to act, to mold the world in the light of his own desire—in short to be a hero.

—Sigmund Freud, "Psychopathic Characters on the Stage," 1905

Where once the dime and nickel novels suggested ways of crime to unbalanced youth, the motion picture has come to make a more ready and more potent appeal. The printed word is never so ardent with an impressionable mind as the acted word.

—Richard Barry, *Pearson's Magazine*, 1911

The young men who opened fire at Columbine High School, at the movie theater in Aurora, Colo., and in other massacres had this in common: they were video gamers who seemed to be acting out some dark digital fantasy. It was as if all that exposure to computerized violence gave them the idea to go on a rampage—or at least fueled their urges.

—Benedict Carey, *New York Times*, 2013

Imagine you were asked to create a profile of the prototypical spectator using the above seven epigraphs. Demographically, the subject is young and most likely male. Intellectually, he is underdeveloped. Emotionally, he is imma-ture, exhibiting a tendency toward emotional and behavioral extremes. He finds it difficult to distinguish between representation and reality, more often attaining catharsis through projection and identification than through lived

experience. These qualities make him susceptible to wild emotional vacilla-
tions, misprision, and injury. In short, he is a potential danger to himself and
to others.

Of course, creating a composite from these fragments that span over
two millennia is ridiculous. It is impossible to assemble any sort of accurate
representation from them. But in many cases, at least up until the twentieth
century, such scintillae are all we have. Unlike the spectacles they watched,
those who witnessed the plays, pageants, public trials, executions, corona-
tions, and funerals of the past have largely formed the faceless backdrop of
historical inquiry. In part this lacuna is due to a scarcity of records: actual
descriptions of spectators at state, religious, and entertainment productions
are few and far between. To study and make claims about them, then,
becomes what Dennis Kennedy calls "a problem in metaphysics, [and] writing about them may border on the impossible."[1] Exerting an equally powerful
influence on the study of spectators and spectatorship, however, is the widely
held prejudice that the spectator is the product of modernity and its concomitant technologies of representation: photography, film, television, and, most
recently, the computer.[2] In her history of spectatorship studies, Michelle
Aaron places what she calls "the birth of the spectator" in the late 1960s.[3]
While some theorists place the origins of spectatorship as a topic of inquiry
slightly earlier, there is, in general, a critical consensus that spectatorship as a
discourse did not come into being before the twentieth century.[4]

But whereas formal theoretical approaches to and detailed statistics about
spectatorship may be the domain of the twentieth and twenty-first centuries,
discourses on the topic are not. Meditations on the dangers of looking (especially the sort associated with entertainment spectacle) exist in abundance
throughout the history of Western culture. While the seven epigraphs with
which I begin frame their anxieties about spectators through their unique
historical and cultural contexts, certain constants emerge: the spectator is
male, young, highly impressionable, and potentially dangerous. These are
not, however, qualities we can assign to actual historical viewing subjects;
that is, the spectator of Augustine's gladiatorial arena is not the same as "the
young men" in the *New York Times* article that merge the fantasy violence of
video games with the incarnate act of shooting high school classmates or
movie patrons. Rather, such qualities stand in for the spectator these writers
imagine, project, and sometimes fear. While "real" spectators may be historically contingent and temporally circumscribed, ideas about them can (and
do) cross such boundaries, accruing various resonances along the way. These

ideas form a different sort of spectatorial presence, one that is discursive rather than material. Often indiscriminately conflated with the real bodies and psyches that attend the theater, sports arena, or movie multiplex, the discursive spectator is a repository of a culture's ideas and anxiety about viewing and interpretive practices, particularly those associated with popular entertainment. And, while entertainment media, exhibition technologies, and viewing practices have changed dramatically from the era of Plato to post-modernism, anxieties about spectatorship have remained remarkably consistent. The discursive spectator, then, provides an alternative starting point for tracing a history of spectatorship—one organized by conceptual and ideological structures rather than practice-oriented ones—of which the twenty-first century is only the most recent part.

This study explores a particular moment in that history, that of early modern England. Walter Benjamin has argued that film's development and ascendancy in the twentieth century both responded to and caused "profound changes in the apperceptive apparatus."[5] Sixteenth-century England also witnessed a surge in a particular form of mass entertainment: professional drama.[6] I argue that as the commercial theater developed and prospered as a for-profit endeavor, a cultural need arose to find new ways to describe the sort of looking that playgoing both catered to and fostered. The narratives that evolved in response produce what I call the early modern discursive spectator—a figure generated largely through early modern cultural anxieties and fantasies about spectators rather than through empirical observation and thick description of actual audience behavior. Finally, I claim that the early modern discursive spectator did not merely develop alongside the phenomenological one, but played as significant a role in shaping early modern viewers and viewing practices as did changes to staging technologies, exhibition practices, and generic experimentation.

As the opening epigraphs suggest, I am not making the case that the early modern period marks the origin of either the discursive spectator or theories of spectatorial dynamics. As Jonas Barish states, such concerns about the effects of entertainment media "go back as far in European history as the theater itself can be traced."[7] Renaissance England did, however, produce a great deal of writing on the theater and its effects on audiences. While theater had been a part of English culture since the early twelfth century,[8] the sixteenth century saw massive changes in theater's production and regulation, including the building of London's first amphitheaters, the proliferation of professional playing companies, and the imposition of laws regulating them.

The years between 1576 and 1642, therefore, are some of the earliest for which we have an abundance of materials that refer both directly and indirectly to theater spectators.[9] As London's professional theater industry took hold and flourished, those involved in the business of the stage developed a pre-occupation with shaping, even controlling, consumer tastes and habits. Simultaneously, moralists and magistrates attempted to discipline—morally, behaviorally, and geographically—London's many theatergoers. Such mobilizations of (and resistances to) commercial, moral, and social pressures on theatergoers mark the early modern period as a particularly significant one in the development and coherence of the discursive spectator. As Jean-Christophe Agnew puts it, "Elizabethan and Jacobean theater . . . did not just hold the mirror up to nature; it brought forth 'another nature'—a new world of 'artificial persons'—the features of which audiences were just beginning to make out in the similarly new and enigmatic exchange relations then developing outside [as well as inside] the theater."[10] While Agnew's "artificial persons" refer to the emergent early modern English professional identity of the actor, another such presence is perpetuated by the professional theater, one Agnew tacitly references: "Inside the banquet hall and guild hall of the sixteenth century, the players experimented sporadically with dramatic forms, developing new conventions that would enable them to communicate with an audience that was at once physically present and psychologically distant."[11] It is precisely this "psychological distance"—the inscrutability of any individual's or group's particular affective and psychological templates, desires, and limits—that gives rise to the cultural projection I call the discursive spectator.

The vast temporal expanse covered by the seven introductory epigraphs signals another of this project's deep investments, which is to consider the discursive spectator's transhistorical presence and potency. While focused primarily on the discursive spectator's early modern incarnation, this study also looks backward to earlier manifestations and forward to later ones. In part, I use the early modern discursive spectator's past and future as a framing mechanism; however, I also move between modern spectatorial theories, many of which deal with modern forms of media and entertainment, and early modern ideas about the theatrical spectator, placing them in conversation with one another throughout the book. That I do so may raise the charge of "unhistoricism," a methodological stance recently cited by Valerie Traub as trending in both queer and early modern studies (and, most particularly, the conjunction of the two). While, as she carefully articulates, "unhistoricism" or "teloskepticism" encompasses numerous critical viewpoints and concerns, it represents, in short, a heuristic method that advocates reading against chronological sequencing as a means of averting teleological narratives of queer identity.[12] While *A Monster with a Thousand Hands* takes as a given that "the spectator" has a discursive (as well as a material) history, it is not an archaeological or genealogical project. Rather, this study understands the discursive spectator as an entity that consists of multiple, sometimes contradictory narratives, some of which have long and relatively consistent half-lives and some of which emerge and disappear within a given era. To imagine the discursive spectator via a framework in which "one model . . . is superseded by another, which may again be superseded by another [and] the superseded model then drops out of the frame of analysis,"[13] is to ignore the ways this figure replicates its own discursive DNA and resists historical pressures. For, even when the discursive spectator *responds* to historical events (such as those that occur during the sixteenth and seventeenth centuries in London's theatrical exhibition, practice, and culture), *how* it responds defies tidy articulation along an axis of historical contingency. While cultural debates about the entertainment spectator tend to become reinvigorated by new or newly popularized entertainment media, the discourses on which they rely tend to recycle long-extant and pervasive biases. The discursive spectator's existence, then, forms along trajectories similar to those Annamarie Jagose claims for queer temporality; in other words, this figure is better understood as a series of "recursive eddies and back-to-the-future loops"[14] rather than a neatly progressing construct that reaches its apotheosis in the era of mass media.

If certain aspects of the discursive spectator can best be described and explored synchronically, a diachronic perspective better serves others. Far from challenging or rejecting historicism, I rely on many of its paradigms in order to flesh out the discursive spectator's travels through a specific period, one that, for my purposes, is demarcated via the rise of the English professional, for-profit theater, and its subsequent cessation during the English Civil War.[15] In addition to demonstrating certain historicist "hallmarks" (for example, the acceptance of periodicity and the use of a range of discursive production as a means of taking the discursive spectator's measure), the book's organization follows a predominantly chronological framework. While this schema runs the risk of suggesting a teleological narrative, it also allows for a more thorough examination of the ways in which the discursive spectator shifts, accrues, and pares resonances even within a relatively short period. To read chronologically does not necessarily imply reading teleologically; that is, to study a concept, discourse, institution, narrative, category, or tradition diachronically does not go hand-in-hand with accepting and propagating a narrative of destiny. Indeed, the call-and-response nature of discursive production often requires placement within a linear time frame in order to bring the smaller epiphenomena that have occurred (and continue to occur) in the discursive spectator's history into clearer focus.[16] Much like an electrocardiogram, which measures the pattern of an individual's heartbeat over a short period in order to pick up irregularities in the heart's sinoatrial current, a chronological approach allows for attentiveness to shifts, both major and minor, in the early modern spectator's discursive presence during roughly a sixty-year period. While such shifts do not add up to a tidy developmental narrative, they provide a means of demonstrating this figure's fluidity (a quality that renders it an ideal surface for registering cultural projections about theater audiences) and attaining a clearer understanding of the discursive spectator's role in shaping spectatorial practice as it manifests in phenomenological experience and the empirical world.

My approach, then, differs from "strict" historicist methods in two primary ways. The first is that with the exception of the first chapter, the majority of my archive derives from material written for and about the theater, as opposed to reaching outside of it to other kinds of cultural institutions. The second, and more significant, is that I am less interested in what the early modern English discursive spectator tells us about something *other than* itself; that is, I do not investigate it in the service of another, larger construct or industry, such as early modern subjectivity, religion, sexuality, affect, cognition, or even the theater itself. Instead, this study advances two primary goals, neither of which, I have come to find, are adequately served by espousing a single methodology. The first is to demonstrate the discursive spectator's value as a topic of study, one that has been largely overlooked and unarticulated in both early modern discussions of theater audiences and audience studies more generally. The second is that rather than privileging a historical narrative's elucidation, I model an interpretive method—a way of reading— that takes the discursive spectator as its primary topic, and then I explore what this readjustment of focus reveals about early modern spectatorship and the scholarly biases, blind spots, and (over)investments found in much of early modern audience studies.

Those looking for a book that focuses heavily on the historical conditions of possibility and production that "produce" the early modern discursive spectator will not find it here. This is not to say that such a study would be unproductive or ineffective: certainly, I hope that others *will* take up and offer other perspectives on the discursive spectator. As Traub posits, "Readings . . . are not the same thing as history,"[17] a claim with which I wholeheartedly agree. However, readings can provide effective starting points for reimagining the kinds of histories we currently tell about the spectator and (re)discovering new material in those we have previously inscribed. The subsequent section looks at some of these narratives via their enunciations in scholarly discourse, which, for the most part, have been trifurcated into the areas of demographic studies, theoretical investigations reliant on modern and postmodern theoretical axioms, and affective inquiries seeking to understand how audiences responded to early modern drama.

A View of the Field

This study participates in a methodological incentive posited by Jeremy Lopez in his 2008 book *Theatrical Convention and Audience Response in Early Modern Drama*. Pointing out that the emphasis on audience demographics has become "unnecessarily paralyzing, making it seem as though we cannot talk about the effects of a play on an 'audience' until we understand the exact composition of that audience," Lopez calls for a more capacious model for studying early modern theatergoers.[18] And, in point of fact, most early critical work on early modern theatrical audiences tended to fixate on "Shakespeare's" audiences and approach the topic using a predominantly demographic approach. Among the most influential of these are Alfred Harbage's *Shakespeare's Audience* (1941), E. K. Chambers's *The Elizabethan Stage* (1974), Ann Jennalie Cook's *The Privileged Playgoers of Shakespeare's England* (1981), and Andrew Gurr's *Playgoing in Shakespeare's England* (2004).[19] Painstakingly stitching together the few scraps of extant evidence about London's theater audiences, these scholars provide us with a relatively comprehensive picture of who might have attended one of Shakespeare's plays at the Globe or one of John Marston's at the Children of Paul's. While their work provides an invaluable snapshot of these audiences of the past, it does not account for the ways that the spectator is as much a cultural idea as a material presence.[20] Recent studies on the early modern audiences, however, attempt to understand and re-create what audiences thought and felt when watching drama (particularly Shakespeare's works). While the desire to unearth and interpret early modern audience response is not new, earlier approaches to this question relied on contemporary theoretical models of spectatorship. Prevalent in the 1990s,[21] this set of inquiries oriented itself toward psychoanalysis and film studies, perspectives that offered alternatives to the dominant practice of demographic historicism. By applying contemporary theories of identification, particularly those derived from Freudian and Lacanian psychoanalysis, these studies sought to elucidate the spectatorial dynamics of the past via ideas produced in and by a more proximate historical era, that of the early and mid-twentieth century. Yet another approach (and the one with the broadest reach, in that such studies began as early as the 1970s and continue into the present moment) looks to historicize audience experiences, viewing practices, and affect.[22] These studies rely on period-specific methods of exploring audience response, ones that offer alternative inroads into and archives for the "who, what, where, and how" of early modern theatergoing that are somewhat less restricted by the limits of demographic data. These include explorations of linguistic (such as puns), representational (such as allegory), and staging (such as the thrust stage) conventions; stage properties; costume; spatial orientation; cognitive structures; embodiment; and affective systems of meaning and exchange.[23] Rather than canvass all of these studies here, I discuss a detailed example of the approaches that attempt to resurrect spectatorial experience with an eye toward clarifying *Monster*'s contribution to early modern audience studies.

Barbara Freedman's *Staging the Gaze: Postmodernism, Psychoanalysis, and Shakespearean Comedy* (1991) remains one of the most ambitious studies of early modern spectatorial dynamics to date.[24] Working primarily within Lacanian psychoanalytic paradigms and apparatus theory,[25] Freedman also draws on feminism, structuralism, and cultural materialism to flesh out a theory of "Elizabethan spectator consciousness," which she defines as "an epistemological model based upon an observer who stands outside of what she sees in a definite position of mastery over it."[26] According to Freedman, rather than participating in this model of spectatorship, Shakespearean comedy exemplifies the theater's participation and role in the cultivation of a subversive, counterhegemonic gaze, one that works to destabilize the spectating subject's illusion of control by staging blindness and misprision as forms of percipience.[27]

Freedman's contribution to early modern audience studies has been somewhat undervalued,[28] perhaps because of its challenge to historicism, which attained a near-hegemonic methodological dominance in the 1990s. Taking on Stephen Greenblatt's claim that the structures of Renaissance identity render psychoanalysis "marginal or belated" as a heuristic for early modern literary study,[29] Freedman makes a case for psychoanalysis's efficacy via history. Her opening chapter focuses on Italian humanists' distinction "between the eye, which sees, and the mind's eye, which sees that it can never see itself seeing," a distinction she likens to the split subject of psychoanalysis.[30] And, while she uses methodological tools sharpened by film theory, she does not buy into them wholesale; for example, Freedman critiques film theory's overinvestment in the line between live and filmed performance, stating that this binary has obscured the ways in which the theatrical and cinematic gaze might be related.[31]

My study shares Freedman's belief that historical and theoretical inquiry are not mutually exclusive, that so-called "modern" theoretical concepts and lexicons can, when used with care, provide vital access points into productive investigative templates for historically antecedent phenomena. My use of history, however, diverges from Freedman's. While *Staging the Gaze* tends to engage with history in order to demonstrate historicism's inevitable imbrication with, even reliance on, theory, Freedman's readings of Shakespeare's plays seem far less interested in continuing the negotiation between history and theory than does her initial chapter. This methodological fade-out makes the insightful historical analysis of her first chapter seem as if it appeared only to get the monkey of historicism off her back. In addition, this bifurcated structure also places many of Freedman's insightful readings in the service of a theoretical *telos* from which she initially takes some pains to distance herself: that psychoanalysis is the most accurate lexicon for expressing and understanding early modern spectatorship.

Freedman's book emerged in a moment in Renaissance studies during which scholars tended to position psychoanalysis and historicism not only as antithetical methodologies but as ones that required defending. Much of the work from this period contains elaborate defenses about how historicism or psychoanalysis constitutes a privileged or superior way of exploring early modern subjectivity, culture, and, most particularly, Shakespeare's plays. Current scholarship in the field tends to move more freely between these and other methodologies. As noted in Carla Mazzio and Douglas Trevor's introduction to *Historicism, Psychoanalysis and Early Modern Culture,* more recent work demonstrates "less intent on upholding particular models of analysis than on rethinking and recasting their effects, [and] many contemporary critics have come to resist the labels that once accompanied certain sets of topical interests and reading strategies."[32] Mazzio and Trevor's description of this more self-reflexively hybrid critical approach aptly depicts the one on which this study draws. Rather than a defense of historicism or psychoanalysis, *Monster* understands and engages with these perspectives as dialectically intertwined and mutually constitutive of one another. In addition, as noted earlier, the discursive spectator's history often presents itself as a series of variant iterations, a temporal model in which psychoanalysis is well-versed. Freud understood such recursive phantasms as the principal dynamic that undergirds individual and cultural behaviors and representations; in psychoanalytic theory, the repression of foundational traumas—sexual, generational, ethnic, and national—forms the template from which all identity arises. While this study focuses on a discursive rather than identitarian construct, the process of recursive sedimentation Freud describes as constitutive of individual and collective identity offers an architectural paradigm for understanding the discursive spectator's history.

In addition to privileging psychoanalysis, Freedman also adopts apparatus theory's initial myopic focus on the visual realm of experience. Early proponents of apparatus theory treat film as if it is *only* visual technology, overlooking the potentially subversive or contradictory effects of sound, including film score, language, ambient noise, and sound effects. While many film scholars have since challenged this bias, there is still a pronounced tendency to talk about cinema as a primarily visual medium.[33] It is a bias Freedman seems to accept, reading Elizabethan entertainment culture as one similarly focused on the visual. While Freedman's study predates those scholars whose work has fleshed out the sensory environment of the early modern theater,[34] there is ample evidence in the texts with which she works that the theater was an experience in which the ear was at least as important as the eye. Often, theatrical spectatorship was described through sensory synecdoche, as if to suggest that the theater's communicative potency was such that the division between the senses melted away. Rather than limiting my analysis to issues of the gaze, I look at Renaissance spectatorship as an act that, up until the seventeenth century, tended to be represented as engaging the full palate of the senses.

Mentioned earlier, Jeremy Lopez's study *Theatrical Conventions and Audience Response in Early Modern Drama* has played a significant role in reinvigorating early modern audience studies. In particular, Lopez's exploration of frequently deployed dramatic conventions as a viable repository for analyzing audience experience opened up new and fertile archival terrain. Like Freedman, Lopez wants to think about the productive possibilities offered by "dehistoric[izing] audience response." Rather than doing so in order to propose an alternative theoretical narrative, Lopez argues for creating an alternative history of spectatorship based in "the continuing vitality of a theatrical tradition."[35] Given this claim, it may seem counterintuitive that Lopez's study focuses primarily on once-popular plays that have largely been ignored in studies of early modern drama; he does so, however, in order to move beyond the scholarly tendency to focus on Shakespeare's audiences. His engagement with underexplored plays provides a much-needed corrective to audience studies, a field that has often been pursued in the service of understanding more about Shakespeare (the author, the "man of the theater," the genius) than about audiences.

Lopez's argument that the most vital and productive of repositories for understanding English Renaissance audiences are "the plays they watched" is one with which I largely agree; indeed, this book uses seventeenth-century plays and masques as its primary archival source. However, Lopez's claim that "Elizabethan and Jacobean drama seems to be very sure of the response it wants from its audience as a whole at any given moment" often gets conflated with the implied one that what a play or playwright wants to communicate to its audience is what it or he accomplishes. For example, in a reading of the players' scene in *Hamlet*, Lopez moves immediately from a claim about the scene's (or its author's) intentions to one about the certain achievement of these communicative goals: "Twenty-eight purple lines into his Hecuba-speech in *Hamlet*, the Player is interrupted by Polonius: 'This is too long' (2.2.456). The audience, having been taught that nothing that Polonius says can be taken seriously, laughs. . . . It is notable that the audience has this kind of laugh at this point because it is prepared for quite the opposite reaction."[36] Lopez might be right in his assumption that the audience would have laughed at this point in *Hamlet*. However, as he earlier states, we cannot and do not *know* what early modern spectators thought and felt or how they reacted while watching this scene.[37] While such fluidity is part of Lopez's project of proposing a history traced through theatrical traditions, ones that help create the audiences with which they communicate, the assumption that the spectator any given playwright wants is the one he gets is problematic. Unwittingly, Lopez resurrects the idea of the passive spectator, an entity that becomes imprinted with whatever message the play (or text or film) wants to send, a bias that undermines his goal of "better understanding the audiences of the English Renaissance."[38]

The tendency to conflate "real" spectators with imagined or projected ones is not unique to Lopez's work; indeed, most studies that seek to theorize the spectator rely on this fallacy to some extent. Certainly, real and theoretical spectators do align at times, and conventions that repeat in a given historical period and extend beyond it suggest a kind of communicative reliability. However, in positing the premise that early modern drama "was extremely self-conscious [and] demanded an equal self-consciousness from its audience as well," Lopez not only avers that the relationship between play (text) and audience is one of predictable cause and effect, he also enacts his early criticism that much of the work on early modern audience ends up in the service of an author, a play, or drama more generally. In fact, one might say that Lopez is not particularly interested in audiences in *Theatrical Convention and Audience Response*; rather, they provide the means by which he can posit the importance of noncanonical (and particularly non-Shakespearean) drama. More accurate, however, would be to say that insofar as Lopez is interested in audiences, he is interested in them as a construct—a projection—of early modern theater practitioners and plays and of contemporary scholars: "The audience I imagine in chapter 1 is the audience I imagine Elizabethan and Jacobean dramatists to have imagined, for which the effects I describe would have been most effective."[39] Such "imaginings" suggest another entity, one that Lopez tacitly acknowledges but does not explore: a category of inquiry made up of the projections addressed and created by early modern cultural institutions, including the law, education, the Church, and, of course, the theater.[40] It is precisely this entity to which *Monster* is devoted.

Most recently, studies such as Tanya Pollard's *Drugs and Theater in Early Modern England* (2005), Charles Whitney's *Early Responses to Renaissance Drama* (2006), Matthew Steggle's *Laughter and Weeping in Early Modern Theatres* (2007), Bruce Smith's *Phenomenal Shakespeare* (2010), and Allison P. Hobgood's *Passionate Playgoing in Early Modern England* (2014) have sought to augment our understanding of early modern theater audiences by bringing embodied spectatorship to the table, or, in Smith's words, "projecting ourselves in the historically reconstructed field of perception as far as we are able."[41] Historicizing affective structures that the early modern theater helped shaped and was shaped by, these studies approach this shared aim using somewhat different archives and approaches.[42] To a large degree, however, they share two basic claims: that while we cannot decisively "know" what audiences thought and felt while watching plays, there is more valid evidence about audience response than has been acknowledged, and that early modern audiences played an active and crucial role in shaping the period's drama. Methodologically hybrid and argumentatively bold (particularly in their defense of phenomenological rather than material or strictly historical archives), these interventions provide a response to the often-repeated charge put forth by performance studies scholars: that historicist approaches to early modern drama tend to forget the very thing that makes theater theater—the vital presence of living bodies onstage.[43] This approach's insistence on the significance of (and possibility of accessing) individual and collective processes of reception and response brings a more animate and tangible practice to the field of early modern audience studies.

Despite the valuable insights advanced by these projects, a clear-cut problem persists, one that Hobgood addresses in *Passionate Playgoing*: "How can we *actually know how participants felt* during or after a performance of *Macbeth* in the early seventeenth century" (original italics)?[44] Following Bruce Smith's charge that we take more literally the "stories" early modern subjects, especially playwrights, told about "what was happening in their bodies and brains when they looked, listened, read, and loved,"[45] Hobgood claims that "the faultlines between early modern humoral theory, philosophical and medical treatises, pro- and anti-theatrical literature, and drama of the early modern period contain a productive narrative about what it might have felt like to participate in early modern theatergoing."[46] Such fault lines are, no doubt, productive places for excavating early modern spectatorship, but they are still the fault lines between *narratives* rather than experiences. More significantly, while each of the archives from which Hobgood draws (humoral theory, philosophical and medical treatises, pro- and antitheatrical literature, and drama) are cultural fields that would, certainly, have a modicum of interest in representing spectators' experiences, reportage is by no means their primary aim. Instead, they are complex, multifaceted discursive structures, a fact that Hobgood acknowledges when she states that her study "explores [the experience of] spectatorship by examining, in great part, early modern *ideas* about emotion."[47] If we imagine plugging in another ineffable, volatile, entangled human experience, such as the trauma of witnessing an accident, and study it via the same cultural structures Hobgood uses for her analysis of spectatorial experience (medical, philosophical, moral, and representational), few, I think, would claim that even a thorough canvassing of these discourses would provide an accurate understanding of traumatic *experience*. Such study certainly would produce some forms of comprehension—empathic identification, intellectual analysis, historical situatedness—but not actual knowledge of how it *felt*, something into which Hobgood claims her research can provide genuine insight: "I rethink early modern theater-going—what it *felt like* to be part of performances in English theater—as an intensely corporeal, highly emotive activity characterized by risky, even outright dangerous bodily transformation" (my italics).[48] However, as Cathy Caruth intuits, most corporeal, highly emotive experience "is not locatable in the . . . original event . . . but rather in the way that its very unassimilated nature . . . returns to haunt the survivor later on."[49]

As this study invests in those hauntings, which often take shape in the form of discursive presences, it may read as antithetical to more embodied and affective hermeneutic approaches. In other words, the discursive spectator may seem too spectral, too exsanguinated, to provide any insight into "real" audiences of the period. And, in one sense, it is. As stated earlier, *A Monster with a Thousand Hands* is not a study of the phenomenological audiences of early modern England but rather of the culturally constructed figure of the spectator. But despite this perspective, this study does concern real audiences: one of its central claims is that cultural discourses about entertainment spectatorship play a significant (and undertheorized) role in shaping individual and cultural interpretive practice and affective response. As Stephen Purcell has said of contemporary audiences that attend Shakespeare's plays, "Ideas about the nature of Shakespearean spectatorship circulate widely in culture more broadly, and audiences will inevitably arrive at a Shakespearean performance with certain preconceptions about what their role is likely to involve."[50] The sources I draw evidence from are similar to (and often the same as) those used by Whitney and Hobgood, including an admixture of more traditional historicist sources (sermons, antitheatrical treatises, legal and medical documents, and correspondence) and less material ones (such as what Whitney terms "allusions," or references to audiences or their experiences found in various representational genres). But whereas Whitney and Hobgood seek to flesh out what Steven Mullaney has called an "emotional logic"[51] of playgoing in the early modern period, I trace an alternative but intersecting history of how early modern English culture imagines, projects, represents, and circulates ideas about theater spectators and the dynamics of theatrical spectatorship.

The Sense of an Audience: Archives, Modes of Evidence, and Ways of Reading

Almost without exception,[52] scholarship on early modern audiences draws heavily on antitheatricalist writings—one of the richest representational repositories of the Renaissance theatrical spectator. This relatively abundant resource, however, presents several challenges. Like English playwrights, English antitheatricalists display a tendency to "borrow" heavily at the levels of polemic and phrasing from one another and from earlier classical and medieval moralists.[53] Jonas Barish, for example, calls a particular section of William Prynne's *Histrio-mastix* "overflow[ing] with an inky gutter of references to Tertullian, Cyprian, Chrysostom, Augustine and 'sundry' other Fathers."[54] Such redundancy mirrors a concern regarding contemporary scholarship that uses this moralist discourse: since nearly all work done on early modern audiences relies heavily on this archive, it becomes difficult to avoid retreading old ground. It is, therefore, worth taking a moment to clarify the use of antitheatricalist writings in this project. Most obviously, as this study is about spectatorial discourses (rather than spectatorial practice or affect), the parroting of classical and contemporary sources that occurs in antitheatricalist treatises becomes an important piece of evidence rather than an idiosyncracy that requires a disclaimer. That is, such repetition aptly demonstrates the presence and potency of certain discourses about theater spectators (re)circulating in early modern England. That Prynne and other antitheatricalists echo various medieval philosophers (who in turn had cited classical ones) to convey the idea of the vulnerable spectator suggests both that this discourse has a history that precedes the early modern period and that these writers, on some level, relied on these earlier discourses in order to craft their own "take" on the discursive spectator. That Prynne and other antitheatricalists echo one another demonstrates one channel through which ideas about theatrical spectators were circulated and reified. These authorial and cultural redundancies provide opportunity to examine precise patterns of repetition and deviation to better understand the conceptual cynosures around which the early modern discursive spectator tends to orbit.

In addition to moralist discourse against the theater (and the counterdiscourse of protheatrical defenses), I draw upon writings produced by other cultural institutions concerned with early modern theatergoers' behavior (such as the legal apparatus and the Anglican Church) and upon the few examples of spectatorial testimony found in correspondence and personal records. However, insofar as the discursive spectator is concerned, there is no more significant archive than the plays and entertainments written for audiences (and often for specific ones). Rather than provide a survey of early modern plays' references to their audiences, such as is found in appendix 2 of Gurr's *Playgoing in Shakespeare's London*, I use a selection of plays and court entertainments to explore developments in the discursive spectator that occur over a limited period of about thirty years. Just as the rise of the English professional theater is a gradual process that takes place over more than a century, English writing about the theater and those who watched it was a work in progress.[55] I do not therefore claim that the early modern period had one cohesive version of the discursive spectator. Rather, I begin by identifying several pervasive discourses about theatrical spectatorship in circulation at the end of the sixteenth century and follow them through the first decades of the seventeenth. While the late sixteenth century saw massive changes to London's theatrical landscape, the seventeenth century also saw numerous changes in early modern theatrical culture, albeit more in degree than kind. A proliferation and diversification of playing venues, innovations in staging conventions, and alterations to the theatrical patronage system during this period suggest and promote greater cultural and artistic interest in the spectator. With the reopening of the boys' companies at Paul's and Blackfriars at the turn of the century, the occupation of the Blackfriars by the King's Men in 1608, and the building of the Cockpit Theater in 1616, more variety, both in genre and venue, became available to playgoers. James I's queen, Anna, an avid patron of the arts, ran a court newly devoted to the production of entertainment spectacle. Under her supervision, the court masque developed into a multimedia event featuring dazzling visual effects that were eventually exported onto the public stage. And, while royal patronage was still a significant means of financial support for playing companies, customer revenue became increasingly important to their survival.[56] In other words, the seventeenth century marks an apogee in "the artist's push-pull relationship with his audience."[57] As competition for playgoers became more intense, schemes for attracting audiences diversified. Generic experiments accelerated as playing companies attempted to attract particular "types" of audience. The satiric, bawdy plays featured by the children's companies, for example, targeted a more select audience, or, in more mercenary terms, one that could afford to pay three times as much for admission.[58] Cultivating a more "sophisticated" audience, however, had its drawbacks; one less-desirable epiphenomenon of the satiric trend was audience backlash. Jokes made at the expense of other playing companies, public figures, and even the audience itself "localized the battlefield . . . by turning the device against the playwrights themselves."[59] Finally, as many playwrights began imagining their work as potentially having two lives—on stage and in print—the reader emerges as a significant asymptote to and influence on the theatrical spectator.

My goal in this study is not to canvass all of the ways in which Tudor-Stuart England thought about the large and unwieldy category of spectatorship, even theatrical spectatorship. Therefore, the book takes a suggestive rather than comprehensive approach. Focusing on the final decades of the sixteenth century, Chapter 1 explores the cultural terrain in which the early modern professional theater took root and held. It is, of course, a terrain undergoing seismic shifts, and, as I argue, the rapidity and magnitude of the English commercial theater's rise generate new ideas (and modifications to existing ones) about and language for describing theatergoers. In particular, the word *spectator* enters the English language during this period, in Sir Philip Sidney's poetic opus *The Countess of Pembroke's Arcadia.*[60] Surveying a variety of texts (sermons, legal documents, treatises, essays, poetry, and drama) that reference or explicitly deliberate on the spectator, I identify three pervasive suppositions circulating during the late sixteenth century: that the interpretive exchange that occurs between the play and the spectator is often understood as a violent, even traumatic, interaction; that spectatorship, as a communal act, produces creative energy that mimics the generative force usually associated with the divine; and that spectatorship is not governed by the sensory binary of audial-visual, but is an experience that activates multiple sense perceptions.

The subsequent chapters take the discourses elucidated in the first and investigate one way in which they progress over the seventeenth century's early decades. Focusing specifically on representations of theatrical spectators found in cultural production designed for entertainment, edification, and pleasure, I demonstrate how certain discursive shifts may be as readily explained by changes in how spectators are linguistically represented and disseminated, particularly by those writing for and about the theater, as by changes in technologies of stagecraft, spectacle, and exhibition. In particular, I focus on subgenres that become cynosures for experiments in form and staging and emerge as highly popular during the early seventeenth century: children's company satire, dramatic romance, and court masque. Chapter 2 explores Francis Beaumont's satire (and notable commercial flop) *The Knight of the Burning Pestle.* Written for the Blackfriars' boys' company, *Knight* is often cited as a play before its time—one that prefigured the radical meta-theater of Brecht and Beckett. Rather than explore the play as a reliquary of audience response and tastes during the early seventeenth century (or try and pinpoint the reason for its failure), I consider the ways in which *Knight* engages with the figure of the violent spectator. Instead of dramatizing the

widely circulated cultural narrative of the theatergoer who sees acts of violence, sedition, and lust acted out on the stage and becomes indelibly
imprinted by them (a transfer demonstrated by an acting out of similar acts
in the real world), *Knight* portrays a revelatory variant of this figure: the
spectator who enacts violence on the vehicle of representation itself. I argue
that this incarnation of the violent spectator appears on the early seventeenth-
century stage as a response to new commercial pressures (both real and perceived), proliferation of venues, and alterations in audience behavior.

Chapter 3 explores the nascent role of the dramatic reader's influence on
the discursive spectator. Taking up Lukas Erne's argument that Shakespeare's
later works were written for both readers and spectators,[61] I look in detail at
two of Shakespeare's dramatic romances that are particularly interested in the
figure of the reader: *Pericles* and *Cymbeline*. Rather than ask how this double
focus affected Shakespeare's writing, however, I focus on how this reimagining of receptive possibilities reinvigorates a particular (and long-standing)
tension in the discursive spectator's shape, which is the play between spectating as a communal or individual activity. Specifically, I revisit a (teleological)
bias repeated by early modern and modern theorists of audience: that with
the approach of modernity and its attendant subjective and technological
revolutions, the viewing collective or audience of the early modern period
transforms into the "isolated watcher," or spectator.[62] In addition to making
the argument that individual and collective models are in play in the early
modern period (and throughout history), I look at the ways in which Shakespeare's romances, albeit narratives written for the stage, represent spectatorship as a fundamentally individual act, at least if it is being done well. Both
Pericles and *Cymbeline* attempt to model "proper" spectatorship, a practice
often tied to reading in both plays. In doing so, they suggest that spectatorial
fashioning is not only desirable but possible, a shaping fantasy that parallels
the concomitant introduction of certain textual apparatuses used to influence
early modern readers in the early seventeenth century. However, this chapter
concludes by suggesting how such disciplinary conventions fail as often as
they succeed in shaping spectators and how discursive and material spectators
as frequently conflict as align.

I continue studying the discursive spectator as an entity poised between
the worlds of page and stage in Chapter 4, which traces changes occurring
within the descriptive lexicon of spectatorial processes over a thirty-year
period. I revisit the archive of the Jacobean court masque, a site widely identi-
fied as a flashpoint for the evolution of a more spectacularized theatrical

practice and visually oriented spectator. Critics have tended to focus on Inigo Jones's innovations in set design and lighting as the primary catalyst for this turn. Jones's stagecraft, however, was not exported onto the public stage until the 1630s (and not consistently until the Restoration), while changes in descriptions of viewers and viewing practices are evident in the first decade of the seventeenth century. I argue that Jones's collaborator and artistic rival, Ben Jonson, played the more significant role in generating these discursive changes. The concatenation of Jonson's practical need to find a descriptive lexicon for Jones's stagecraft and his anxiety that the masque's spectacle consistently trumped its poetry generates one of the more profound changes to the seventeenth-century discourse on spectatorship: the representation of looking and listening as separate, even oppositional, interpretive activities.

Jonson spent much of his career seeking his "ideal consumer,"[63] and he understood the masque genre, both in its performed and written form, as a potential instrument for inculcating "learning and sharpness" in his audience.[64] The attempt to negotiate between the "understanding"[65] spectator the writer wants and the obtuse one he fears is a dynamic shared with the other plays discussed herein: all imagine the possibility of spectatorial fashioning via disciplinary conventions that promote certain behaviors and interpretive practices while holding up others to ridicule and condemnation. My argument here turns on the premise that these projections play a significant role in shaping how audiences act, think, and respond, which in turn (re)shapes the way dramatists imagine and represent their audiences. The circulatory passages through which these ideas and practices flow is where the discursive spectator lives and breathes, the place where it forms the connective tissue between ideas and anxieties about the spectator and real viewing subjects.

In his treatise on modern theater audiences, Herbert Blau notes that the audience "is always already a deceit, another fantasy of perversion (or perverse fantasy), an obligatory scene in the theater that from its very beginning theater wished it could do without."[66] Whether fantasy or phantasm, the spectator is not merely the witnessing body (or the body witnessing) performance, but an entity that determines the very conditions of theatrical production. If, as Peter Handke writes, "the audience does not yet exist"[67] until it is addressed by a play, I would argue that a play does not, indeed cannot, come into being without first imagining an audience, *its* audience. Tellingly, the words *spectator* and *spectre* are etymological kin: both derive from the Latin root *spectāre*. Embodied as the "beholder, onlooker, or observer,"[68] the spectator also haunts the theater's moral and creative landscape as an "apparition, phantom, or ghost, especially one of a terrifying nature or aspect."[69] Unstable, protean, and capricious, the spectator seems as much eidolon as entity. And yet this shadow presence—this apparition—remains long after the onlookers go home. Writing commendatory verses for colleague John Fletcher's failed play *The Faithful Shepherdess*, actor Nathan Field gives this phantasm a name and shape: "[T]he monster clapt his thousand hands / And drownd the sceane with his confused cry." Field's refiguring of Plato's metaphor for the crowd— the many-headed monster—offers some insight into what was at stake for those invested in the art and commerce of the early modern theater; less clear is what has been at stake in eliding or ignoring the discursive spectator over centuries of scholarly inquiry into that institution.[70] In the chapters that follow, I trace the discursive spectator's imprint on some of the cultural productions that shaped and were shaped by this figure in order to better understand its influence on those involved in producing the early modern theater, those who attended it, and those who have pursued and continue to pursue it as an object of study.

CHAPTER I

Toward a Theory
of Discursive Spectatorship

Near the turn of the twentieth century, a young Russian journalist began a short piece for the *Nizhegorodski listok* newspaper with the following description:

> Last night I was in the Kingdom of the Shadows. If only you knew how strange it is to be there. It is a world without sound, without colour. Everything there—the earth, the trees, the people, the water and the air—is dipped in monotonous grey. Grey rays of the sun across the grey sky, grey eyes in grey faces, and the leaves of the trees are ashen grey. It is not life, but its shadow, it is not motion but its soundless spectre.[1]

His observations echo a number of modernity's oft-cited maladies: a decrescence of human experience via exposure to the industrialized workplace and landscape, an anesthetized perceptual *habitus* owing to urban life's sensory overstimulation and relentless pace, and subjective erosion augmented by the inexorable force of mass labor's and culture's hegemonizing engines. But, although written by the young Maxim Gorky (who became one of Russia's most outspoken voices against some of these pressures) in late imperial Russia, it is not a day-in-the-life account but a review of the newest invention from the Continent, the Lumière cinematograph.[2] From Gorky's description, this novelty does not sound as if it would have much of a draw: why would people go see a lifeless effigy of their already diluted existence? Nor does Gorky mention any compensatory gratifications here—such as those Tom

Gunning describes in his theory of "the cinema of attractions"—there are no foreign lands or fantastical fictions.[3] Instead, it depicts what for many would be familiar scenes: city streets bustling with people and carriages, trains rushing to various destinations, and a group of men at a bar drinking and playing cards. The only pleasure it seems to offer is the thrill of witnessing another new form of optical wizardry and the concomitant satisfaction of affirming humankind's relentless march toward "progress" via technological advancement.

Despite his initial description of the less-than-scintillating panorama, Gorky's narrative suggests that eventually the cinematograph's spell takes hold of him. While the adjective "grey" predominates in the first paragraph (shown above), the second demonstrates a surprising about-face: "The extraordinary impression it creates is so unique and complex that I doubt my ability to describe it with all its nuances."[4] Despite this new medium's communicative limitations, it manages to create a surprising and novel *vraisemblance*:

> Suddenly something clicks, everything vanishes and a train appears
> on the screen. It speeds straight towards you—watch out! It seems
> as though it will plunge into the darkness in which you sit, turning
> you into a ripped sack full of lacerated flesh and splintered bones,
> and crushing into dust and into broken fragments this hall and this
> building, so full of women, wine, music and vice. . . .
>
> This mute, grey life finally begins to disturb and depress you. It
> seems as though it carries a warning, fraught with a vague and sinis-
> ter meaning that makes your heart grow faint. Strange imaginings
> invade your mind and your consciousness begins to wane and grow
> dim.[5]

Contrasts abound in Gorky's account. Despite his claim that the medium creates only a pale facsimile of human existence ("this mute, grey life"), it also encompasses the ability to render mass and acceleration through affect rather than physics. Watching the image of a moving train, Gorky becomes pulled suddenly into incarnate sentience, as the experience renders him acutely aware of his existence as flesh-and-blood organism, "a ripped sack of lacerated flesh and splintered bones." And, while he similarly imagines the exhibition hall "crushing into dust and broken fragments," Gorky also becomes newly sensitized to the edifice as reliquary of some of human culture's most vital pleasures, "women, wine, music, and vice." This early version of "the movies," a silent, black-and-white, two-dimensional, mobile, and highly selective narrative form, both enervates and overstimulates Gorky. Although limited to communicating primarily through the visual codes of movement in grayscale, this technology causes him to imagine pain, experience fear, and become absorbed to the extent that he can only describe it through the metaphor of losing consciousness. The "movement of shadows, only shadows" initiates a new level of perceptual acuity in Gorky, one that makes the old ("you anticipate nothing new in this all too familiar scene")[6] foreign, strange, new.

Let me turn to a different account of shadows, this time, of the ilk mentioned in *A Midsummer Night's Dream* ("The best in this kind are but shadows" [5.1.208])[7] and found in sometime actor, playwright, and moralist Anthony Munday's account of the early modern stage:

> For the strangest Comedie brings greatest delectation and pleasure.
> Our nature is led awaie with vanitie, which the auctor perceiving
> frames himself with novelties and strange trifles to content the vaine
> humors of his rude auditors, faining countries never heard of; mon-
> sters and prodigious creatures that are not: as of the Arimaspie, of
> the Grips, the Pigmeies, the Cranes, & other such notorious lies.
> And if they write of histories that are knowen, as the life of *Pompeie;*
> the martial affaires of *Caesar,* and other worthies, they give them a
> newe face, and turne them out like counterfeites to showe them-
> selves on the stage. It was therefore aptlie applied of him, who lik-
> ened the writers of our daies vnto Tailors, who having their sheers
> in their hand, can alter the facion of anie thing into another
> forme, & with a new face make that seeme new which is old.[8]

At first glance, the differences between Gorky's and Munday's two descriptions seem more abundant than their likenesses. Rather than depicting the familiar (city life, people leaving a factory, transportation methods), Munday describes fantastical portrayals that stretch credulity. Gorky's account suggests a singular perspective and subjectively isolated experience, whereas Munday's implies a collective one, both through his use of the plural pronoun—"our" natures and "our" days—and his reference to the amassed "auditors." A closer look at these accounts, however, reveals certain symmetries. Gorky's place of exhibition, filled with women, wine, music, and vice, resonates with Munday's description of the theater crammed full of "rude auditors." Additionally, Munday understands the theater as a place where vice flourishes and in which women are rendered particularly vulnerable: "The Theatre I found to be an appointed place of Bauderie; mine owne eares have heard honest women allured with abhominable speeches. Sometime I have seene two knaves at once importunate upon one light huswife, whereby much quarel hath growen to the disquieting of manie."[9] Despite the "greyness" that pervades much of Gorky's narrative, the cinematograph provides him with a profoundly, if terrifyingly, embodied experience; Munday also represents London's professional theaters and plays themselves as exceptionally somatic. His claim that the theater caters to its audiences' "vaine humors" suggests the early modern period's understanding of playgoing as an inherently embodied undertaking: "humors" invokes both "mood" or "inclination" and the body's governing fluids. While Munday mentions plays' sometimes fantastical plots, he also discusses another genre—the history play—in which "the life of Pompey, the martial affairs of Caesar" are given "new faces, and turn[ed] . . . out like counterfeits," which sounds akin to Gorky's "familiar" scenes made *unheimlich*: "You anticipate nothing new in this all too familiar scene, for you have seen pictures of Paris streets more than once. But suddenly a strange flicker passes through the screen and the picture stirs to life."[10] Indeed, Munday's description of playwrights as "tailors" (or "play-patchers" as Tiffany Stern calls them)[11] brings to mind early filmmaking, which was far more about editing than original narrative. Finally, although the cinematograph is an almost entirely new entertainment technology in the late nineteenth century and plays in the late sixteenth century were not,[12] both Gorky's and Munday's descriptions discuss forms of entertainment that are novel to the culture that produces them. The cinematograph is new in that it introduces the quality of movement to photographic representation; the late sixteenth-century theater is new in that it presents secular dramatic material written by professional writers and acted by professional actors for profit. Most significantly, both commentators see these communicative mediums as having the ability to mesmerize their onlookers, transporting them to something akin to an alternative reality. Gorky describes his mind being "invaded" by "strange imaginings" and his consciousness "wan[ing] and grow[ing] dim," and Munday speaks of the auditors' "nature" being "led away with vanity." This potency, according

to both commentators, functions like sorcery (or chicanery). Gorky calls it
"Merlin's vicious trick,"[13] and Munday imagines the playwright as a kind of
puppeteer who manipulates not only his art form but his audience: "Our
nature is led awaie with vanitie, which the auctor perceiving frames himself
with novelties and strange trifles."

How might we read these similarities? As proleptic? As a form of transhistorical continuity in terms of audience reception? Perhaps. Alternatively,
these two commentaries, much like the epigraphs with which this book
begins, demonstrate another kind of connection, one that is discursive rather
than affective or material. Certainly, discursive tendencies can be discerned
between these writers and their historical contemporaries. The version of
Gorky's article cited above appears in a contemporary scholarly collection
that collates it with other early twentieth-century articles that review the
Lumière cinematograph. The editors attribute the manifold parallelisms
between Gorky's description and others' (for example, O. Winter's 1896 article on the cinematograph for *New Review* and an unattributed 1898 article for
Punch articulate the machine's effect in ways that echo Gorky with surprising
precision)[14] to discursive influences, or "schools of critical thought" such as
"the photographic and scientific community, the entertainment sector, and
. . . most vividly, the general press and general public."[15] As for Munday,
some scholars have claimed that the "plaigiaristic" nature of the antitheatricalists' writings makes them unworthy of serious consideration.[16] My interest
in these iterations, however, is not in gauging their originality as a means of
determining either their earnestness or worth; rather, I take them as traces of
the Western entertainment spectator's discursive history, a history to which
Gorky and Munday are subject. That is to say, many of the homologies
between their claims, such as their agreement that popular mass entertainment "tricks" its audiences into confusing the fictional with the real, have
had a potent and transhistorical hold on the Western cultural imaginary.
Both authors, however, are not mere repositories and perpetuators of this
history but contributors to it. For, while Munday and Gorky repeat certain
"tenets" of mass culture, they adapt others to fit the descriptive needs engendered by their particular historical, cultural, and technological moment.
Pulled between these two modes of representation (the chronic and the adaptive), these two social critics' interpretations similarly display twinned anxieties. One prevalent concern is iterative: it centers on a culturally inculcated
view that entertainment "spectacles" have a profound, perhaps irrevocable,
impact on those who watch them. The other, and less immediately apparent,

is adaptive: both critics endeavor to find adequate terminology to describe the experience these novel diversions create and the sort of interaction they invite or produce (a lexical challenge suggested by both writers' excessive use of metaphor). A pattern emerges that links these two writers, immutably separated by time and space: both bear witness to cultural moments where a need arises to resurrect long-standing cultural myths about spectators while finding new ways to understand, discuss, and represent the act of spectatorship.

The link I have outlined here is a tenuous one: large, loose and, some might even say, naïvely ahistorical. I begin with this connection, however, to highlight the continuities across time in the spectator's discursive history, ones that have been obscured by critics' tendency to highlight the differences between modern and premodern spectatorial practices, practices they imagine as being initiated and shaped by technology and exhibition. Consider, for example, Andrew Gurr's claims about the essential differences between early modern and contemporary audiences:

> "Audience" is a collective term for a group of listeners. A "spectator" is an individual, seeing for him or herself. Modern playgoers are set up, by their physical and mental conditioning, to be solitary spectators, sitting in the dark watching a moving picture, eavesdroppers privileged by the camera's hidden eye. In fundamental contrast, the early modern playgoers were audiences, people gathered as crowds, forming what they called assemblies, gatherings or companies. They sat or stood in a circle round the speakers who were enacting what they came to hear and see. An audience comes to hear, and therefore it clusters as closely as possible around the speaker. Spectators come to see, and so they position themselves where they can confront the spectacle.[17]

Although Gurr begins by comparing early modern and modern playgoers, he moves quickly to associating modern spectators with film, saying they are "eavesdroppers privileged by the camera's hidden eye." His elision of film and theater, or more accurately, his tacit claim that "modern" spectators are shaped by cinema, illustrates the ways that studies of spectatorship (and even the term *spectator* itself) has been overdetermined as a modern phenomenon. Despite the fact that he later acknowledges the use of *spectator* by early modern writers, Gurr makes the case here that by and large, the term is anachronistic as a referent for early modern theatergoers. Like many cultural theorists, Gurr understands twentieth-century spectatorship as image- rather than language-driven, fostering a sense of private, even voyeuristic looking and interactive only in a virtual sense.

Gurr's demarcation points to a question that drives much of this study: how did early modern playwrights see the difference between "an audience" and "spectators"? Did they adhere to Gurr's neat sensory and subjective taxonomies, or were they less clear about such differences? Why did the term *spectator* appear in the English language during the late sixteenth century at all: what conceptual work might it signify? In order to begin addressing such questions, I explore some of the term's earliest instances and contexts in order to trace certain discursive threads that begin to coalesce around the figure of the spectator during the final decades of Elizabeth I's reign. Three of the most widely repeated conventions are as follows:

- Spectatorship constitutes a dynamic exchange between the theatrical event and the individuals experiencing it. Frequently, it is portrayed as a violent, even traumatic, experience.
- Spectatorship suggests a collective experience shared by a community of interpreters. The energies generated by this community are believed to contain a creative spark that imitates or mimics the divine.
- Spectatorship is not an experience relegated to the sensory binary of audial-visual, but is imagined and articulated as one that activates multiple senses for the spectator.

Although distinct, these "tenets" do not exist in isolation. Rather, they intersect at a larger early modern concern about the spectator, one still highly topical at the beginning of the twenty-first century. Each of these concepts represent an initial attempt by early modern writers to articulate the theater's unique ability to create something that could (a) seem more real to the spectator than reality itself, and (b) cause the spectator to want (or even at times attempt) to inscribe this alternative reality onto the world in which he or she lived. In other words, what was it about the particular interaction between theatrical performance and the theatrical spectator that opened up a space where the imaginary could, even if only temporarily, become confused with or mistaken for the real? To use a contemporary analogy, film and television are often seen as particularly effective mechanisms for the dissemination of ideology because of how they manipulate the viewer's point of view. Techniques such as continuity editing, camera angle, and film speed create a uniquely "real" experience for the spectator, one designed to enhance perceptual experience and detail. But the early modern professional theater, using what we would today call "minimalist" sets and other nonrealistic conventions (such as having boys play women and the doubling and tripling of roles), would seem to provide clear signposts of the theater's fictionality. As Philip Sidney points out in his *Apologie for Poetrie*, "What child is there that, coming to a play and seeing *Thebes* written in great letters upon an old door, doth believe that it is Thebes?"[18] Clearly the potency of the theatrical experience for the early modern spectator was not based on the sort of verisimilitude created by modern viewing technologies. Was it, then, that the theater engaged the spectator's imagination through completely different channels, or was it that verisimilitude itself meant something different to the early modern spectator?

The three concepts of spectatorship outlined above provide a starting point for exploring these questions. Rather than attempting to excavate actual spectatorial experience, I assess how those who thought and wrote about this figure imagined and tried to articulate and control that experience. As with the case of Gorky, some of this narrative comes from "real" or perceptual experience. Many of the individuals writing about the theater (whether for or against) were themselves theatergoers; certainly Elizabethan and Jacobean playwrights attended the theater, and many of the "antitheatricalists" were former playwrights and actors. Some of the narrative, however, comes from preexisting ideas about the spectator that arrives in the sixteenth century through oral (folklore, gossip, sermons) and written discourse (moralist and philosophical treatises, romance, and classical drama). Therefore, while my project seeks to articulate an early modern theory of discursive spectatorship that is my own, the ideas from which it is constructed are theirs. Found in a range of late sixteenth-century writings on and for the theater, these texts grapple with the figure of the spectator and the "new" experiences of looking that developed alongside the rise of the professional theater in early modern England. For those writing against the theater, the sorts of interpretive exchanges that occurred in the playhouse were seen as potentially subversive and ultimately detrimental to the individual and society. For those invested in and writing for the stage, this dynamic was not only celebrated but, as my later chapters explore, feared, as the energies generated when spectators and drama met in the theater were not easily predicted or controlled. Before

turning to those writers who were engaged actively in this debate, I first visit
the site where the term *spectator* emerges: a prose romance penned by one of
the most spectacular figures of the Elizabethan court.

The Active–Passive Spectator and the Rhetoric of Violence

Gurr's claim that the collective term *audience* triumphed over the solitary
spectator in early modern references is only partly accurate. While *audience*
may have been used more frequently than *spectator*, both are found regularly
in writings about the stage and other forms of early modern spectacle.[19] The
term first appears in the sixteenth century: the *Oxford English Dictionary* cites
Philip Sidney as the first Anglophone author to use *spectator* in *The Countess
of Pembroke's Arcadia.*[20] It appears with greater frequency as the late sixteenth
century (and playgoing culture) progresses, and, by the end of the first decade
of the seventeenth century, is used regularly to refer to theater audiences and
other groups gathered together for the purpose of looking. For early modern
writers who settled on *spectator* as another way of representing the "audiences," "beholders," and "onlookers" of their culture, this term did not evoke
the same sorts of meaning we assign it from our twentieth-century critical
perspective. But how did it function for them? Gurr suggests it filled a particular need in the vocabulary of playwrights concerned with the interpretive
tension between looking and listening, particularly by those who used it to
deride audiences that preferred the visual side of stagecraft to linguistic art-
istry. Citing Ben Jonson as chief among detractors of those who come primarily to look rather than listen, Gurr states, "Every time Jonson called his
auditors 'spectators,' as he almost invariably did, he was covertly sneering at
the debased preference for stage spectacle rather than the poetic 'soul' of the
play, which he claimed they could only find by listening to his words."[21]
Jonson, of course, is something like an early modern version of Mikey from
the Life cereal commercials of the 1970s—he hates everything—and therefore
is not the most objective of cultural witnesses. But Gurr claims that Jonson
is by no means the only critic of the "barren spectators"; apparently, many
of Jonson's contemporaries shared the view that poetry was losing out to
spectacle.[22]

   In claiming, however, that even in the early modern period the term
spectator was tied inextricably to the visual, Gurr contradicts his initial claim
about the difference between Renaissance audiences and contemporary ones.

If early modern playgoers "were audiences," and an audience "comes to hear," why did there emerge a need for a term that separates lookers from listeners? Neither Sidney nor Edmund Spenser, two of the earliest English writers to use the term, wrote for the stage; therefore, it is unlikely that the competition between sight and hearing that obsessed Jonson and his contemporaries would have held the same charge for them.[23] Gurr himself expresses some confusion over Sidney's use of *spectator*, since he assumes the poet would naturally privilege hearing over seeing: "Curiously the first writer to use the term 'spectator' appears to have been that most critical of educated and gentlemanly playgoers, Philip Sidney."[24] Gurr does not delve further into this question, making it seem as though "spectator" was simply another neologism generated during a particularly fecund epoch for the English language. However, *spectator* functions neither as a mere writerly synonym nor a term coined to designate a particular sort of playgoer. Unlike other neologisms of the period that spring fully formed into the English language, *spectator* is a translation and a very literal one at that. Before Sidney's rendition, the Latin *spectator* was usually translated as "beholder" or "looker-on."[25] For example, in an account of the festivities orchestrated for the Duc d'Alencon's visit to Antwerp in 1582, Arthur Golding translates those that stand and watch the extravagant spectacles as "beholders."[26] Sidney uses *beholders* seventeen times in the *Arcadia,* whereas *spectator* appears only twice. The question is, why did it appear at all? What representational lacuna does *spectator* fill for Sidney?

Similar to Golding's usage, Sidney's uses *beholder* to describe onlookers; for example, in Book I, *beholders* describes those who watch the portrait pageant held by Phalantus of Corinth to choose the most beautiful of eleven noble women. His first use of *spectator*, however, occurs during a narrative detour in which Sidney attempts to elucidate a complex dynamic of witnessing, one generated by a singular perspective and charged with psychic drama. Having lost his kingdom through his bastard son's treachery, the usurped king of Paphlagonia (Leonatus) provides his betrayal's backstory through narrative flashback. The "real-time" action begins when Leonatus's recreant son Plexirtus discovers that his father and younger (and legitimate) brother are still alive and have reunited. In something of a panic, Plexirtus sets out to find and kill them: "But by and by the occasion was presented: for *Plexirtus* (so was the bastard called) came thether with fortie horse, onely of purpose to murder this brother; of whose comming he had soone advertisement, and thought no eyes of sufficient credite in such a matter, but his owne; and therefore came himself to be actor, and spectator."[27] In terms of signification,

Sidney's use of *spectator* appears to function in contradistinction to *actor*, an entity that represents the passive and impressionable side of this subjective equation. As both *actor* and *spectator,* Plexirtus should form a holistic specta-torial entity, an interpretive version of Aristophanes's sexually unified origin-ary beings.[28] Instead, the two terms butt up uncomfortably against one another in the phrase, creating a sense of fragmentation rather than unity. In part, the narrative itself generates this dynamic. We already know that Plexir-tus is a study in contradictions: he seems loyal, humble, and temperate but in reality is duplicitous, proud, and ambitious. But the interpretive yin and yang that Sidney seems to want to portray here feels odd, in large part because he tries on the new term *spectator* rather than using the tried-and-true *beholder*, a substitution that hints at a desire to represent something other than neatly opposing modes of interaction. What that is, exactly, is unclear; however, a kind of *anschauung* undergirds both *actor* and *spectator* here. Plex-irtus does not merely set out to get rid of his annoying little brother but sets out to see what he needs to see: he "thought no eyes of sufficient credite in such a matter, but his owne." Plexirtus is "actor" in that he seeks to confront the sight of his younger brother's material reality; he is "spectator" in that his witnessing this physical entity is the *sine qua non* for Plexirtus's subjective and psychic alteration from king into illegitimate usurper. The visual, then, becomes the epistemological channel that bridges the active and passive modes occupied by "actor" and "spectator" in this passage. Perhaps, as Gurr claims, the emergence of *spectator* as a term reflects a corresponding rise or reaffirmation of sight as the preeminent sense through which individuals came to know the world in the late sixteenth century. However, a question remains as to why Sidney did not rely on the more customary *beholder*, a term that would have evoked visual experience equally well.

One possibility is that Sidney attempts to express a relationship between acting and looking organized around a schema other than that offered by oppositional or complementary polarities. His statement that Plexirtus became "actor, and spectator" follows an equally enigmatic lead-in phrase: "*and therefore came him selfe to be* actor, and spectator" (my italics). On the one hand, Plexirtus's "coming to be" is literal in that he comes in his own person to see for himself what he has heretofore only heard. On the other hand, the phrase "came him selfe to be" gives the figurative sense that a transformation has taken place in Plexirtus, not one that is physical or moral but experiential. Plexirtus's actions here follow a specific, if empirically topsy-turvy, trajectory in this passage: he does not see and then desire but desires and then sees. The reverse cause and effect described here seems to initiate a particularly powerful generative force, one that, to use Stephen Greenblatt's phrase about subjectivity in the period, is "resolutely dialectical" in nature.[29] When Plexirtus comes to be actor and spectator, he undergoes a transformation that is neither enacted upon him by outside forces (such as God or nature) nor completely generated by his imagination or psyche. Rather, the act of "coming of himself to be" necessitates being active and passive simultaneously. It is a chaos of agency, a collision of imaginative and experiential selves, a doing and a being done to. Rather than expressing polarities of experience (active/passive), Sidney struggles to express what happens when these seemingly divergent energies are yoked together, a struggle revealed in the very structure of the phrase. Sidney describes Plexirtus's active transformation (the creation of himself as both actor and spectator) through the passive voice: he "comes to be." When Sidney transports the term *spectator*, then, from one language to another virtually unchanged, it is not because he is running low on vocabulary but because he is trying to communicate something more turbulent and more subjective than *beholding* designates.

The disruptive rhythms generated by this primal chaos of *dasein* offer a kind of cultural seismograph, one that gauges moments during which the discursive spectator gains (or, more accurately, regains) traction in a given historical period. In 1584, when Sidney grasps for a signifier that encapsulates late sixteenth-century dynamics of reception, particularly those surrounding fictional representation, the sixteenth-century English incarnation of the spectator is still inchoate in form and concept but rapidly materializing in various discourses found in the period. Several other late Elizabethan writers echo Sidney's use of the term in that they use it to describe an event that changes the viewing subject's identity in some fashion. In his epic romance *Vertue's History,* Francis Rous describes a scene of exquisite horror:

> Of bloody gusts, and those vermilion swordes,
> Which dide themselues in brothers broken hearts,
> How swimming blood in streets made flowing fords,
> And ruthfull turmoyles rose in diuers parts
> I meane to sing.[30]

He then calls upon a nameless "spectator" to avenge these wrongs: "Which while these things were done spectator [*sic*] stoode: / Lift up blacke Nemesis thy glowing eyes." Again, the observer described here is one who is called to occupy the positions of both actor and spectator, to witness and then avenge. Even closer to Sidney's usage is the example found in Samuel Daniel's *Poetical Essays*: "O faithlesse Cosen, here behold I stand / Spectator of that act my selfe haue plaid."[31] Daniel's speaker addresses his cousin who has betrayed him ("thou dost me wrong / T'usurpe the government I held so long"), and, while the narrative situation is a reversal of Plexirtus's, his spectatorial positioning is similar in that it is only in the seeing of his betrayer that the reality of his new identity (betrayed, powerless) becomes fully realized.[32]

There is another connection between these examples in that they all describe acts of violence. Sidney's spectator sets out to see, then murder, his father and brother; Rous's witnesses a bloodbath, and Daniel's has been betrayed and overthrown by a family member. These scenarios do not simply describe instances of witnessing violence; rather, they suggest a process whereby this witnessing causes the subject to alter not only at the internal, psychic level (à la psychoanalysis) but at the manifest, social one. When Plexirtus sees his father and brother, he is forced to see himself as a traitor and parricide (a destiny he intends to fulfill) rather than as a legitimate ruler. Rous's spectator witnesses actual violence, an experience that turns him into "Nemesis," the classical goddess of vengeance. And Daniel uses the term *spectator* to describe the moment where Richard II realizes he is no longer king of England—the moment that Shakespeare portrays by having Richard call for a looking glass because he cannot imagine he will recognize himself bereft of his majesty and having relinquished his divine right. In addition to describing an action that demands a play between active and passive modes of interaction, it seems that *spectator* also suggests a viewing subject that is altered by what she or he sees, not gently or subtly, but suddenly and violently.

While none of the above examples specifically references the theater (although Daniel's uses a theatrical metaphor), each seeks to describe a sort of looking that produces similar cathartic effects that dramatic performance was imagined to produce. These writers' use of the newfangled *spectator* suggests their efforts to articulate certain shifts occurring around the figure of the beholder. Whereas Sidney, Rous, and Daniel describe an interpretive site involving concurrent modes of active and passive interpretation that result in psychic trauma, others try to elucidate the convergence of individual and group consciousness that the theater could facilitate. This play between individual and communal forms of address was not unique to the theater but was related to that which took place in various other contexts, such as public executions and the Anglican Mass. Indeed, one of the most common complaints that city magistrates and clergy alike made against the theater was that it drew people from the churches and into the theaters, a charge that was taken seriously enough to result in the 1569 banning of plays on Sundays. Of equal concern, however, was the belief that the theater, like the Mass, harnessed the combined imaginative and affective energies on which it drew in ways that could animate narrative to the point where it came dangerously close to reality. This generative potency was one point on which both late sixteenth-century protheatrical and antitheatrical treatises concur; as Charles Whitney has put it, the theater's potency was largely understood as both "a challenge to be overcome [and] a positive resource, a part of what energized a theater and extended its impact beyond the time and place of performance."[33] And, although anti- and protheatrical writers differed on whether this was a quality to celebrate or fear, both see the spectator as a catalyst that ignites the spark of life inherent in stage drama, an ability that imitates, even challenges, the prerogative of divinity itself.

Words Meet Flesh: Communities of Theatrical Looking

The stage's ability to tap into the imaginative potency inherent in any given audience made it a cause for civic and ecclesiastical concern. However, a more immediate and acute problem was the theater's ability to draw crowds out of the churches and into the playhouse. Complaints of this nature can be found in the *Stationers' Register* from the 1590s, stating that plays withdrew "all sorts in general from their daily resort to sermons and other godly exercise."[34] Often the subject of sermons and other forms of moralist literature, this cultural anxiety pervades Anglican preacher John Northbrooke's 1577 screed against "idle pastimes": "And by the long suffring and permitting of these vaine plays, it hath stricken such a blinde zeale into the heartes of the people, that they shame not to say and affirme openly, that Playes are as good as Sermons, and that they learne as much or more at a Playe, than they doe at Gods worde preached. God be mercifull to this Realme of Englande, for we begynne to haue ytching eares, and lothe that heavenly Manna, as appeareth by their flowe and negligent comming unto Sermons, and running so fast, and so many, continually unto Playes.&c."[35] Northbrooke's tendency toward hyperbole is hardly unique among antitheatrical writers; for example, William Burton's 1595 sermon contains similar rhetoric: "As wise as they are, they can be at playes by candlelight, & heare them vntil midnight, and that without any inconvenience too, and sweare by their trothe they finde more edefying in one play, then in twenty sermons."[36] Northbrooke's metaphorical tendencies, however, demonstrate a level of expressiveness not seen in other iterations of the theater-as-replacement-for-the-Mass discourse.[37] For example, Northbrooke's claim that the English "lothe" the heavenly manna that is the word of God parallels the intractable Elizabethans with the ungrateful Israelites, who, when God fed them with heavenly food while they wandered the desert, complained of the monotony of their divinely-provided diet: "And the mixed multitude that was among them fell to lusting: and the children of Israel also wept again, and said, Who shall give us flesh to eat? / We remember the fish, which we did eat in Egypt freely; the cucumbers, and the melons, and the leeks, and the onions, and the garlick: / But our soul is dried away: there is nothing at all, beside this manna, before our eyes."[38] Like the Israelites before them, the English risk God's favor by pursuing the spices of life and valuing earthly pleasures (even those enjoyed under the yoke of physical or spiritual enslavement) over freedom.

In inferring this connection between the English and the Israelites, however, Northbrooke gestures toward something that exists at the core of the way early modern culture imagined theatrical spectatorship. By comparing the English, who run from the church and into the theater, to the Israelites, who eschew the food of God and long for well-fed slavery, Northbrooke delineates English theatergoers as a unique community of believers, even if their belief constitutes heresy. Such kinship manifests not only through ties of race, culture, nation, and religion, but is forged anew through a "blind zeal" for the theater. Northbrooke's articulation of the theatergoing public as a community is reinforced through his portrayal of England's playgoers as a people who speak and think as one: "They shame not to say and affirm openly that players are as good as sermons, and that they learn as much or more at a play than they do at God's word preached."[39] The fact that a similar dialogic form is used in the biblical passage from which Northbrooke's metaphor derives (the Israelites are depicted as collectively voicing their complaint) does not, I would argue, render it unimaginative or derivative. Rather, Northbrooke selects material that reflects something about the theatrical spectator that he intuits and indirectly expresses.

The theater's popularity, however, raised a more profound metaphysical issue than the fact it resulted in poor church attendance. The communal force Northbrooke's early treatise suggests was noted by both the theater's proponents and detractors. Whereas the antitheatricalists saw this force as one that needed rechanneling back into the devotional sphere, those who wrote for the stage tended to imagine it as a force that could make or break the theater's creative and financial success. Whether playwrights imagined their playgoers primarily through these mercenary terms is unclear; however, they often articulated the spectatorial energy generated between audience and performance as one that contained something ineffable and incredibly potent. Thomas Nashe's 1592 social satire, *Piers Penniless His Supplication to the Devil,* suggests this generative ability: "How it would have joyed brave Talbot, the terror of the French, to think that after he had lain two hundred years in his tomb, he should triumph again on the stage and have his bones new embalmed with the tears of ten thousand spectators at least (at several times), who, in the tragedian that represents his person, imagine they behold him fresh bleeding!"[40] Nashe describes a traditionally Aristotelian catharsis here in that he describes a spectacle (the bleeding Talbot) that creates a burst of emotion in the onlookers. These spectators, however, play a large role in creating what they see, as Nashe's rendition imagines the onlookers' collective response as the animating force behind Talbot's revivification. While Nashe restricts the "miracle" of Talbot's resuscitation to the sphere of theatrical make-believe (a device Shakespeare will push to its limits in the final scene of *The Winter's Tale*), his metaphor of the body "new embalmed" with the spectators' tears smacks as much of baptism as of funerary rite, of bestowing new life as of raising specters from the past.

Although Nashe here speaks as a proponent of the theater, he follows antitheatricalist discourse in partaking of devotional imagery to craft his defense. Drawing on the iconic image of the wounded-then-resurrected body as a metaphor for the potency of the theatrical experience, Nashe may simply be throwing the antitheatricalists' high-flown rhetoric back in their teeth via the mechanisms of satire. Entitled "The Defence of Plays," this segment of *Piers Penniless* responds directly to the flurry of antitheatrical tracts generated during the last two decades of the sixteenth century. Although Nashe stops short of definitively referencing the paradigm of Christian martyrdom, his description of Talbot through terms that emphasize both corporeal ephemerality (entombment, embalmment, bones, and blood) and the capability of

transcending such limitations (triumph, joy, and new life) contains resonances from biblical renditions of Christ's burial and resurrection. What better way to contest, even enrage, moralist critics of the theater than this
skillfully veiled blasphemy used in praise of the theater and, moreover, by
using an image saturated with popish resonances?

There may, however, be more at work here than Nashe's wit. The Christian echoes found in this passage owe more to the Church's performative
traditions than its scriptural ones. Although all of the four gospels contain a
scene where the Marys go to anoint Jesus's body (only to find it missing),
this moment is glossed over rather quickly in each.[41] This narrative was,
however, a popular one within the tradition of liturgical drama, which elabo-
rated and expanded on it to include responses from the congregation. Consider this version from a twelfth-century Easter Mass:

> *To them let the deacon representing the angel answer, saying:*
> Whom do you seek, O trembling women, weeping at this tomb?
> *And they to him:*
> We seek Jesus of Nazareth who was crucified.
> *To them let him add:*
> He is not here whom you seek, but going quickly tell his disciples
>   and Peter that Jesus is risen.
> *After this, as they draw near, let him rise and raise up the curtain and*
>   *expose the sepulchre to view, and say to them:*
> Come and see the place where the Lord had been laid, alleluia,
>   alleluia . . .
> *This said, let the whole community sing together, saying:*
> Tell us, Mary, what did you see on the way?
> *And let one of the three who visited the sepulchre say in a clear voice:*
> I saw the sepulchre of the living Christ, and the glory of his rising.[42]

Of course, it is unlikely that Nashe had any familiarity with this particular
text or with liturgical drama at all: it seems to have largely disappeared from
the Mass even before the English Reformation.[43] However, Nashe's portrayal
of Talbot's onstage revivification shares something with the *Visitatio Sepulchri*
other than tearful onlookers and a martyr who triumphs over death: both
illustrate an innate understanding of the importance of the spectators' role in
the (re)generative process itself. In each case, of course, this process is imaginative. The spectators witness only a re-creation rather than an actual creation. This caveat, however, should not lessen the force generated by this act:

as David Bevington points out, liturgical dramatization "was not intended as a mere imitation of an action, but as a demonstration of the living reality of Christ's resurrection."[44] In order for this demonstration to work, however, the presence of the congregation was essential. Composed of both imagination and faith, their participation *is* "the living reality" found in the ritual. Nashe describes his theatrical spectators through similar, if more secular, terms. Like the congregants who come to witness and participate in the ritual reenactment of Christ's death and rebirth, Nashe's spectators come to see the dead Talbot live, speak, and, indeed, die again. And, although one instance constitutes a religious ritual and the other an afternoon's entertainment, in both cases it is the convergence of the spectators' shared emotion and cultural beliefs that transforms a simple mimetic act into something that contains the spark of life itself.[45]

That the professional theater became a site where certain cultural conflicts previously negotiated largely through Catholic ritual were revisited and reevaluated has been argued previously.[46] However, the ways in which these changes played a role in shaping discourses about theatrical spectatorship has not been sufficiently explored. Part of the communicative need that the term *spectator* fills is the idea of an individual engaged in a secularized hermeneutic, one who could both partake in the emotion generated through the shared presence of other spectators while also engaging in a unique "individual" experience.[47] Thomas Kyd's narrative framing of his highly popular play *The Spanish Tragedy* suggests this dialectic. When Andrea's ghost sits down with Revenge to watch "the miserie" of the play unfold, they become part of the interpretive community the play's audience constitutes. Yet they also remain individual forces, ones that create meaning inside the play in that they participate in its creation both structurally and narratively. Kyd returns to this framing device periodically throughout *The Spanish Tragedy*. Like any bored onlooker, Revenge falls asleep during the lengthy third act, and Andrea throws a fit when he thinks things are not going quite the way he wants: "Awake, Revenge, or we are woe-begone!" (3.15.17).[48] But for every moment in which these characters perform stereotypical behaviors associated with inattentive or overly invested audience members, there is another in which they actually motivate certain actions within the play. Andrea's desire for divine justice sets the revenge plot in motion, and his call for aid is answered by none other than Revenge: "Be still Andrea; ere we go from hence, / I'll turn their friendship to fell despite / Their love to mortal hate, their day to night" (1.5.5–7).[49] How, exactly, Revenge accomplishes this is left unclear, as the play does not show him doing anything except watching and taking catnaps: it seems his very presence is sufficient to set events in motion. Through the act of spectating, Andrea and Revenge can bring to life "the mystery" and the tragedy of life, or, when metadramatically considered, the play itself.

I am not suggesting this framing device is crafted merely (or even primarily) as a meditation on the spectator. Seneca's *Thyestes,* which clearly influenced the content and structure of Kyd's play, also begins with a postmortal conversation between a ghost and a personified minor deity.[50] As Megaera (one of the Furies) drags Tantalus from his insatiate existence, she calls on Thyestes to "vexe" his mortal house with "rage of furyes might."[51] Tantalus is initially a completely unwilling participant; despite Megaera's command, he tries to flee back to his lake of eternal torment. Finally, tortured into submission, he enters his grandson's house to continue the cycle of despair his own actions initiated long ago.[52] Numerous differences exist between the Senecan narrative and Kyd's play. Rather than remaining onstage to watch and comment on the action, Tantalus and the Fury disappear after the first scene and do not return. Tantalus is also forced to participate in a divine act of vengeance against his family rather than being granted the honor of watching his own personal vendetta acted out in the mortal realm. Kyd's alterations to Seneca's model cannot, of course, be traced to a single influence or cause, but I would argue that the changes he makes to the immortal characters' roles respond to the period's shifting ideas about the theatrical spectator. In extending the role of the framing narrative to one that remains physically and dialogically present for the entirety of the play, Kyd comments on the nature of the early modern theatrical space itself. But his commentary is not about the stage exactly; that is, it is not about what can be created on the platform at the Curtain or the Rose. Rather, Kyd dramatizes an extradiegetic space, one related to the new and relatively uncharted territory evolving for the theatrical spectator. Occupied by Andrea and Revenge, this spectatorial terrain is essentially a medial one. It is neither heaven nor hell; it calls neither for direct action nor quiescent acceptance from its participants. Shaky ground though it may seem, this emergent space is imagined as offering a certain amount of fluidity in terms of spectatorial positioning. In it, one can be (in Sidney's terms) both actor and spectator, or, in Kyd's implicit articulation, both a member of the community of interpreters and a unique interpretive subject.

Gluttonous Eyes and Ticklish Ears: The Spectator's Synaesthesia

Northbrooke's early attack on the professional theater spearheaded a deluge of similar critiques. As the sixteenth century came to a close, these focused less on the general evils committed by London's populace and more on those committed at the theater, particularly via its detrimental influence on those in attendance. As Jeremy Lopez has pointed out, one of the most pervasive rhetorical devices for critiquing the theater was the dietary metaphor.[53] For example, Northbrooke succinctly metaphorizes scripture as "manna from heaven," and earlier in his treatise, he represents the problem of church attendance as a sort of a feast or famine binary: "The Church is alwaye emptie and voyde, the playing place is replenished and full: we leave Christ alone at the aultar, and feede our eyes with vaine and unhonest sights, and with filthie and uncleane playes."[54] His use of the idiomatic expression "feede our eyes" is particularly apt considering the subject matter. After all, Christ himself used a gastric metaphor to express the most profound of metaphysical transformations, when he tells his bewildered disciples, "Take, eat; this is my body."[55] In describing the flock's departure from Christ's altar to feast on the epicurian pleasures offered by the professional theater, Northbrooke draws attention to the communal nature that both the liturgy and the theater were understood to share but positions them as antithetical.[56] The fellowship offered at the modest table of Christ is, in effect, broken by the desire to feast in gluttony at the trough of the professional stage. At the same time, Northbrooke plays off a sensory prejudice extant since antiquity, which considers sight and hearing as "higher" planes of sensory experience while taste and smell are "lower" forms.[57] By aligning theatrical and gustatory experience, Northbrooke reinforces his initial condemnation of the theater. Not only does it lead one away from the divine realm and into the merely appetitive, but it does so by appealing to the lowest rungs of the sensory register.

In conflating high (sight) and low (smell and taste) sensory experiences, Northbrooke initiates a mixed metaphor that becomes something of a touchstone in antitheatricalist discourse. Stephen Gosson offers a more elaborate version in his 1579 *The Schoole of Abuse*:

> There setchey abroche straunge consortes of melody, to tickle the
> eare; costly apparel, to flatter the sight; effeminate gesture, to ravish
> the sence; and wanton speache, to whet desire too inordinate lust.

Therefore of both barrelles, I iudge Cookes and Painters the better
hearing, for the one extendeth his arte no farther then to the tongue,
palate, and nose, the other to the eye; and both are ended in out-
warde sense, which is common too us with bruite beasts. But these
by the privie entries of the eare, slip downe into the hart, & with
gunshotte of affection gaule the minde, where reason and vertue
should rule the roste.[58]

Like Northbrooke, Gosson begins with a common sensory idiom to begin
his metonym. He also brings together taste and sight by yoking together cook
and painter in order to emphasize the theater's power to appeal to man's
baser sensory appetites. There are, however, two key differences between the
metaphors. The most immediately obvious is the extreme to which Gosson
takes his comparison; it is a synaesthetic maelstrom compared to Northbrooke's brief and tidy idiom. In Gosson's account, sight and hearing are
nearly personified: melodies "tickle" the ear, the sense is "ravished," and sight
is lent a sort of consciousness in that it can be "flattered." Later, he claims,
"I judge cooks and painters the better hearing," a somewhat bewildering (if
surprisingly playful) way of describing a rather puritanical anxiety about the
theater as a sort of *Hamlet*-like poison poured into the ear. Less immediately
apparent is Gosson's downgrading of sight in the sensory hierarchy to a rung
somewhere closer to the ones that taste and smell occupy. Claiming that
those arts directed at taste, smell, and sight have, as their end point, the
stimuli of the "outward sense" at which they are directed, Gosson states that
it is drama's use of language that makes it particularly dangerous. In targeting
the ear, playwrights wield a weapon that is far more subtle, as it is through
this orifice that they gain access to the deep recesses of the spectator's heart
and mind. Whereas Northbrooke understands the eye as the primary portal
through which temptation and corruption enters the spectatorial vessel, Gosson sees the ear as the more vulnerable aperture.

Perhaps these discrepancies result from the different foci of the two passages. Northbrooke expresses a distinctly religious concern posited through
Christian imagery, whereas Gosson addresses a more nationalistic and gendered set of anxieties through secular terms: "Our wrestling at arms is turned
to wallowing in ladies' laps; our courage to cowardice; our running to riot,
our bows to balls, and our darts to dishes. We have robbed Greece of gluttony, Italy of wantonness, Spain of pride, France of deceit, and Dutchland

of quaffing."[59] Perhaps they are related to Gurr's claim that the late sixteenth-century stage was a place where English culture began transitioning from one that was equally sensitive to audial and visual stimuli, to one that, at least within the realm of the theater, privileged sight over sound. Neither of these explanations, however, adequately addresses the way in which these two writers commingle sight and hearing with taste, smell, and touch in order to illustrate the mechanisms of engagement the theater exploits. Rather than describing the theatrical experience as one that pulls the spectator between the poles of audial and visual experience, Northbrooke and Gosson imagine it as a site of sensory interplay, even chaos, one that Carla Mazzio aptly designates as a kind of synaesthetic disorder.[60] Although the antitheatricalists do imagine this sensory intermingling as a sort of malaise fostered by the theater, they do not imagine it as a distressing experience for the spectator. Instead, it seems they see it as an encounter that allows for a vertiginous loss of self in a somatic tangle, one they fear the spectator finds uniquely pleasurable.

Mazzio reads this sensory phenomenon as related to the overlooked significance of touch in early modern scholarship, claiming that touch "disrupted the boundaries between the senses themselves."[61] Making the argument that Gosson's metaphor can be unpacked if we consider touch as its connective tissue, Mazzio contributes to a larger scholarly discourse surrounding sensory hierarchies in the Renaissance, which have gone some way toward excavating the ways that the "lower" senses of touch, taste, and smell dictated lived experience in the early modern world.[62] These studies provide a useful corrective to the often *a priori* scholarly assumption that one's worldview in the early modern period (as well as in our own) is dictated mostly by what one sees. But it also leads to a phenomenological question: was the synaesthesia described by Northbrooke and Gosson a sensation they had actually experienced while at the theater? Did they understand the combination of verse, singing, costume, gesture, vocal inflection, stage properties, live bodies, and that elusive thing we call imagination as conspiring to create a truly *multisensory* experience? If not, what is it about the multisensory metaphor that for many of the antitheatricalists at least, captures something essential about what happens to the spectator when he or she engages with a play?

Difficult to parse, the multisensory metaphor can function on both the figurative and literal planes. The word *metaphor*, from the Greek *metapherein*, means "to transfer," and in this sense, the antitheatricalist metaphor functions straightforwardly in that it transfers the sensibilities of one organ of perception to another: the ears feel, the eyes taste.[63] In this respect, Mazzio's claims about touch are persuasive: the senses become so close that they actually make linguistic and (perhaps) experiential contact. Metaphor, however, is more than a mere figurative conduit; it is often used to express evanescent, difficult, or as yet unarticulated concepts, or as one critic puts it, "Metaphor is the dreamwork of language."[64] This innate ambiguity makes metaphor an especially apt vehicle for describing an event that cannot be seen but can only be intuited or felt. If the antitheatricalists are trying to put into language—to make visible—what occurs within the theatrical spectator when he or she watches a play, this interaction can only be represented, hence known, through approximations.

The work performed by the multisensory metaphor in late sixteenth-century accounts of the theater, then, happens somewhere between what it allows for figuratively via substitution and what it allows writers to express about what specifically is unique about the early modern theatrical experience. Like much of antitheatrical discourse, synaesthesia has a long history in Western thought; like much of the antitheatricalists' rhetorical and conceptualizations, this one is indebted to its classical precedents. While the *Oxford English Dictionary* cites 1891 as the term's first use in psychology, and 1901 in literary criticism,[65] Daniel Heller-Roazen traces *synaesthesia* back to classical philosophy, particularly Aristotle's concept of the "common sense":

> The distant origin of the modern "synaesthesia," the Greek term
> was no neologism when the thinkers of late Antiquity bestowed
> upon it a technical sense in the doctrine of the soul. In the classical
> varieties of the language, admittedly, the noun appears to have con-
> stituted something of a rare expression; but it is not without signifi-
> cance that the verb from which it was drawn, *sunaisthanesthai,* can
> be found in two passages of Aristotle's own treatises. Formed by the
> addition of the prefix "with" (*sun-*) to the verb "to sense" or "to
> perceive" (*aisthanesthai*), the expression in all likelihood designated
> a "feeling in common," a perception shared by more than one.[66]

This "common sense" may appear tangential to the antitheatricalist usage, which more closely follows Galen's concept of *sunaisthēsis* as a sensation "that reaches a single body all at once, while consisting, in effect, of multiple physiological affections."[67] However, the idea of the communal extant in Aristotle's formulation lingers quietly in antitheatrical discourse, particularly in its presentation of the theater as a force capable of rapidly generating spontaneous (if highly unstable) forms of community. Steven Mullaney has recently argued that the early modern theater "embodied thoughts, contradications, and social traumas of its audiences—and that could serve as a catalyst for the making of various publics and counterpublics, imagined communities, and collective identities."[68] Like many arguments about early modern audiences, particularly those focused on unearthing early modern spectatorial responses, Mullaney's glosses over the discursive history of this narrative. The antitheatricalists seek refuge in the spectator's discursive past at this historical moment precisely because of social concerns about the theater as a heterogeneous physical space in which different classes and genders mingle indiscriminately and an imaginative space in which individual viewers merge into a potent, affectively connected entity. The sensory fluidity expressed via the multisensory metaphor allows for the expression of a (recurrent) historical anxiety over the spectator's supposedly unbounded involvement in what she or he sees. At the same time, it attempts to represent the "effects" of the professional theater on those who watch it, one of which is articulated, via the multisensory metaphor, as a state of imaginative and affective rapture.

Regardless of whether early modern theatergoers were inclined toward synaesthesia at the theater or otherwise, the multisensory metaphor's discursive circulation becomes apparent when one considers the ways in which both antitheatricalists and playwrights engage it. For every naysayer, there is a proponent who responds in kind:

> I have had a most rare vision. I have had a dream past the wit of man to say what dream it was. Man is but an ass if he go about t'expound this dream. Methought I was—there is no man can tell what. Methought I was, and methought I had—but man is but a patched fool if he will offer to say what methought I had. The eye of man hath not heard, the ear of man hath not seen, man's hand is not able to taste, his tongue to conceive, not his heart to report what my dream was.[69]

Bottom's much-discussed bungling of Corinthians 2:9 aptly demonstrates the synaesthetic metaphor's discursive saturation; as Jennifer Waldron states, "Shakespeare cleverly manipulates the same kind of perfectionist Protestant tropes as did these antitheatrical writers."[70] When Northbrooke speaks of visual gluttony, Gosson of feeling ears and hearing palates, or Shakespeare of hearing eyes and speaking hearts, they may not literally suggest that the theatrical spectator experiences sensory substitution, fusion, or confusion. Rather, they participate in a discursive tradition, one newly invigorated by the early modern professional theater. But, as with other antitheatricalist tautologies, this one should not be dismissed as simply a colorful turn of phrase that becomes a rhetorical banner under which early modern cultural critics and proponents of the theater mobilize. While these articulations of multisensory experience remain deeply rooted in a discursive tradition, they also demonstrate innovation in honing their subject by focusing on a particular cause of synaesthesia (the professional theater) and in deploying synaesthesia as a literary device.

*   *   *

All three tenets discussed above illustrate another, related strain extant in sixteenth-century spectatorial discourse. Like the play between active and passive (or violent and complacent) and communal and individual that the theater supposedly facilitated in the spectator, the multisensory metaphor similarly suggests the possibility of movement between phenomenological (what one sees and hears) and associative (other sensory experiences seeing and hearing can invoke) modes of experience. In doing so, it exposes another space where theater's detractors understood the spectator as particularly vulnerable. Not only was the theater understood to erode the boundaries between perceptory modalities; it facilitated a possible further categorical breakdown between real and imaginary. Religious and civic voices alike echoed this particular complaint against playgoing, claiming that life, in truth, often imitated art. In addition to addressing the problem that the theater lured men away from their work and their God, a lord mayor's petition against playgoing, dated February 25, 1592, states, "The youth is greatly corrupted and their manners infected by the wanton and profane devices represented on the stages."[71] Earlier critics such as Plato and Augustine believed that the theater cultivated undesirable tendencies in the spectator because it enacted *mimesis*: its aim was simply to imitate the already less-than-absolute or ersatz world created by man. Sixteenth-century commentators, however, feared that the theatrical experience could (and ultimately would) cause the spectator to lose the ability to separate the factual (the social order as it existed) from the fictional (the world as it might otherwise be). And, while these anxieties were consistently posited through language that emphasized the spectator's vulnerability and intellectual and moral frailty, such phrasing often was juxtaposed with the language of agency and imaginative fecundity. Anthony Munday's *A Second and Third Blast of Retreat from Plays and Theaters* illustrates this paradox of the spectator as an entity both vulnerable to influence and willful in her inscription of individual desire:

> This inward fight hath vanquished the chastitie of manie women;
> some by taking pittie on the deceitful teares of the stagelovers, have
> bene mooved by their complaint to rue on their secret frends,
> whome they have thought to have tasted like torment; some having
> noted the ensamples how maidens restrained from the marriage of
> those whome their frends have misliked, have there learned a policie
> to prevent their parents, by stealing them awaie; some seeing by
> ensample of the stage plaier one carried with too much liking of an
> other man's wife, having noted by what practise she hath bene
> assailed and overtaken, have not failed to put the like in effect in
> earnest, that was afore shown in jest.[72]

It is the inward fight that vanquishes, the imaginative self, gestated through acts of playgoing, that battles the moral one established and reified through forms of sociocultural discipline. The chaste woman becomes a whore in an instant; the jest written for a simple laugh turns deadly. Like Nashe's half-ludic, half-horrific image of the bleeding Talbot, Munday's account shows a world where the impossible can occur in a moment's time and sometimes even the participants are not entirely aware of what they do. It is no accident that Gosson, himself a former playwright, references the Christian doctrine of free will in his refutation of stage playing. Chastising those women who display themselves in the dangerously public space of the theater, he warns, "Thought is free: you can forbidd no man, that vieweth you, to noate you, and that noateth you, to judge you, for entring to places of suspicion."[73] While his anxiety about women's mobility outside the patriarchically controlled sphere of the home is not unique, Gosson's opening gambit of "thought is free" articulates a new danger generated by the collision of theatrical spectacle and spectator. It is no longer free will that leads "the simple gazer" astray but "free thought" or interpretive license.

That the theater could open up a space of phenomenological instability was an idea shared by theater's proponents. While the antitheatricalists understood this potential as one that placed the spectator in spiritual and sometimes physical jeopardy, those on the opposing side claimed this quality was what made the theater an ideal mechanism for disseminating social, moral, and civic values to a wide audience. Replying to Gosson's *Schoole of*

Abuse, Thomas Lodge claims that the long-standing aim of theater is to provide a mirror through which men are shown their worldly infirmities, and in
doing so, it opens the door for self-rapprochement and reform: "For sayth
[Horace] ther was no abuse [depicted in plays] but these men reprehended
it. a thefe was loth to be seene one there spectacle, a coward was never present
at theyr assemblies, a backbiter abhord that company . . . a harlot woulde
seeke no harbor at stage plais, lest she shold here her owne name growe in
question: and the discourse of her honesty cause her to bee hated of the
godly."[74] Philip Sidney offers a similar defense of the theater, stating that its
mimetic powers naturally created analogies between the macrocosm of character typologies and the microcosm of spectator as individual-in-the-world:
"The Comedy is an imitation of the common errors of our life, which he
representeth, in the most ridiculous & scornefull sort that may be. So as it is
impossible, that any beholder can be content to be such a one."[75] As late as
1612, Thomas Heywood is still defending his craft using similar logic, if more
high-flown terminology: "So bewitching a thing is liuely and well spirited
action, that it hath power to new mold the harts of the spectators and fashion
them to the shape of any noble and notable attempt."[76]

It may seem as though the agential and sensory confusions particular
to drama are disruptions that speak only to *how* the theater communicates
with its audience. But both antitheatricalist and protheatricalist ideas about
the spectator link the concepts of sensory and subjective fluidity through
the rhetoric they use to describe these interpretive phenomena. Although
each uses different formulations to describe how theatrical spectatorship
"worked"—how it communicated with or to its audiences, preyed on or
activated their imaginations, and authorized or damned them—they express
and explain these dynamics both through metaphor and as metaphor. Sometimes, as in the case of Northbrooke's and Gosson's sensory metonym, metaphor is used both as the rhetorical mode of expression and as a crucial
component of the thing being expressed. Others see it as a major key in
which drama plays on the instrument of spectatorial imagination. Munday,
Lodge, and Sidney all see metaphor as a mode intrinsic to both dramatic
communication and spectatorial interpretation in that what is shown through
the world onstage is then transferred by the individual to him- or herself and
the world that he or she occupies. The clearest articulations of this principle,
however, are found in the writings of early modern playwrights themselves.
As early as 1566, George Gascoigne prefaces his *Supposes* by providing the law
students for whom it was written with an "explanation," not only of his play

but of drama in general: "But, understand, our Suppose is nothing else *but a mistaking of the imagination of one thing for another*" (my italics).[77] Thirty years later, Shakespeare opens his final play of the *Henriad* by similarly addressing the Bankside audiences:

> And let us, ciphers to this great account
> On your imaginary forces work.
> Suppose within the girdle of these walls
> Are now confined two mighty monarchies.[78]

This "metaphorical principle" then is one inextricably linked to the period's ideas about how theatrical spectatorship functioned and why it was so potent, addictive, and potentially dangerous to both individuals and society itself.

As the sixteenth century moved toward a close, the theater's cultural foothold became more secure. Correspondingly, the antitheatricalist movement diminished to the point of near silence. With two notable exceptions, post-Elizabethan treatises against the theater go out with more of a whimper than a bang. The two surviving tracts from the Stuart period (I. G.'s 1615 *A Refutation of the Apology for Actors* and William Prynne's 1633 *Histrio-mastix*), while similar in style and form to those written in the last decades of the sixteenth century, demonstrate some shifts in the spectator's construction within the seventeenth-century cultural imaginary. While not interested in precise demographic specimens, these later treatises describe spectators that are already becoming taxonomized through stereotypes. Whereas Northbrooke and Gosson describe the theater's siren call ensnaring the elusive essence of men's souls, I. G. and Prynne portray a character that sounds suspiciously like the ubiquitous groundling. I. G. claims that early modern theater audiences are made up of "in general the vulgar sort," while Prynne delineates them more specifically as "*ordinary Spectators, what are they but ridiculous, foolish, vaine, fantasticke persons, who delight in nothing more then toyes and vanities?*" (original italics).[79] Such typecasting was not limited to antitheatricalist discourse; playwrights took full advantage of circulating spectatorial stereotypes to create cutting-edge humor that walked a fine line between satirical in-jokes for and outright mockery of their audiences.[80]

As literary representations of the spectator transitioned from elusive substance to stock characters, other changes appear as well. The idea that the spectator was a site where certain experiential polarities (such as active vs. passive and collective vs. singular), as well as the full spectrum of the senses

were engaged simultaneously does not disappear during the seventeenth century, but other competing, even contradictory models develop alongside
them. For example, the multisensory metaphor becomes largely condensed
during the seventeenth century. Instead of describing the theater as a place
where the senses conjoin in cacophonous harmony, playwrights and antitheatricalists begin to articulate the spectatorial experience as one dominated by
the eye and ear. I. G. condemns "the profane spectacles presented in the
theaters, to the as [*sic*] profane sights of all that go to be spectators of them,"
and Prynne separates the dangers of the playhouse into that which hurts the
eyes (such as viewing lewd, impious, or tyrannous acts and effeminate and
lavishly dressed actors) and that which injures the ears (blasphemy, obsceni-
ties, and love songs).[81] But while the earlier synaesthetic metaphor fades, the
premise behind it—that the theater has the power to construct an experience
for the spectator that causes the line between imaginative and physical perception to bend, if not quite break—does not. Unlike Gurr, who sees the
sensory division of sight and sound as a place of contest between poetry and
spectacle, I see these later paraphrases of the multisensory metaphor as an
impulse to control the evanescent spectator and the unwieldy interpretive
energies this figure was thought to be capable of generating.

    The following chapters focus on how a particular group that had a vested
interest in the spectator imagined and attempted to shape this figure. Like
the antitheatrical polemicists, early modern playwrights exhibited an anxiety
that the spectator could not be known or effectively controlled. But they also
demonstrated a desire to encourage and harness this energy, for it was, finally,
the lifeblood of their trade. Whereas late sixteenth-century writers focused
primarily on "what" and "how" questions about spectatorship (such as what
made theatrical spectatorship a unique type of interaction and how the theater communicated with the spectator), by the seventeenth century, playwrights were experimenting with ways of influencing and shaping real
spectators via their product. The discursive spectator, therefore, has a stronger
presence in drama during the seventeenth century than it had previously,
particularly in two genres: the dramatic romance and the court masque.
While not new, these forms are rich sites of generic and formal experimentation during the seventeenth century's early decades; both also reached new
heights of popularity during that period. But before turning to the work of
two playwrights, Shakespeare and Jonson, whose work in these respective
genres were popular successes, I look at one of the period's documented
failures, Francis Beaumont's *The Knight of the Burning Pestle*. Beaumont's

play holds a mirror up to the early modern audience by dramatizing the behaviors of two citizens attending the theater. Harmless though this might seem, Beaumont's bitingly satirical portrayal was not met favorably: the dedicatory epistle written for the play's publication claims that it was "utterly rejected" at its premiere. *Knight* offers a rare extant instance of an early modern play that both takes the spectator and spectatorial resistance as its principal subject and is met with actual resistance from its audience. As such, the play is the site of a collision between the discursive and the phenomenological spectator, one that bears traces of the subjective conflict that *Knight* parodies: the moment where the real viewer faces a reflection over which she or he has no immediate control and does not recognize.

CHAPTER 2

The Blood of the Muses

Violent Spectatorship and Authorial Response in *The Knight of the Burning Pestle*

I have heard
That guilty creatures sitting at a play
Have by the very cunning of the scene
Been strook so to the soul, that presently
They have proclaimed their malefactions
        —William Shakespeare, *Hamlet*, c. 1602

In short, he so immersed himself in these romances that he spent
whole days and nights over his books; and thus with little sleeping
and much reading, his brains dried up to such a degree that he lost
the use of his reason. His imagination became filled with a host of
fancies he had read in his books—enchantments, quarrels, battles,
challenges, wounds, courtships, loves, tortures, and many other
absurdities. So true did all this phantasmagoria from books appear
to him that he counted no history in the world more authentic.
        —Miguel de Cervantes, *Don Quixote*, 1605

Written within a few years of each other, the Western literary tradition's most
famous ghost story and its first best-seller contain variations on one of the
Renaissance's most prevalent spectatorial themes: the spectator who cannot
or will not differentiate between the representational and the real. Toward

the end of the "rogue and peasant slave" monologue, Hamlet recounts an oft-cited theatrical yarn, where an onstage event (usually a violent act) ignites the sleeping conscience of an audience member and drives him or her to confess a similar transgression, a scenario later played out in the play's third act.[1] An extreme version of Aristotelian catharsis, this model imagines the theater as the affective analogue of the poison poured into Old Hamlet's ear—an elixir that seeps into the viewer's moral substrate, forcing that which has been kept hidden into the light. Violence subtends multiple experiential planes here: ontic, theatrical, and psychological. A murder is committed in the real world; later, the perpetrator sees the act mimicked onstage and belatedly feels remorse via traumatic recall. Less apparent is the violence inherent in the spectatorial process itself. An incisive rather than blunt force, the theatrical illusion infiltrates the spectator's psyche, a procedure that might result in a socially efficacious purging of excess emotion or a bringing forth of monstrous secrets.

The second version, exemplified by one of *Don Quixote*'s early passages, describes the more widely circulated version of this paradigm, in which the viewer or reader becomes overly invested in the fictional world presented. Despite satirizing this figure, *Don Quixote* cannot fully disarm its potential destructiveness: Quixote may be a charming eccentric, but he also forcibly attempts to reinscribe the world according to his own fantasies.[2] As in the *Hamlet* example, violence here permeates the imagined relationship between fictional entertainment and its consumer. In this case, however, representation pathologically overtakes the consuming subject's phenomenological template, changing the way she or he interacts with the world. When such alterations exceed the bounds of an individual's imagination (as they do with Quixote), they spill into the world of action, sometimes humorously and harmlessly, sometimes violently and irrevocably.

Issues of spectatorship also connect *Hamlet* and *Don Quixote* via a representational genealogy in which both connect to one of seventeenth-century England's most extended representations of theatrical spectatorship—Francis Beaumont's *The Knight of the Burning Pestle*. When Hamlet inquires of Rosencrantz why the players are traveling, he replies,

> There is, sir, an aery of children, little eyases, that cry out
> on top of question and are most tyrannically clapp'd for it.
> These are now the fashion, and so berattled the common
> Stages—so they call them—that many wearing rapiers are
> afraid of goose-quills and dare scarce come thither.[3]

Almost universally glossed in modern editions as referring to London's children's companies, which were popular during the late sixteenth and early seventeenth centuries, this passage is also frequently cited as referring to the so-called War of the Theaters, or Poetomachia.[4] While this passage predates Beaumont's ill-starred play, *Knight* was written for the Blackfriars children's company—the battleground on which the Poetomachia was largely fought—and may have been one of its residual casualties.[5] Although lasting for only a brief period at the sixteenth century's end, some of the behaviors generated by this "war" (such as railing) persisted, particularly among the children's companies' audiences. *Knight*'s aggressively satirical tone and treatment of spectatorial "types" suggest a template forged in a combative atmosphere; indeed, as Michael Shapiro has argued, the play's staging of resistance could be an elaborate metadramatic mechanism that attempts to disrupt the potential for audience hostility.[6]

If *Hamlet* provides insight into the theatrical culture in which *Knight* participated, *Don Quixote* plays a role in its composition and legacy. Several of *Knight*'s scenes suggest *Don Quixote*'s influence, such as the mirroring of Don Quixote and Sancho Panza through the Citizen and his apprentice, and the Knight's onstage confrontation with Barbaroso, the barber-giant.[7] More directly, the First Quarto's (1613) dedicatory epistle mentions Cervantes's novel directly: "Perhaps it will be thought to be of the race of *Don Quixote*."[8] Publisher Walter Burre likely referenced *Don Quixote* for publicity—by 1613 the novel was an international success[9] and Thomas Shelton's English translation had appeared in 1612—but there are other reasons Burre might construct *Knight*'s genealogy to include *Don Quixote*. Significantly, the very identificatory template imagined in the novel (and mirrored in its commercial success) is that which *Knight* seemed unable to cultivate in its theater audience—a potent, unswerving absorption in the world presented to the viewer or reader. By bringing *Don Quixote* and *Knight* into the same orbit, Burre imagines a space where identification can be reforged, where a play that fails on the stage may find a new, more appreciative audience in print. Who might be included in that audience, however, is highly ambiguous—a reality highlighted by the passive locution of Burre's sentence: "Perhaps *it will be thought to be* of the race of *Don Quixote*" (my italics). The sentence's subject, of course, is the play, but "it" can only wait and hope to "be thought to be of" by an oddly absent entity—a presence that hovers uneasily in the statement like the vestiges of a now-absent god in the temple ruins of a long-vanished culture.

As argued earlier, this inchoate figure can be read as symptomatic of a discourse in flux, one struggling to incorporate changing ideas about theatrical spectators as watchers, readers, and consumers. Of particular interest to me in the above examples, however, is the way these writers recalibrate violence not only as something that may occur within the viewing-reading process itself—that is, something that may occur within the spectator's imagination when it engages with certain kinds of representation—but something that is acted out within and on the artistic product itself. *Hamlet, Don Quixote,* and *Knight* all contain scenes depicting the cessation or destruction of their respective mediums. Claudius's act of *dramatis interruptus* in act 3, scene 2, may testify to his burdened soul, but it also disrupts and ends *The Murder of Gonzago.* Don Quixote's housekeeper burns his library, and *Knight's* entire premise swerves on the systematic dismantling of a play by audience members. And, if it is true that *The Murder of Gonzago* serves its purpose and does not really need an ending, that Cervantes's novel is saved from burning by a literature-loving priest, and that *Knight* ultimately proves an interesting, if Frankensteinian, production, these outcomes do not fully efface the images of violence enacted on the vehicle of representation.

While hardly ubiquitous, the destruction of books and plays (imagined or enacted) is seen with some frequency, particularly in the first decades of the seventeenth century. The senate burns Sejanus's books, and Prospero drowns his. Although found mostly in prologues and paratextual apparatuses, the image of the wounded, even slaughtered, play abounds during this period; for example, in his commendatory epistle to Fletcher's 1608 stage failure, *The Faithful Shepherdess,* Jonson refers to the play as a "murdered poem."[10] This trope (if one can call it such) becomes more pronounced if one includes its reverse—moments where artistic objects come to life or are anthropomorphized, such as Imogen's reading of Tereus's tale moments before Iachimo enters her bedchamber, or Middleton's claim that "plaies in this citie are like wenches new falne to the trade, onelie desired of your neatest gallants, while they are freshe."[11] Whether suggestive of a fantasy or anxiety (or some admixture thereof) on the part of these authors, a figurative trend emerges where they describe their "works" (in the Jonsonian sense) as sentient, visceral, and, most important, mortal.

I highlight this descriptive tendency because it offers an alternative lens through which to consider the link between psychic and material violence often imagined as part and parcel of the theatrical spectator's experience. It also offers another hermeneutic by which to explore *Knight,* a text that has tended to serve primarily as a litmus test for seventeenth-century theatrical tastes and reception.[12] I am less interested here in why the play "failed" than why Beaumont wrote a play that explicitly dramatizes audience resistance. Michael Shapiro sees *Knight* as the (unsuccessful) apogee of a "neutralizing" strategy that playwrights developed in response to the coterie audiences' habit of "celebrat[ing] themselves at the expense of the play."[13] But, as Jeffrey Masten has pointed out, the play is also one of the clearest articulations of a discourse expanding to include the idea of drama as a commercial product subject to consumer desire.[14] In "The Audience as Patron: *The Knight of the Burning Pestle,*" Alexander Leggatt argues that the primary anxiety to which the play responds is, "How does [the playwright] resist the tyranny of the audience and maintain the right to work on one's own terms, when the audience is paying the bills?"[15] But whereas Leggatt understands this dynamic to signify the play's "demystify[ication of] theatre by presenting it as a cash transaction,"[16] I see it as elucidating a variant of the early modern discursive spectator. Earlier versions of this figure (including many classical models) imagine the link between violence and spectatorship through a cause-and-effect model in which dramatic and literary fiction had the potency not only to penetrate the viewer's imagination but also to lacerate his or her subconscious, a psychic injury that could result in violent acts committed in the material world.[17] By the seventeenth century, however, an offshoot of this discursive figuration appears: the spectator that unleashes his or her destructive energies on the object of representation.[18] This spectatorial revenant begins to haunt seventeenth-century theatrical discourse (particularly that generated by playwrights) owing to a combination of real and perceived commercial pressures, proliferation of venues, and alterations in audience behavior.

Recently, Tiffany Stern has reinvigorated the question of how the acquisition of the Blackfriars playhouse by the King's Men shaped dramatists' conception of their plays and audiences in the early seventeenth century.[19] Focusing on material details, such as lighting, scent, perspective, and audience demographics, Stern argues that this event marks a significant period of generic, scenic, and spatial experimentation for seventeenth-century playwrights. In making these claims, Stern suggests that playwrights understood this moment as one imbued with tremendous opportunity. New visual effects (such as candlelight glinting on rich embroidery) and spatial arrangements (such as audience members sitting closer to and on the stage) reinvigorated theater practitioners' creative faculties, resulting in a new set of communicative conventions for a wider range of audiences. If such changes brought new inspiration and opportunity, they also brought forth new uncertainties. I am not as convinced as Stern that playwrights saw the expanding heterogeneity of their audiences only through the lens of opportunity; rather, the inchoate nature of that terrain also caused them to experiment with intra- and extra-diegetic means of controlling what John Day called "the confused audience" in his 1606 play *The Isle of Gulls*.[20] *Knight* provides prime examples of two mechanisms—one narrative and one discursive—through which playwrights attempted to exercise discipline on theatergoers: satire and taxonomy. The first is not new: satire has long functioned as a form of counternarrative to the stories society likes to tell itself, a cutting-but-sanctioned genre that exposes a culture's underbelly, particularly those parts that hegemonic narratives seek to conceal. The second, if also not novel, acuminates in the early modern period, particularly via emerging class distinctions. Long before the early modern period, "the rabble" had been associated with violent and hyperidentified spectatorship; *Knight*, however, provides a variant on this discourse, in which the spectator presents not only a social or a political danger but also a commercial one. In response to this threat, the play attempts a taxonomic discipline in which disruptive spectators who imagine themselves as authorized to judge or confound a play because they are, as Leggatt says, "paying customers," come face to face with their real social limitations.[21] This confrontation shatters both their pleasure in the imaginative mobility offered to them via playgoing and in the social narrative we now call upward mobility. In *Knight*, the character-spectators respond to such assays with another set of experiments involving conventions of interaction, appreciation, and censure.

Rather than attempt to link these behaviors to actual spectatorial practice, this chapter focuses on metadramatic and paratextual representations of subversive audience behavior in order to shed light on one of seventeenth-century England's most significant contributions to the discursive spectator's history. Taking *Knight* as a test case, the following analysis investigates the Citizen and his wife as representational fields onto which certain spectatorial uncertainties, anxieties, and desires are projected and enacted. While the Citizen and his wife embody certain social stereotypes, such as the (potentially) socially mobile but culturally impoverished merchant class, both also echo certain creative concerns, such as the playwright and his work devolving into mere instruments of consumer tastes. Kathleen McLuskie has drawn attention to the "complicate[d] . . . relationship between consumers of theatre and its development as a form of commercial entertainment": this complexity, created by the unstable energies generated by playwright-consumer relationship, is that which *Knight* articulates as a form of aggression.[22] The play presents violence as a force generated by *both* the increased opportunities and the increased pressures of the professional theater's expanding commercial arena, a push-pull dynamic between the drive for artistic expression and the equal (and at times competing) drive for commercial success.

If such concerns proleptically smack of Walter Benjamin's misgivings about mechanical and mass reproduction, it is because both germinate from the same seed: an anxiety about a shift in the locus of control. Both scenarios imagine a world in which the artistic object loses its ability to discipline the spectator's movement and taste; instead, the artistic product becomes an entity moved and shaped by mass demands.[23] The forces of consumerism are not articulated as unilateral but as circulatory; that is, violence becomes an essential ingredient in both communication and interpretation. Writing at the commencement of the most brutal world conflict in history, Benjamin describes twentieth-century spectatorship through terms that seem forged at the fires of modern martial technologies, impersonal, efficient, and anesthetizing:

> From an alluring perspective or persuasive structure of sound the
> work of art of the Dadaists became an instrument of ballistics. It hit
> the spectator like a bullet, it happened to him, thus acquiring a
> tactile quality. It promoted a demand for film, the distracting ele-
> ment of which is also primarily tactile, being based on changes of
> place and focus which periodically assail the spectator. The painting
> invites the spectator to contemplation; before it the spectator can
> abandon himself to his associations. Before the movie frame he can-
> not do so. No sooner has his eye grasped a scene than it is already
> changed. It cannot be arrested. . . . This constitutes the shock effect
> of the film, which, like all shocks, should be cushioned by height-
> ened presence of mind. By means of its technical structure, the film
> has taken the physical shock effect out of the wrappers in which
> Dadaism had, as it were, kept it inside the moral shock effect.[24]

Benjamin's primary critique here is that film, unlike Dadaist art, "assails" the spectator incessantly, leaving no moment for contemplation and critique, a practice he imagines creates a viewing subject endlessly hindered by a kind of affective aphony. Bearing the indelible imprint of twentieth-century history and technology, Benjamin's traumatized spectatorial subject seems isolated by its precise contingencies. But, as Ellen Mackay has aptly demonstrated, the ballistics metaphor pervades both anti- and protheatrical writings about the early modern theater.[25] Citing authors such as Stephen Gosson, who imagines the theatre's "gaul[ing]" effect on the spectator's imagination as a "gunshotte of affection," and Thomas Heywood, who anecdotally narrates an event wherein a troupe of marauding Spaniards is put to flight by the mere presentation of a stage battle, Mackay maps a discursive tradition that articulates the theater's affective powers as containing the potential to "impact [its] beholders like gunfire."[26]

Benjamin's critique of modern spectatorship, however, is as much about a particular representative technology as about affective impact in that it meditates on how different presentations of a similar subject matter collate different spectatorial communities. The work of art-ritual interpellates the few, the believers, while the film speaks to the masses, oddly enough, through a pretense of interpellating the individual: "Fascism [a political ideology for which film is the disseminating apogee] sees its salvation in giving these masses not their right but instead a chance to express themselves."[27] Film, as a representational medium, here aids in fascism's subversion of genuine mass liberation (in this case, the failure to abolish private property) for something more illusorily liberating—the chance to express or recognize oneself in an image writ large for all to see. More similar to this aspect of Benjamin's critique is one found in the 1610 dedicatory epistle to Edward Sharpham's play *Cupid's Whirligig,* which describes the ability of another kind of apparatus—a paratextual one[28]—to communicate both with the masses and with the solitary reader: "Sir, I must needs discharge two Epistles upŏ you the one the Readers, that should be like haile shot that scatters and strikes a multitude, the other dedicatory, like a bullet, that aimes onely at your selfe."[29] While all of the above examples imagine popular entertainment as both affective and physical forces with ample potential to wound, Benjamin's and Sharpham's address an additional complexity: the question of how certain mass communicative-artistic media emplace spectators in various kinds of ideological (or imagined) communities via an appeal to them as individual subjects. Unlike Benjamin, whose concerns ultimately reside in mass culture's large-scale social effects, or Benedict Anderson, who explores how such communities are formed (particularly in the service of nationalism),[30] Sharpham displays far less certainty that they exist or, if they do, that he has any concrete understanding of their constitution. Stating that his opening address "*should* scatter like hail shotte*," Sharpham quickly moves into the imaginative realm of interpellative failure, via images of the play's alternative future in obscurity. It might, he acknowledges, reach only a single individual—its dedicatee, Robert Hayman—in which case the play "cannot live above an hour." From the vantage point offered by Sharpham's cultural nexus of time, place, and profession, no certainty about imaginative communities' cohesiveness as an object of study or manipulation exists, at least with regard to the theatrical marketplace.

The idea that the theater could produce communities antagonistic to its aims and successes coheres in the early seventeenth century, and its material-ization shapes many of *Knight*'s concerns. What sets *Knight* apart from con-temporaneous send-ups of London's theatergoing "types"[31] is its extended representation of audience perception and response or, more broadly, the way it imagines the theater to access and engage the spectator through a dynamic Masten calls "contentious collaboration."[32] Depicting this process as one marked by violence and cognitive dissonance (rather than the lulling seduction imagined by the phrase "willing suspension of disbelief"), the play dramatizes its own vulnerability and reckless dismemberment. However, *Knight* also imagines an equally violent response in that it seeks to enforce the yoking of spectatorial and social taxonomies as a means of audience disci-pline. Rather than the by-product or result of theatergoing, then, *Knight* presents violence as one of the primary energies generated by the interaction of spectator-consumer and play.

"To Thine Own Censure": Alienation, Disidentification, and Aggression as Audience Response

To yoke alienation, theater, and spectatorship invariably invokes Brecht. The theatrical praxis of *Verfremdungseffekt* sought to estrange the spectator from the kind of well-oiled (hence unproblematized) identification that Brecht believed bourgeois modes of popular theater cultivated.[33] Encompassing the potential to transform complacent viewing practices into active, critical engagement with theatrical spectacle, alienation cultivated a politically active cultural con-sciousness and subject. But while Brecht saw *Verfremdungseffekt* as a positive force, he still imagined it as something that is *done to* the spectator: "The audience [is] hindered from simply identifying itself with the characters in the play. Acceptance or rejection of their actions and utterances [is] meant to take place on a conscious plane, instead of, as hitherto, in the audience's subconscious."[34] In crafting a theatrical strategy that sought to shatter the spectator's identificatory processes, Brecht posits that "right looking" *requires* a kind of psychic disruption or estrangement: "The spectator was no longer in any way allowed to submit to an experience uncritically (and without practical consequences) by means of simple empathy with the characters in a play. The production took the subject matter and the incidents shown and put them through a process of alienation: the alienation that is necessary to all understanding."[35] Epic theater, then, impedes sentimental cathexes fostered in the spectator's subconscious by thrusting them into the light of consciousness, a process that recalls one of the most influential Western narratives of spectatorship—Plato's cave. Like the poor, tethered captive who, even once unbound, must be forcibly dragged from his familiar realm of darkness into the dazzling-but-agonizing sunlight, Brecht's spectator may ultimately benefit from *Verfremdungseffekt,* but the mechanisms by which such transformation occur must traumatize before they enlighten.

Multiple studies of the influence of early modern drama—particularly Shakespeare—on Brecht exist,[36] and clearly the alienation depicted in (and ostensibly generated by watching) *Knight* could be placed on a genealogy of theater's affective strategies that includes Brecht's *Verfremdungseffekt.* However, *Knight* depicts alienation both as a mark of spectatorial agency—an always available strategy of rejecting identification with what is presented onstage—*and* as an identificatory disruption that could be punitively deployed against the spectator.[37] Although not a term associated with Brecht, identification is an essential part of *Verfremdungseffekt* in that the spectator must decathect from character and narrative and counteridentify with a more politicized, less strictly self-referential entity. *Knight,* however, proposes a viewing subject that disidentifies (a term I discuss subsequently) with the character presented onstage as his or her analogue and counteridentifies with a kind of theatrical *imago*—a self-image created through idealized fictional representations gleaned from various theatrical and literary influences.

If, in theatrical parlance at least, *alienation* inevitably raises specters of Brecht, *identification* cannot help but signify the term's psychoanalytic lineage. Freud's most expansive work on the subject can be found in *Group Psychology and the Analysis of the Ego.* Stating that in its most basic form, identification is "the earliest expression of an emotional tie with another person," Freud goes on to suggest how continuous identificatory dissolutions and reconstructions continuously (re)constitute the subject over time: "[Iden-tification] may arise with every new perception of a common quality shared with some other person who is not an object of the sexual instinct. The more important this common quality is, the more successful may this partial identification become, and it may thus represent the beginning of a new tie."[38] Jacques Lacan's narrative of primary identification—the mirror stage—foregrounds deficit more than Freud's in that identification becomes an illu-sory mechanism by which the subject attains a sense of wholeness, a kind of signifying potency that exists only in the Real.[39] While the spectatorial identification depicted in *Knight* shares qualities with both Freud's and Lacan's concepts (it is both mobile and partly generated by a desire to experi-ence or "see" a more idealized version of the self), it is forged more via theatrical archetypes than familial or corporeal ones. If, as Diana Fuss sug-gests, subjectivity can be understood as "the history of one's identifications," *Knight* proposes a spectatorial subject constituted by the history of its *literary* identifications—cathexes that have been largely formed from the material provided by early modern commercial entertainment.[40]

The final "modern" theoretical concept I use here—disidentification—functions more as an informing concept for my argument than a key term. Judith Butler sees disidentification as a potential strategy for subverting hege-monic identificatory templates, one that may allow the subject to open ave-nues of subjective and political resistance.[41] José Esteban Muñoz subsequently claims that disidentification is an inherently political act, arguing that it "nei-ther opts to assimilate within such a structure nor strictly opposes it; rather, disidentification . . . works on and against dominant ideology."[42] It is the term's deep investiture in the arena of identity politics that renders it particu-larly difficult in both an early modern context and with regard to this play. While *Knight* is marked by class stratification and its attendant frictions, the play is not overtly interested in the political implications of this agential expression on the part of the citizen class: what the Citizen initially protests is not the plight of his class but its theatrical (mis)representation. Despite this difference, *Knight* does dramatize an extended act of spectatorial resis-tance, and this portrayal of agency, however satiric and constructed, resonates with Butler's and Muñoz's concept. Not simply a psychic turning away from "the uneasy sense of standing under a sign to which one does and does not belong,"[43] disidentification entails the moment when the subject attempts to invoke or generate a counterdiscourse as a means of enacting an alternative signifying register.

Of course, *Knight*'s disidentifying subjects are representations of spectators: they cannot "realize" or "enact" anything except within theatrical space
in which they are given voice. However, the appearance of characters who
assert their right to have a say about what they see because they have "paid"
in a play largely about early modern spectatorial practice aptly demonstrates
the discursive spectator's imbrication with the figure of the consumer, at least
in the mind of those writing for the early modern stage. Indeed, Alexander
Leggatt has surmised that the play's failure resulted from its insistence on the
theater as a commercial industry as much as an artistic enterprise (if not more
so), thereby reducing the relationship between spectator and play to a mere
"cash transaction."[44] While not yet associated with capitalist economic structures and commodity fetishism, the term *consumer* was extant in the Renaissance, and its most common early modern usage suggests a similar mindless
appetitiveness: "a person or thing which devours, wastes, or destroys."[45]
Whereas the most common (and transhistorical) discourse about the violent
spectator articulates this figure largely via the hypodermic model (what the
spectator sees, she or he might do), the consumer-spectator model imagines
violence as a form of spectatorial agency, where the spectator can reject, even
destroy, the product for which she or he has paid.

The play begins by dramatizing versions of both discursive models (the
hypodermic and the violently agential). The boy who delivers the play's prologue manages only three lines of introductory verse before being vociferously
interrupted by an audience member: "Down with your title, boy; down with
your title!" (Ind. 9). The heckler, whom we soon learn is a grocer and avid
theatergoer, charges the company with marking London's citizens as targets
for disrespect, even mockery. What causes him finally to act on his frustra-
tion, however, is rather more complex: "This seven years there hath been
plays at this house; I have observed it, you have still girds at citizens, and
now you call your play *The London Merchant*" (Ind. 6–9). His claim that the
theater actively "studies" for material designed to "abuse your betters" (17)
suggests a kind of spectatorial victim complex: the grocer has been "abused"
by having to witness the misrepresentation of a figure with which he identifies. Almost the exact obverse of the alienation produced in the Lacanian
mirror stage, where the child sees a more perfect version of itself in its reflection, the commercial stage offers the Citizen a representational corollary that
he perceives as diminished and incomplete. The stage surrogate he will propose, however, skews in the opposite direction. While the Citizen insists on
a degree of verisimilitude—"I will have a citizen, and he shall be of my own

trade" (30)—he chooses his young apprentice to play the part and states that grocer-character must "do admirable things," actions that turn out to be steeped in the romantic ideals of nobility, chivalry, and self-sacrifice.[46] Book-ended by a structural fantasy (the younger man destined to follow in the Grocer's footsteps who has the potential to "do great things" in his profession and on the stage—the two arenas in which the Citizen is most invested) and a historical-mythological one (the medieval icon of the knight), the self-image the Citizen stages suggests that theatrical spectatorship functions as a kind of vicarious ego trip.[47] The model of spectatorship parodied here suggests a highly individuated form of spectatorial cathexis, one in which the viewer desires a characterological model with which she or he can readily identify. However, this paradigm shifts uneasily with the Grocer's rather extreme man-ner of protest, which echoes the militant, often political, protester's battle cry: "Down with your title, boy; down with your title!" Despite this provoca-tive rhetoric, this act of public resistance finds no echo in the audience. As the Grocer's protestations do not originate in any sort of shared public senti-ment (at least none made manifest in the play), we might well ask what sort of authority sanctions his right to interrupt and alter this stage production at will?

One possibility is that the Citizen functions allegorically. Elias Canetti cites discontent as a primary facet of the social taxonomy loosely termed "the crowd": "One of the most striking traits of the inner life of the crowd is the feeling of being persecuted, a peculiar angry sensitiveness and irritability directed against those it has once and forever nominated as enemies."[48] Reducing the "boundless hate of a confused audience"[49] to a single voice may constitute a narrative exercise that serves an authorial fantasy of control, but an additional specter haunts this character's construction. While Beaumont portrays the Citizen and his wife as the sole dissenters in *Knight,* he underpins their right to disrupt the production with an alternative form of authority: money. As Leslie Thompson has noted, the play obsessively meditates on playgoing as a form of commercial exchange,[50] an emphasis most pronounced in the play's opening where the connections between theatrical performance and money occur on multiple planes. On hearing that the company is with-out shawms (double-reeded instruments), the Citizen states he will pay for them himself "rather than we'll be without them" (101). In response to his wife's proposal that their apprentice play a role in the "new" play, the Citizen recalls that Rafe "should have played Jeronimo with a shoemaker for a wager," a bet with money at stake (85–86). The injunction therefore suggests that the theatrical enterprise's components (actors, company, props, plays) are commodities available for hire, an exchange system that extends beyond the professional domain and spills over into the amateur one (Rafe would play Jeronimo for a wager). In making these connections, *Knight* suggests that playing, in *all* its forms, is imagined as inextricably linked to forms of monetary exchange.

*   *   *

The Induction's conflation of confrontational and commercial dynamics is not limited to the Citizen's complete rejection of the original play; he also violates the performance space. His actions here initially seem more in line with the hypodermic model, as the Citizen's aggressive behavior follows from what he witnesses onstage. However, his responses are again directed at the social microcosm of the theatrical product (the play) rather than the wider world. And, while articulated through embodied (he climbs onto the stage from "below") rather than linguistic resistance, this representation of the Citizen's actions is informed as much by cultural narratives about disruptive theatergoers as by actual audience behavior. While the space of the stage in the hall playhouses was, in a sense, regularly "transgressed" by the practice of stool sitting, where certain members of the audience would seat themselves on the stage platform, the play articulates the Citizen's incursion into both narrative and performance space as a conscious attempt to ameliorate the psychic injury he feels the theater perpetually enacts upon him.[51] It is not until some fifty-one lines after his initial complaint that he calls for stools so he and his wife can be seated on the stage, suggesting that during the majority of his confrontation with the Boy (lines 4–55), he stands and faces him in a posture of conflict. Such positioning would also serve to reproduce the divide between the majority of the "real" audience watching the play from the dramatic action, creating a visual metaphor for the sort of estrangement that the Citizen protests. By the time he and his wife are seated, the Citizen has successfully renegotiated what he is going to see, suggesting that his move to this more marginal area indicates a willingness to return to the customary sphere of audience participation. However, in doing so, the couple flaunts two further conventions: the privilege of sitting onstage costs extra, and women did not usually participate in this form of audience behavior.[52] Thompson notes the discrepancy between the couple's original seats and their new ones, but claims that the act of switching seats suggests "the implication that [they] too had paid to [sit in this space]."[53] The play, however, makes no note of such a transaction, suggesting the Citizen feels entitled both to make decisions about what he sees and what he pays for. The theatergoer becomes the customer; the satiric acrimony directed at the spectator is met with countermoves of the professional theater consumer.

This tension provides the armature around which the play is structured. Rather than disposing with the original city comedy entirely, the company moves haphazardly between the two narratives. Similarly, the play alternates between configuring the citizens through consumer and hypodermic models of violent spectatorship. Transitions between the plays consist mostly of the couple's vocal demands to see more of "their" production. While some of these interruptions take the form of innocuous commentary, "How likest thou this, wench?" (2.91), many devolve into physical threats made against the playhouse or players: "Sirrah, you scurvy boy, bid the players send Rafe, or by God's—and they do not, I'll tear some of their periwigs behind their heads" (Int. 1, 11–13).[54] The Citizen's recourse to intimidation tends to occur when the stage action moves too far afield from the couple's desires—a visceral reaction that functions as a structural asymptote to *The London Merchant*'s forward motion despite the Citizens' multilateral resistance strategies. At other times, however, the Citizen's acrimony seems directed at a different sort of disenfranchisement, one connected to the egoic rupture the play illustrates in its first scene. In act 4, at his wife's suggestion, the Citizen demands an elaborate romance scenario as a vehicle for Rafe, and his request meets not only with resistance but condescension:

> Boy: Sir, if you will imagine this to be done already, you shall hear
>   them talk together. But we cannot present a house covered with
>   black velvet and a lady in beaten gold.
> Citizen: Sir, boy, let's ha' as you can then.
> Boy: Besides, it will show ill-favoredly to have a Citizen's prentice
>   to court a king's daughter.
> Citizen: Will it so, sir? You are well read in histories! I pray you,
>   what was Sir Dagonet? Was he not prentice to a Citizen in
>   London? Read the play of the *The Four Prentices of London* where
>   they toss their pikes so. I pray you, fetch him in, sir; fetch him
>   in. (42–52)

What piques the Citizen's full-blown anger is not the company's refusal to comply with the couple's vision for the scene—"We cannot present a house covered with black velvet and a lady in beaten gold"—but the Boy's refusal to comply with his vision of *himself*. "It will show ill-favoredly to have a grocer's prentice to court a king's daughter." The first rebuff still allows for creative authority: the Citizen is told only that he will have to imagine or mentally create the material setting of what he wants to see. The second, however, abruptly shut downs both his imaginative agency and his identificatory fantasy of class mobility[55] by shutting down the subversive play of identity the performance has heretofore allowed. This sudden intrusion of a social discourse with teeth (that of class taxonomy—a grocer's apprentice cannot court a king's daughter) into the more flexible parameters of the play world delivers a jolt that converts the Citizen's willingness to collaborate into angry opposition. Unlike the resistance he musters when his creative will is thwarted (surly threats and bullying), here he initiates a full-stop refusal of the representation with which he is confronted, a response that recalls his embodied resistance in the Induction.

While both sorts of resistance the Citizen mounts enact potential modes of spectatorial defiance, they are not the same. The Citizen's threats posit a performative self, one that participates, albeit disruptively, in the discourse set up by both the fictional world of the play and the larger theatrical community (spectators, playwrights, and players), but does not extend beyond it. His response *is* defiance, his aggression confined to a linguistic exchange that deals exclusively with and takes place within the theater. However, the Citizen's actions in the Induction and the act 4 confrontation are motivated by something extratheatrical: a need to resist something that comes dangerously close to the Citizen's self-image, something that threatens dissolution of the self rather than its construction. At such moments, the Citizen moves from the language of intimidation to that of alteration and from the act of voicing dissatisfaction to that of disidentification. He first forces a change of course for the play's narrative and, in the later scene, challenges the social narrative the play attempts to impose on his protagonist (and by extension, on him). Using the combative image of the apprentices "tossing their pikes" from Thomas Heywood's 1594 *The Four Prentices of London,* the Citizen authorizes his projected self-image using a theatrical (rather than sociological or historical) archive. In doing so, he performs a different act of aggression, one that mimics the sort he imagines the play and the theater more generally to have performed on him.[56] The Citizen's primary complaint against the entire "citizen play" genre is that it presents him with an image of himself with which he does not want to identify and from which he feels alienated. He counters this experience by publicly insisting on an alternative version—a *bricolage* of fragments (images, narratives, and language) left in his memory from previous theatrical experiences. While some of this material, such as the militant apprentices from Heywood's play, provides the Citizen with positive identificatory templates, some of it must, by default, come from the flotsam left in the wake of the multiple misrecognitions he has witnessed over the course of years. The process through which the Citizen constructs his counterimage, then, does not establish or recover some sort of originary identity but suggests a tenuous, post-traumatic piecing together of self. And while this "refashioning" dynamic suggests the sort feared by social authorities, here it is inextricably bound to class identity and the imaginative maneuverability that resides at the consumerist fantasy's heart.

The process articulated above echoes one that Cynthia Marshall identifies as shaping early modern subjectivity more generally: "What a culture in its official versions of itself is suturing together and publicly solidifying—such as the outlines of the individual subject in early modern England—texts designed for entertainment or mediation might be busily undoing . . . the formation and dissolution of the self are locked in a profoundly paradoxical tension."[57] Significantly, a similar "paradoxical tension" informs *Knight*'s version of the violent spectator, one illustrated by the choice of Heywood's *Four Prentices* as the Citizen's self-fashioning ur-text. His brief reference to the pike-tossing apprentices comes from a scene in Heywood's play where two brothers (one a grocer's apprentice and one a goldsmith's) meet abroad after being separated during their service in the First Crusade. Since each believes the other is dead, they do not recognize each other and end up fighting in single combat for their respective lieges. The "tossing of pikes" that the Citizen calls upon to conjure up images of valor and solidarity actually precedes a critical rift in Heywood's play: the moment when the brothers viciously turn on one another, intent on destroying that which is nearest to their own selves because they have fallen so deeply under the sway of their new identities as men of courage and military prowess. In referencing this scene, the Citizen (and the play) suggests that the construction and destruction of identity are inevitable by-products of theatrical spectatorship. Further, it implies that as the spectator forges new avenues of identification, even those constructed from the baseless fabric of cultural or theatrical representation, she or he risks losing a vital part of the self through the act of willful forgetting.

Palimpsestic and volatile, this identificatory model shares certain qualities with Freud's theory of mourning and melancholia. As Tammy Clewell notes, "The work of mourning . . . entails a kind of hyperremembering, a process of obsessive recollection during which the [subject] resuscitates the existence of the lost other in the space of the psyche, replacing an actual absence with an imaginary presence."[58] If one substitutes "mourning" with "spectatorship" and "psyche" with "theater" here, Clewell's statement provides a surprisingly accurate account of *Knight*'s dramatization of the Citizen's identificatory processes. However, the Citizen's response to those moments when the play and performers sunder his identificatory cathexes more resembles the behavior of the melancholic. The primary difference between the mourner and the melancholic exists in their response to the lost object of desire. Irrevocably torn from the loved object, the mourner, over time, moves through the violence of loss and reinvests in a new, different object; the melancholic remains fixated, assuaging his pain by feasting on it: "The ego wants to incorporate this [lost] object into itself. . . . It wants to do so by devouring it."[59] Rather than replace the love object, the melancholic consumes it, an act that ostensibly destroys in order to preserve. By "incorporating" the lost object, the consuming subject becomes reconfigured, producing a subjectively hybrid entity. But rather than fully merge into a unified psyche, this "new" egoic mutation exists in a state of discord with itself, endlessly simulating the acts of violence that formed it in the first place: "If the love for the object . . . takes refuge in narcissistic identification, then the hate comes into operation on this substitutive object [now the self], abusing it, debasing it, making it suffer and deriving sadistic satisfaction from its suffering."[60]

Despite the historical chasm stretching between Beaumont's Citizen and Freud's melancholic, juxtaposing them illuminates a connection between the way in which violent spectatorship's psychic and material realms were imagined to coexist. Like the melancholic, who attempts to regain control over that which she or he has lost by consuming it, the Citizen tries to master his theatrical representation by enforcing his status as consumer.[61] And, similar to the miscegenated and self-loathing construct produced by the melancholic's consumption, the new representational entity created by the spectator-consumer in *Knight* also ends up being constituted through fragmentation and rupture. Owing to the Citizen's intervention, the amalgamated play's narrative structure is, by default, organized around the principle of fragmentation; notably, the play seems to turn against itself whenever one of its diegetic trajectories begins to develop. From the Citizen's first interruption of *The London Merchant*, to the multiple interjections made by him and his wife, to the awkward segueing between the parallel plays, *Knight* disrupts any possibility of forming the sort of cathexes with its own audience that the Citizen so desperately wants to cultivate. The play's fractured rhythms produce yet another layer of audience alienation, this time one that has the potential to traverse the representational realm. As Leggatt points out, "[In *The Knight*] the audience that rebels is not the real one but . . . the real audience watching the rebellion is made to think of its own role and responsibilities."[62] By corralling its "real" spectators firmly in the metaspectatorial realm, one where they are pushed to focus more on themselves than on what occurs in the play, *Knight* seems to want to offer little room for either interpretive agency or affective investment.

By making this claim, I may seem to stand in agreement with critics who claim that *Knight* was a commercial failure largely because its audience was "not ready" either for the self-reflexive viewing practices it demands or the sophisticated commentary on the nature of spectatorship it offers.[63] More germane for my argument here, however, is that the play's purposeful alienation of its audience entails yet another kind of violence that may be deployed against the spectator. Twice in the play, the Boy addresses the "real" audience: once at 3.298, "I pray, gentlemen, rule him," and once at 4.53, "It is not our fault, gentlemen." While these asides could be seen as attempts to include the audience, they function equally effectively as a means of silencing them. In asking the "gentlemen" to intervene in the contest of wills between the company and the couple, the Boy places the real audience in a double bind. On one hand, the Citizens are ruining (or at least altering the experience of) the play they paid to see. Audience intervention was not uncommon in the early modern theater, particularly when one of the spectators was acting disruptively, a reality that Heywood mentions in *The Gull's Hornbook*: "But if the rabble, with a full throat, cry: 'Away with the fool!' you were worse than a madman to tarry by it."[64] In the case of *Knight*, however, any intervention by "real" spectators would inevitably associate them with the Citizen and Wife, two characters the play holds up as targets of ridicule owing to their spectatorial naïveté and lack of theatrical etiquette. Later, when the Boy states "it is not our fault, gentlemen," a comment that follows closely on his act 3 plea for help, his abdication of responsibility for what is happening onstage seems to implicate not only the Citizen and his wife but the play's entire audience. If it is not the company's fault, whose is it? The citizen couple's? The protocapitalist system of theatrical patronage where audiences arguably have a "right" to interfere with a production because they are paying for it?

Or does the play insinuate that the audience has a responsibility not only to exhibit a modicum of self-control but to police each other? If so, whose behavioral standards should set the precedent and why? If one of the real spectators *were* to do something, would they not simply be replicating the very behavior they were opposing? Despite its exploration of spectatorial agency, the play does not make a space for the real spectators' voice(s), but places them in a similarly disenfranchised position as that to which the Citizen claims to have been subject in the play's opening. It is not, perhaps, that the early seventeenth-century audience did not "get" what the *Knight* was trying to communicate but that they got it all too well.

Parthenogenesis, Plague, and Bad Press: The Afterlife of Performance

The combative dynamics that structure *Knight's* play text also inform its paratexts. As Masten points out, the 1613 quarto introduces the play via a complex genealogy, in which publisher Walter Burre's dedicatory epistle suggests a commercial narrative structured along the *bildungsroman's* trajectory: the play is an "unfortunate child" whose parents immediately expose him to the "wide world" because he "was so unlike his brethren" (4–5).[65] Having been nearly "smothered" by rejection, the "ragged" infant is rescued and "fostered" by Burre, who keeps it in his care until it can "speak for itself" (14–17). After several years, Burre claims that *Knight* was "desirous to try its fortune in the world" (18); however, he fears it may once again be "slighted and traduced" (20) by an unappreciative and ignorant public. In framing the play as an entity with tragic origins and a potentially brutal future, Burre linguistically and narratively echoes its communicative dynamics. His rendition of *Knight's* origins tells a story of violent reception and rejection, near-destruction, and finally, a search for acceptance that seems destined for further repudiation. Punctuated by terms such as "exposed," "smothered," "antipathy," "misprision," "revenge," "challenge," and "breaking," the dedicatory epistle both narrates *Knight's* commercial failure and places the blame for its theatrical demise squarely on the shoulders of its callous spectators.

If Burre's version of the commercial theater depicts it as a heartless and capricious realm of existence, it is also a relentlessly patriarchal one. The (male) author as parthenogenetic source of his work appears widely in Western literature;[66] however, Burre adapts the usual consanguinities by adding two surrogate fathers and a sibling. After being "relieved and cherished" (10–11) by patron Robert Keysar and "fostered privately" (14) for two years by Burre, the play again sets out to try its fortune. Should it fail, the epistle mentions a possible plan B: "If it be slighted or traduced, it hopes his father will beget him a younger brother" (20–22), a surrogate-sibling that must somehow demonstrate his brother's true nature by making "the world" see the error of its earlier judgment. How, exactly, that will occur remains unspecified, but Burre's language suggests a sort of chivalric tournament in which the winner's point-of-view will, by fiat, be accepted.[67]

While Burre's use of the paternal *topos* fits his primary aim—to present the play as a misprized work of greatness—it sits less comfortably as an introduction to a play rife with mother-son relationships. *The London Merchant* focuses on Mistress Merrythought's relationships with her two sons. Foregrounding the worn meme of divided affections (she despises the elder and favors the younger), the narrative makes this schism manifest by dividing the sons in terms of legacy: Mistress Merrythought has "laid up" for her younger son and informs her elder that he must go to his father or shift for himself.[68] Maternal and financial connections also permeate the Citizens' play; here, they surface in the relationship between Nell, the grocer's wife, and Rafe, her husband's apprentice. While not her biological child, Nell constantly refers to Rafe as a foster son for whom she is responsible both physically and fiscally. Her motherly pride in Rafe's stage talents is evident throughout the play; she frequently refers to him as "our Rafe" and "a good boy."[69] As the couple's "man,"[70] Rafe's relationship to them is necessarily structured around the concept of exchange; however, the Wife's free-handed generosity toward Rafe over the course of the play, as demonstrated through her insistence on paying the fictional "debts" incurred during his stage sojourn ("Rafe shall not be beholding . . . give him his money, George" (3.174–75)) suggests a relationship based as much on genuine affection as conscription.

Laurie Osborne reads Burre's excision of the play's maternal dynamics as a reauthorizing tactic, one informed by the play's relationship to and portrayal of female theatrical spectatorship: "Even while [Burre's] dedication adopts the prevailing rhetoric of Nell's motherly support of Rafe, it omits all maternal or feminine reference. . . . The effect of this strategy, as I read it, is an attempt to retrieve the powers over the fortune of *The Knight of the Burning Pestle* from the hands of the female audience within the play, and, very possibly, the female audience outside the play."[71] Following a line of critical discourse initiated by Jean Howard and Stephen Orgel—that women's presence as theatergoers and entertainment consumers was pervasive and anxiogenic in the early modern era—Osborne sees Nell as "reveal[ing] the potential power of the paying audience—most definitely including the women—over what is represented onstage."[72] Toward the essay's close, Osborne shifts to the play's historical context, revisiting Marion Taylor's hypothesis that *Knight*'s failure may have been prompted by Lady Arbella Stuart's displeasure at the play's mocking reference to one of her former romantic attachments.[73] In addition to providing a concrete example of women's potential power over theatrical representation, Osborne suggests this narrative might explain Burre's systematic exclusion of women from *Knight*'s network of preservation. Yet Burre's epistle never suggests that the play fell into political disfavor; rather, he attributes its failure to "the wide world," a phrase that more recalls the combined, undifferentiated forces from Shakespeare's "wooden O" than individual, gendered, or aristocratic displeasure. And while the epistle may excise the maternal aspects of *Knight*'s lineage, it does not, like many of the period's writings, demonize women as spectators, spectacles, or paying customers.[74]

My claim here is not that either Burre or *Knight* seeks to protect women (either real or representational) from the violence that shapes its spectatorial dynamics. Indeed, *The London Merchant* diegetically subjects both Luce and Mrs. Merrythought to the emotional cruelty and mistreatment often understood (for women at least) as an inevitable epiphenomenon of marriage,[75] and Nell's affective response to moments when the play threatens violence against women mimics actual physical suffering. As critics such as Howard, Orgel, and Osborne argue,[76] women's presence in and importance to the early modern professional theater was a source of commercial, legal, and moral anxiety for those who ran and regulated it, and these concerns play a role in *Knight*'s portrayal of female spectatorship. However, critics have tended to use Nell as a fulcrum for measuring whether or how women's presence and participation in the theater subverted patriarchal norms or served to reify them.[77] In doing so, these scholars assign Nell a kind of representational verisimilitude; that is, they seem to suggest Beaumont crafted a female character largely based on empirical evidence of female theatergoers' behaviors.[78] In the analysis that follows, I focus less on how Nell's spectatorial predilections suggest or excavate early modern women's viewing practices and more on the type of violent spectatorship the play associates with her character—both that which is enacted on her as a viewer and that which she enacts on the play. At least as responsible as her husband in reshaping the company's original production, few critics credit Nell with providing a great deal of the imaginative accelerant that kindles the new play into being.[79] In part, this oversight may occur because unlike her husband, who *forces* changes to the play, Nell traffics in the power of suggestion. Rather than the kind of violence perpetuated by the aggressively disruptive playgoer (the Grocer), Nell's presence suggests an alternative form of destruction—that which can be done by popular opinion and word of mouth.

That the success or failure of early modern plays in large part rested on *viva voce* seems indisputable, yet there is little concrete evidence to support this claim. However, as Charles Whitney argues, "Playgoers carry their theatrical experiences with them from the theatre and continue to absorb, assimilate and apply them. In the early modern period, this process generated much of the publicity of the stage, not the least being imitation and casual discussion of dramatic material."[80] Whitney's claim resonates with recent work done on the early modern public sphere and its production. For example, in order to produce the "contact zone where different publics encounter each other . . . irregularly, unpredictably, and at odd angles,"[81] various places for discursive contact (in this case about the public theater) must be in operation: the tavern, the marketplace, and, of course, the theater itself. In fact, Burre's epistle could be seen as metaphorizing the way that information and opinion *about* any given play travels from person to person and place to place. Read thusly, it becomes doubly curious that Burre creates an overwhelmingly masculine narrative in the epistle when the play exercises its anxieties about *viva voce*'s influence primarily through Nell.

Perhaps Beaumont simply draws on the abiding convention of woman-as-gossip, a concept that took a more definitively pejorative turn in the seventeenth century.[82] Numerous critics have shown that "the gossip" represented a ubiquitous threat to male hegemony in the period. As Karen Newman argues, "Talk in women then is dangerous because it is perceived as a usurpation of multiple forms of authority, a threat to order and male sovereignty, to masculine control of commodity exchange, to a desired hegemonic male sexuality."[83] At face value, gossip seems like an innocuous activity; however, gossiping (not unlike spectating) could constitute and promote a danger to the established social order. Certainly, insofar as gossip is an essentially social activity, Nell enacts a more convivial form of spectatorship than her husband. If he is primarily absorbed in controlling and investing in his onstage creation, she regularly addresses the community formed by the various members that constitute *Knight*'s performing and viewing community, actor and audience member alike. And, at the play's close, Nell invites the entire audience to attend her home for "a pottle of wine and a pipe of tobacco," extending a fantasy of near-Arcadian post-show camaraderie. But, while the maternal-hostess stereotype undoubtedly provides some of the material for Nell's template (as it does for so many female characters in Jacobean city comedies), it is worth noting that the play systematically excises her *and* her husband from the sort of *bonhomie* she wants to cultivate. Despite the fact that she addresses the "gentleman" or audience ten times, they never respond or acknowledge her presence, a silence that suggests a fermenting hostility, particularly given the play's portrayal of spectatorship as a network of various aggressions.[84] Taking into consideration *Knight's* emphasis on social isolation (via the play's rejection of the citizen couple's exclusion from the realm of ideal, even acceptable, spectatorship), I use the term *word of mouth* to refer to the (pejorative) discursive channels through which information travels. Additionally, *word of mouth* places emphasis on the affective and informational patterns of circulation and transmission on which this reading focuses, as opposed to *gossip*, which suggests a focus on what is seen and said.

Nell cites a variety of oral networks and traditions over the play's course; tellingly, most of these references correspond to other forms of popular culture. While she has self-avowedly never attended the theater, she seems to know quite a bit about it: she exhorts Rafe to "speak a huffing part" (Ind. 75), asks one of the boy players if he had not been taught by "Maister Monk-ester" (Nathan Field's teacher),[85] and later states that Rafe's performance cannot be matched by any of London's "twelve companies" (2.202). While the play's editors gloss this phrase as referring to the twelve livery companies of London, there may be a play on London's multiple theater companies as well.[86] Nell tends to cross-reference particular narrative episodes in the play(s) with alternative popular culture forms; for example, during Rafe's conflict with Barbaroso, the barber-giant, she reminisces about a "great Dutchman" on display to London's populace[87] and, during the third interlude, asks one of the boys who has come out to dance whether he can tumble or eat fire. In the episode that arguably caused one critic to refer to Nell as having "an inner personality of libidinous violence,"[88] she eggs Rafe on during his combat with Barbaroso by calling out, "There, boy: kill, kill, kill, kill, kill, Rafe" (3.349)—a response that calls to mind the stereotypical bloodthirsty spectators of the bear pits. In part, Nell's motley references remind us that London's popular culture was not restricted to the professional theater; more significant, however, is that most of Nell's references come from things she has heard about rather than seen. She has not seen plays but has heard about them ("I was ne'er at one of these plays, as they say" (Ind. 51–52); she mentions a Scotsman who "they say" was higher than the fabled Dutchman (1.271–72); she supplements Rafe's reference to the "Prince of Portigo" by confiding in her husband that "they say the King of Portugal cannot sit at his meat, but the giants and ettins will come and snatch it from him" (1.231–33). Indeed, Nell uses the phrase "they say" (or a near variant) seven times and, in each instance, uses it to introduce information gleaned from alternate, even competing, forms of entertainment: specialty acts, romance narratives, impromptu amateur performances.[89] Additionally, she mentions other forms of oral dissemination of information and narratives, such as criers (2.348) and folklore (see n. 80). Her suggestion that Rafe lead the company's "youths" in a procession "with drums, and guns, and flags, and march to Mile End in pompous fashion" (5.58–59) recalls the means of publicity that Tiffany Stern claims was often used by professional companies: "The actors [would] parade through the city 'crying the play,' which is to say broadcasting the title of the play to be performed accompanied by drums and trumpets."[90] Once, Nell even uses the actual phrase "word of mouth" when she seeks her husband's assistance in making the players "understand" that she tires of *The London Merchant* and wants to see more of Rafe: "I'll see no more else, indeed, la, and I pray you let the youths understand so much by word of mouth" (2.89–91). This moment in the play comes across as odd, as Nell has heretofore addressed the players directly when she wants to communicate with them. Here, however, Nell makes a demand (rather than a suggestion or request), suggesting that in her understanding of communicative emphasis, *word of mouth* contains a kind of *ex cathedra* authority that exceeds her own individual agency.

While Nell's faith in word of mouth suggests its primacy as an informational system in the period, the play also betrays an anxiety particular to those invested in commercial entertainment. Nell does not merely depend on word of mouth as a means of informational access; she accepts the knowledge she receives as reliable. The concern that opinion could function as fact (particularly when it came to adjudicating merit) permeates many plays' paratextual material. The epilogue to *All Is True* states that "those we fear / W'have frighted with our trumpets, so tis clear / They'll say 'tis naught" (3–5), and Jonson's *The New Inn* concludes with a lament that "the play lived not in opinion, to have it spoken."[91] If one way to "kill" a play was by enacting obloquy at its performance, another equally efficient method was to murder it via "opinion" or word of mouth. However, a related anxiety lurks under Nell's cheerful surface: word of mouth provides her with the majority of her preconceptions about what she wants and expects to see. Nell's motley imaginative storehouse (one partly shared by her husband) provides ample fodder for satirizing the gullible and unworldly spectator, but referential malapropisms (such as citing "Rafe and Lucrece" [3.14–16] and Nell's permutation of "Jonah and the Whale" to "Joan and the Wall" [3.279]) suggest more than mere caricature. In contradistinction to the antitheatricalist jeremiad that claimed the spectator functioned as *tabula rasa*—an entity whose imaginative and social structures could be endlessly expunged and overwritten—*Knight* depicts the spectator's referential template as resistant to erasure. Instead, it resembles an inefficiently merged document, scarred by the marks of previous spectatorial encounters. Put in Bourdieuvian terms, this model of spectatorship suggests that the encounter between the spectator's *habitus* and the early modern theatrical field necessitates a kind of conflict. The discourse initiated by early modern playwrights, however, articulates spectators' (or, more accurately, certain kinds of spectators') preconceptions as a form of taintedness, a form of imaginative disease that renders such spectators impure and unworthy of membership among the "full and understanding Auditory."[92] Infection appears frequently as a metaphor for the early modern theater's affective potency, particularly in anti- and protheatrical discourse. This frequent concatenation of contagion and spectatorship has led critics to focus on the contagion metaphor's relationship to cultural anxieties: about the theater as a hotbed of disease (Barroll); about alterations to medical science and treatment (Pollard); about the expanding global nature of English mercantilism (Gil-Harris); about Catholicism's continued seepage into a reformed England (Mackay).[93] Even those few studies that take the contagion metaphor as a serious commentary on spectatorial dynamics tend to focus on its more widely found manifestation—a unidirectional dynamic where the theater "infects" the spectator's psyche, leading him or her to impose the theater's fictions on the world outside it.[94] Both Matthew Steggle and Alison Hobgood offer a more reciprocal version of the contagion metaphor, in which play and audience cross-infect one another. For Hobgood, this metaphor helps articulate "what it felt like to be part of performances in English theater—as an intensely corporeal, highly emotive activity characterized by risky, even outright dangerous bodily transformation . . . [one] that might have happened not just to spectators but to the plays themselves."[95] Initially, *Knight* imagines a similarly reciprocal infectious trajectory where both spectator and spectacle infect one another but concludes by rechanneling that synergy into an alternative one-way dynamic, one where the play remains altered but its spectators do not. Via the figure of Nell, *Knight* posits a different spectatorial phantasm than that personified through the irrevocably altered and emotionally incontinent theatergoer; rather, the play suggests it is precisely Nell's imperviousness to affective transformation that makes her so dangerous (to the theatrical enterprise at least).

Unsurprisingly, given that antitheatricalist writings frequently cited women as most vulnerable to the theater's contagion, many of Nell's most potent affective responses to the play either cause her to confuse fiction and reality or resemble the symptoms of bodily illness. During a scene from *The London Merchant* in which Jasper pretends he is going to kill Luce for revenge, Nell becomes so unsettled that the line between play and real violence dissolves: "Away, George, away, raise the watch at Ludgate, and bring a mittimus from the justice for this desperate villain. . . . O, my heart, what a varlet's this to offer manslaughter upon the harmless gentlewoman" (3.92–96). Soon after witnessing this incident, she exhibits symptoms of physical ailment: "By the faith o' my body, 'a has put me into such a fright that I tremble, as they say, as 'twere an aspen leaf, Look o' my little finger, George, how it shakes. Now i' truth, every member of my body is the worse for it" (3.130–34). But whereas the antitheatricalist version of theatrical contagion ends with the infected (female) subject destroying her lived world "by [attending plays] they have dishonored the vessels of holiness, and brought their husbands into contempt, their children into question, their bodies into sickness and their souls to the state of everlasting damnation,"[96] *Knight* makes no indication that Nell's theatrical experience has had or will have any long-lasting effects; rather, the play concludes with her good-naturedly thanking the "gentlemen" (audience) for their patience and inviting them over to her house for a drink and a smoke. It is, however, her very immutability that presents a larger danger, at least where the theater's interest is concerned. The dual play in *Knight* effectively concludes with a final "death" monologue by Rafe, which, in a sense, gives the citizen couple the final word. Although there are some brief following lines by Merrythought (a character in the company's original play) that make a feeble attempt at advancing some sort of final rapprochement—"Methinks all we, thus kindly and unexpectedly reconciled, should not depart without a song" (5.357–58)—the musicians to whom he speaks ("Strike up then" [5.36]) have been hired and paid by the Grocer. More significantly, Nell gets *Knight*'s actual final lines, and the play makes it pretty clear that whatever has actually happened onstage and regardless of the other spectators' experience, she is quite pleased with what she has seen: "I thank you all gentlemen, for your patience and countenance to Rafe. . . . I refer you to your own discretions, whether you will applaud him or no, for I will wink, and whist you shall do what you will" (Epilogue, 4; 8–10). Despite the company's multiple statements that Nell's disruptive behavior and taste in theater are unwelcome, she has come away seeing what she wanted to see via a combination of consumer demand and willful ignorance. Antitheatricalist Stephen Gosson's warning to female spectators that "thought is free; you can forbid no man vieweth you to note you, and that noteth you, to judge you,"[97] functions with equal validity as a warning to playwrights about their inability to control what spectators take from or do with what they see performed onstage.

Both moralists and theater practitioners fear the spectator—a construct whose processes of engagement remain unseen, unpredictable, and finally ungovernable. Given this parallel, the antitheatricalist narrative of spectatorial violence may share another with *Knight*. Both extend an essentially interior process (the interaction between theater and individual imagination) into the world of visible and tangible action, a representation that allows for an illusion of control, even if the consequences end up being devastating ones. A certain satisfaction is evident in Anthony Munday's tale of the ruinous female spectator who lays waste to everything in her path. Her destruction (as well as that of her husband and children) seems almost trifling compared with what Munday's polemic attains through it—a spectacle of self-undoing that can be used, ideally, as a disciplinary mechanism for those theatergoers whose "damage" remains secreted away in the recesses of their subconscious. This desire to "bring to light" recalls Leontes's actions that set *The Winter's Tale* in motion. His fanatical need to discover and expose his wife's imagined corruption is born from a profound need to make visible something he intuits but cannot witness or even verbalize except via the clichéd trope of adultery. But it is only by translating the "nothing" of his fears into the "something" of infidelity that he can attempt to control it at all. The "real" acts of violence often imagined as the inevitable *telos* of repeated theater attendance in the period, then, reveal something inherent in concerns surrounding the inability to control interpretive practices—an arena in which, as *Knight* would have it, anything can happen. In depicting a spectator who makes his or her imaginative life visible (hence known) by acting it out in the world, both playwrights and those opposed to the theater fashion a discursive spectator who is far more easily manipulated and controlled than the real viewing subjects who attended the theater.

Passion Play: Between the One and the Many

Ben Jonson's commendatory epistle to John Fletcher's 1608 *The Faithful Shepherdess* suggests it met a fate similar to *Knight*'s:

> The wise and many-headed bench that sits,
> Upon the life and death of plays and wits,
> (Composed of gamester, captain, knight, knight's man,
> Lady or pusill, that wears mask or fan,
> Velvet or taffeta cap, cauked in the dark
> With the shop's foreman or some such brave spark,
> That may judge for his sixpence) had, before
> They saw it half, damned the whole play and more:
> Their motives were, since it had not to do
> With vices, which they looked for and came to.
> I, that am glad thy innocence was thy guilt,
> And wish that all the Muses' blood were spilt
> In such a martyrdom, to vex their eyes,
> Do crown thy murdered poem: which shall rise
> A glorified work to time, when fire
> Or moths shall eat what all these fools admire.[98]

Whereas Burre's dedicatory epistle for *Knight* lays the blame for the play's failure on "the wide world," Jonson's directly accuses the audience of destroying the fledgling play. He imagines violent spectatorship as an act for which one might somehow attain revenge: if the play is a "murdered poem," Jonson wishes for a mass slaughter of the Muses themselves in order to "vex the eyes" of those who have brutalized Fletcher's work. While Jonson appropriates the anthropomorphistic trope, he augments it with the possibility of resurrection. In Jonson's eschatological figuration, the martyred play lives again in a kind of literary second coming, but even this moment of glorified triumph is steeped in destruction. The murdered poem ascends amid the material extinction and memorial obscurity of its fellows—those plays whose momentary flash of mass approbation flames out under the discerning eye of a future golden age. However, this dream of impending acclaim relies not only on a dust-to-dust cycle for substandard (if popular) plays but for their admirers as well—those cruel and capricious adjudicators who "saw it half, damned the whole play and more." Like the crowds who, after demanding Christ's death, called out to Pilate, "His blood be on us and our children,"[99] Jonson's vision infers a scene of final judgment for the monster with a thousand hands.

There is another play written around the same time as *Knight* that similarly features an alienated audience, an exile, and a "rebirth" into prominence. Rather than ending humorously, however, this play ends in annihilation: the spurned entity's new community rejects it as wholeheartedly as its original one. Usually categorized as a historical tragedy, *Coriolanus* seems, at first glance, to have little to do with *Knight*. But, in addition to the fact that several critics have read the play as satire (Shaw called it "Shakespeare's greatest comedy"),[100] it deals with many of the same spectatorial issues as does Beaumont's play. In her reading of *Coriolanus*, Cynthia Marshall notes critics' near-universal indifference to its eponymous hero: "[By] withholding the usual means (soliloquy and direct address) of establishing intimacy between characters and audience, Coriolanus himself presents particular difficulties."[101] Coriolanus's refusal in act 2, scene 3, to show the people his wounds is a crucible of this sort of identificatory alienation, one that Marshall argues extends beyond the diegetic audience: "The play implicates an audience's own desire to see Martius' wounds."[102] But the insurmountable divide between what Coriolanus, as one who wishes to be "author of himself" (5.3.36),[103] wants to embody and what the play's multiple audiences want from him suggest a distant history framed around a contemporary spectatorial problem. In other words, *Coriolanus* may represent the most fully fledged personification of the play martyred at the altar of popular opinion.

The "mutable, rank-scented meinie" (3.1.70) so abhorred by Coriolanus reflects a discourse often employed by frustrated playwrights.[104] From Marston's "goose-breaths" to Dekker's "great beast" that breathes plaudities (or derision) on plays' "light commodity of words,"[105] the mass audience was both necessary and potentially devastating to the business of theater. I have been arguing for a reconsideration of the oft-made connection between violence and spectatorship in early modern England as part of a discourse that offered a fantasy of control to both proponents and enemies of the professional theater, by making legible the interpsychic processes inherent in spectatorial engagement. For such a semiotics to function, however, there must be a concomitant rise in the articulation of the audience as a group of individuals. Both *Knight* and *Coriolanus* gesture toward this emergent convention: *Knight* depicts the destruction of a play not at the hands of a group but only two, distinct spectators, and *Coriolanus* attempts to disperse the band of angry plebeians by referring to them as parts rather than a whole: "Go get

you home, you fragments" (1.1.212). Although Andrew Gurr and Karoline
Szatek state confidently that "audiences at the early modern theaters from
Shakespeare's time up to the closure of 1642 were different from modern
spectators in [that] they behaved as crowds, not as individuals,"[106] within
early modern discourse about theatergoers, the individual "spectator" begins
taking on greater form and clarity. It is worth pointing out that both in
Burre's and Jonson's "second life" narratives, the play's performance incarnation is superseded by its textual one. Burre's epistle inserts *Knight* into a
literary rather than theatrical lineage, and Jonson's imagines the slaughtered
play to return as the triumphal "poem" whose corpus survives earthly tor-
ments particular to books (fire and pests). As it became more common for
plays to have a double life on stage and page, the figure of the reader takes
on greater prominence in seventeenth-century drama. In the subsequent
chapter, I explore the ways this figure contributes to a reconfiguration of the
early modern spectator as something that alternates between a member of an
interpretive community and an individual viewer.

CHAPTER 3

The Book of Praises

The Spectator as Reader in Shakespeare's Romances

In the preface to the second edition of *Shakespeare as Literary Dramatist*, Lukas Erne provides two reasons for the book's reprint: influence and controversy. If Erne's argument that "Shakespeare wrote his plays not only with performance but also with a readerly reception in mind" hardly seems controversial at this point in Shakespeare studies, his tale of the monograph's reception suggests otherwise: "Others have passionately disagreed with the book, claiming that the author and all those who agree with him suffer from a post 9/11 trauma, or, as happened at the Blackfriars conference in Staunton, Virginia, in 2011, holding up a copy of the book and pantomiming machine-gunning it."[1] Despite the fact that several other contemporaneous studies made similar claims,[2] Erne's in particular seemed to reignite the long-standing critical feud between performance and literary perspectives on Shakespeare. Perhaps the tipping point was that Erne's central claim is unapologetically about "the" author himself; indeed, his argument hinges on a kind of insight into Shakespeare's inner world—his imagination—a sacred terrain for scholars. Traditionally, it has been less Shakespeare's plays than the man, the writer, and the artist that the camps of performance and textual scholarship seem eager to claim as their own. Either he is the "man of the theater,"[3] who lived only for the ephemerality of theatrical performance and was notoriously diffident about the success and preservation of his work and reputation in print, or he is the crafty businessman, who, like his confederate Ben Jonson, was planning a folio of his own before his death.[4]

This chapter will not settle these arguments. It will, however, take seriously Erne's claim—seconded by numerous others—that Shakespeare's works were, at some point in his career, written for both theatergoers and readers. It has been well established that early modern drama attracted both a substantial spectatorial and reading public and that the "literary" and "theatrical" spheres of early modern entertainment culture became "increasingly porous" as the seventeenth century progressed.[5] As Julie Stone Peters puts it, "Playwrights were highly conscious of their double audience . . . of spectators and readers."[6] More recently, in making a case for the sale of playbills at plays, Tiffany Stern has argued that "published plays anticipate being read by spectators, often the very spectators that watched the piece in the first place."[7] My interest is less in how this reconfiguration of the entertainment marketplace as one that had (at least) two potential avenues for profit and publicity affected playwrights and more in how this reimagining affected and altered ideas about and representations of theatrical spectators. As one critic puts it, "It cannot be extravagant to think that there might be changes in aesthetic consciousness and expectation when poetic dramas, formerly enacted in public space, were rendered privately to the mind."[8] Most work on the intersections of print and drama, however, has focused either on how this interface affected dramatists' understanding of and approach to their craft or on excavating the reading public for printed drama.[9] Strikingly, studies on theater and print cultures' intersections tend to separate readers from spectators—a shadow divide perhaps cast by the long history of demarcation between performance and textual studies.[10] However, when public drama begins to exist in these two incarnations and be written with that doubleness in mind, this re-visioning alters playwright's ideas about their product *and* their audiences. In the *longue durée*, Western discourses about theater spectators had tended to represent them as a singular consciousness—an entity that shares in a unified interpretive and affective experience.[11] Indeed, it is the collective nature of this affective (if imagined) community that rendered it dangerous—a phantasm that produces the image of the viciously unified "playkillers" discussed in the previous chapter. However, as *Knight of the Burning Pestle* suggests, another version of theater audiences is becoming legible in spectatorial discourse—one that fluctuates between a collective model and a more individuated one. For while *Knight*'s failure is placed squarely on the shoulders of "the wide world" by its publisher, the play dramatizes its undoing at the hands of two characters largely delineated through their respective idiosyncracies of expectation, interpretation, and response. This fluctuation between singular and collective modes of viewing is one occurring in discourses about reading practices in early modern

England as well. Heidi Brayman Hackel points out that counter to many literacy historians' claim that silent reading became widespread in the early modern period, both aural (reading aloud either to oneself or to others) and silent reading coexisted in equal measure during the Renaissance and were often discursively intertwined.[12] Tellingly, Brayman Hackel uses *spectator* to articulate the complex mutability inherent in the ways that reading was both practiced and represented in Renaissance England: "Historians of reading might conceive of early modern people as spectators *and* hearers of books."[13]

Rather than a narrative of origins—that the idea of the spectator as individual entity emerges at this historical moment—this chapter argues that this alternative spectatorial model becomes more distinct in the early modern period. Just as scholars have cautioned against inflating a related claim—that the Reformation brought a newly self-conscious subject into being—I would be overstating my case to demarcate the spectator-as-individual's origin in the early modern period. Indeed, classical theories of spectatorship have always moved between collective and individual models. Plato's allegory of the cave depends on both paradigms as much as Theodor Adorno's culture industry does: both require the throng who perceives and experiences in affective concert and the exception that breaks away to see with new eyes.[14] Despite this pattern, audience studies (including work focused on early modern England's theatrical culture) invests heavily in the *telos* that individualized interpretive experience and practice only comes about with the rise of modern exhibition and specular technologies: "Modern playgoers are set up, by their physical and mental conditioning, to be solitary spectators, sitting comfortably in the dark watching a moving picture, eavesdroppers privileged by the camera's moving eye. In fundamental contrast, the early modern playgoers were . . . people gathered as crowds, forming what they called assemblies, gatherings, or companies."[15] My argument here suggests an alternative history for the figure of the spectator, one in which collective and individual archetypes always exist in a dialectical relationship with each other. Rather than functioning as the sole producers of spectatorial practice, I contend that changes in exhibition and technology promote new sorts of instabilities and crosscurrents between extant spectatorial discourses. In the early seventeenth century, the blurring of boundaries between readers and spectators (and between printed texts and performed plays) creates a moment when the largely asymptotic discourses of singular "spectator" and holistic "audience" collide. Such frictions destabilize both models, bringing each into sharper relief as playwrights begin addressing and appealing to their audiences as a group of individuals as much as a collective entity.[16]

The dynamic I herein elucidate is not unique to a single playwright's work; so why focus on Shakespeare?[17] Unlike other playwrights, Shakespeare was famously diffident about publication (or at least he left no record of any such interest);[18] he was, however, the most published dramatist in early modern England.[19] And, late in his career, he turns toward romance or tragicomedy, a widespread entertainment genre that proliferated on stage and page, and, as Sarah Wall-Randell points out, one marked by "a pervasive fascination with books."[20] Inherently intertextual, metatextual, and cross-generic, numerous critics have demonstrated the vast, interconnected web of romance narratives available for both reading and viewing consumption, as well as their immense popularity.[21] Popular throughout the sixteenth and seventeenth centuries, romance experienced an efflorescence during the Jacobean era, a period that, as Brian Gibbons has put it, witnessed an almost kaleidoscopic profusion of the form.[22] Following Fredric Jameson's claim that romance often reemerges to satisfy a cultural need to "express a transitional moment,"[23] scholars have focused either on the way that dramatic romance marks a shift in Shakespeare's career or in larger sociocultural apparatuses.[24] But while many of these interventions note that Shakespeare's romances create a different sort of psychological or affective relationship with their audiences than do the comedies and tragedies,[25] there has not been sufficient consideration of whether such differences might reflect a concurrent destabilization of ideas about audiences themselves.

The remainder of this chapter looks closely at two of Shakespeare's romances as nodal points that render such oscillations in the discursive spectator particularly discernible. While all of Shakespeare's so-called romances contain a version of the "living text,"[26] *Pericles* and *Cymbeline* exhibit a particular fascination with scenes of reading. *Pericles* resurrects a late medieval English author to guide the audience through the play, and *Cymbeline* brings a "literary" scene triply to life, incarnating Ovid's tale of Philomel, Boccaccio's tale of the wager,[27] and Shakespeare's own *Rape of Lucrece*. Both plays also emphasize, even attempt to inculcate the importance of, individual judgment: Phyllis Gorfain has argued that *Pericles* relies heavily on the riddle as a means of "exploring the epistemological problem that knowledge may be no more than perception,"[28] and Leah Marcus notes that *Cymbeline* "repeatedly invites its audience to 'reading' and decipherment."[29] In doing so, these plays share a concern with many Jacobean plays—the desire for what Jonson wistfully called "understanders"[30] rather than mere viewers. But whereas many plays and paratextual apparatuses lambaste the unlearned masses drooling over spectacle and lament their pervasiveness, *Pericles* and *Cymbeline* suggest that spectatorial fashioning is not only desirable but possible, an architectural fantasy that parallels what Kevin Sharpe identifies as rapidly developing textual practices aimed at disciplining, or shaping, early modern readers: "Authors therefore developed strategies to contain the hermeneutic liberties of readers. As well as the content and language of their texts they deployed the material features of writing—the size, format, and typography of the book—its genre and form, to exercise some measure of control."[31] While performed plays could not exert the disciplinary measures of print culture, early modern plays deploy a range of hortatory conventions: asides, prologues and epilogues, and choral invocations. Writing on Ben Jonson's stage comedies, Alison Hobgood notes that the playwright "asks playgoers to resist the overwhelming communicability of sensation and sentiment" or to "feel" the play correctly.[32] Shakespeare's romances, however, experiment with alternative means of "producing" an ideal spectator: devices that attempt to get him or her to interpret (rather than behave, identify, or affectively engage) correctly. As a means of doing so, these plays caution against responding with "passion" and privilege discerning, even distanced, judgment instead. Such emphasis on interpretive choices and their consequences produces a more individuated form of addressing the audience than is found in Shakespeare's earlier plays. The prologue to *Henry V,* for example, imagines the audience as an interpretive collective whose participatory harmony is necessary to produce the play. Like the "one man" that the prologue imagines "divided into a thousand parts,"[33] the individuals that make up the play's audience must merge into a unified imaginative and affective force in order to bring the play to life—a dynamic discussed in detail in Chapter 1. Shakespeare's first two romances, however, offer an alternative version of spectatorial dynamics, where the thousand parts of the audience are often understood and addressed as singular interpretive entities, individuals who can (and should) make interpretive and affective choices rather than an easily manipulated and affectively synchronized body. Or, perhaps more accurately, these plays suggest that whatever synchronicity occurs among viewers stems from a slightly different etiology than that found in the majority of spectatorial models. Rather than imagining the bulk of spectatorial practice and affective response as being generated by repeated exposure to certain kinds of entertainment or ritual spectacle (whether the theater, the bear pit, the civic procession, or the Mass), the model set forth in *Pericles* and *Cymbeline* suggests, even advocates for, a kind of spectatorial ethos—an interpretive morality—that has to be cultivated in the individual viewer.[34] While both plays invest heavily in the idea of "right" spectation, *Pericles* offers the most instruction on what this action constitutes, via a ubiquitous narrator-guide, a hero through whom sight's potential to mislead is explicitly dramatized, and a spectacle that resists visual interpretation.

"Did You Ever Hear the Like?": Sense Education in *Pericles*

Barbara Mowat calls *Pericles* an "exceedingly bookish play,"[35] as it confounds the print-drama binary on multiple levels. Shakespeare's drama[36] appeared on the London entertainment scene around the same time as George Wilkins's prose romance *The Painfull Adventures of Pericles Prince of Tyre*, which was advertised as a "the true History of the Play of Pericles as it was lately presented."[37] Shakespeare's dramatic landscape abounds with reading materials (written riddles, letters, heraldry, and epitaphs inscribed on funerary monuments), much of which demands intra- and extradiegetic decipherment. *Pericles* also signals its literary antecedents more self-consciously than any other Shakespeare play. While Mowat points out that the play is "openly scripted from Gower's *Confessio Amantis*,"[38] the narrative also resurrects the fourteenth-century English poet, intellectual, and moralist John Gower as a kind of impresario. Most obviously, Gower's character serves as a device that bridges narrative fissures opened up by the play's complete disregard of the Aristotelian unities.[39] Given his cultural status as English literary icon, however, Gower wields an undeniable authority, one that extends beyond the bardic function he claims for himself at the play's opening—"And that to hear an old man sing / May to your wishes pleasure bring" (1.0.13–14).[40] Such gratification soon becomes tinged with a hint of decree, as he reminds the audience of the narrative's earlier incarnation as both text and instructional fable: "And lords and ladies in their lives / Have read it for restoratives" (1.0.7–8). In the textual notes to the Arden 3 edition of the play, Suzanne Gossett glosses the term *restoratives* thusly: "Like Gower, who is restored from the grave, the audience will be 'restored' or re-created by the play."[41] But Gower initially presents himself as an agent of such alterations rather than a mere beneficiary of them; after all, it is his work that functions as "restorative" in the line. Signifying the play's literary, didactic, and generic heritage, Gower's presence is rendered as both character and text; indeed, even the language used to describe his resurrection suggests he is not merely "restored from the grave" but transmogrified. His rising phoenixlike from "ashes ancient" resonates both with classical and Biblical images of life's recursivity, but, in more ritualistic and material terms, the suggestion that Gower—an English Catholic who was interred in an elaborate tomb at the Priory of St. Mary Overie in Southwark—had been rendered into "ashes" is a provocative one.[42] Books, however, were often consecrated to ashes (either accidentally or because of censorship), and the spectacle of book burning would have been a common enough sight as James I reinstated public book burnings early in his reign.[43]

Besides performing a choral role, Gower also provides a kind of perceptual gloss for the spectator. His first lines prioritize sound, "To sing a song that old was sung / From ashes ancient Gower is come" (1.0.1–2), an emphasis heightened by the lines' odd syntax in which "song" precedes Gower himself. Such audial privileging occurs throughout Gower's introduction: he mentions song or singing twice more and places the organ of audial reception before that of sight: "To glad your ear and please your eyes" (1.0.4). While this locution introduces a theme the play repeatedly emphasizes—the privileging of sound over sight—it also demonstrates the tension found in *Pericles* between singular and plural forms of spectatorial address. While the possessive pronoun "your" works equally well for addressing a singular spectator or a collective audience, the imbalance between "ear" and "eyes" sits uncomfortably in the line. While "eyes" is necessary for the opening's rhymed tetrameter couplets (the previous line is "Assuming man's infirmities"), the singular "ear" seems purposefully discordant. To be sure, "ear" could signify a hegemonic communicative fantasy, where every member of the audience comprehends uniformly, or it could reinforce the idea that the ears (here presented as a singular entity) are far more trustworthy than the deceitful or "doubled" eyes. However, given that Gower's opening speech is largely about reception, the unequal parallelism may also signify an indeterminacy—a sort of spectatorial presbyopia—in the play's projection of its audience. Moving between a close-up perspective on the individual interpreter and a wide-angle one on a larger theatergoing congregation, the play counterintuitively (at least from a modern perspective) often aligns the "readerly" construct with listening, or the audial realm of interpretation, and the "spectatorial" with visual. However, as mentioned earlier, reading was often associated with the audial realm for both singular and communal readers: "Despite the spread of silent reading, many early modern people—most, if we accept David Cressy's literacy figures—experienced reading primarily aurally rather than visually."[44]

The privileging of the audial in *Pericles*, then, functions both as a means of inculcating a heightened sense of attentiveness and undermining pleasure derived primarily from spectacle.[45] Gower's setting of the scene at Antioch suggests that what is most pleasing to the eye can be damning to the soul:

> This king unto him took a fere,
> Who died and left a female heir
> So buxom, blithe and full of face,
> As heaven had lent her all his grace,
> With whom the father liking took
> And to her incest did provoke.
> Bad child, worse father, to entice his own
> To evil should be done by none. (1.0.21–28)

While arguably necessary to set the stage for Pericles's arrival in Antioch, Gower's preemptive revelation of the incest secret steals a bit of the scene's dramatic thunder and compromises the moment where the "buxom, blithe and full of face" princess appears onstage. Rather than allowing the audience to experience the celestial beauty of Antiochus's daughter before they discover her inner corruption, as Pericles does, the play frustrates this possibility, creating instead a spectatorial experience that merges the polarities of delectation and disgust.[46] The scene concludes with another perceptual mixed message, when Gower points out the row of impaled heads that surround the stage and promises that the dramatic action will now begin. The verbal (and, in the case of modern editions, gestural)[47] emphasis Gower places on the grisly spectacle of the beheaded suitors coincides with his relinquishing of narrative control, imbricating the audience's first unmediated experience of the play's action—the place where narrative and specular immersion could commence—with a visual spectacle seemingly designed to invoke horror and discipline in equal parts. Even from its opening scene, *Pericles* seeks to impede cathexes formed primarily through visual stimuli; even Gower's final injunction to the audience weds the instrument of sight not with enjoyment but discernment: "What now ensues, to the judgment of your eye / I give, my cause who best can justify" (1.0.42).

After the fully fleshed spectacle of the opening scene at Antioch, which includes a masquelike presentation of the princess ("See where she comes, appareled like the spring" [1.113]) and Antiochus's further emphasis on the martyred suitors ("Yon sometimes famous princes [*indicating the heads*], like thyself / Drawn by report, adventurous by desire, / Tell thee with speechless tongues and semblance pale . . . And with dead cheeks advise thee to desist" (1.1.35–37; 40), the play swerves away from showing and toward telling.[48] The devastating famine at Tarsus is depicted through the lachrymose musings of the country's symbolic parents (the governor Cleon and his wife, Dionyza), a rendition that reads more like a private moment of grief than a scene of national disaster: "My Dionyza, shall we rest us here / And by relating tales of others' griefs / See if it 'twill teach us to forget our own?" (1.4.1–3). The tournament scene at 2.2 at Pentapolis shows the king, Simonides, and his daughter decoding the knights' heraldric devices, but the joust itself is marked by only a single stage direction: "*Great shoutes, and all cry,* The meane Knight!" (2.2.58, original italics).[49] Finally, in what Marion Lomax notes as a missed opportunity for a dazzling *coup de theatre*, the spectacular demise of Antiochus and his daughter is rendered through Helicanus's secondhand report rather than as staged spectacle.[50] Equally significant are the numerous scenes of staged reading in *Pericles*. Letters (or more accurately, the reading of them) motivate most of the play's medial action. Pericles ends up being shipwrecked in Pentapolis after reading Helicanus's written warning that the assassin Thaliard had learned of his whereabouts in Tarsus, and he becomes engaged to Thaisa after her father receives her letter that "she'll wed the stranger knight / Or never more to view nor day nor light" (2.5.15–16). Act 3 begins with a dumb show of Pericles being presented with and reading Helicanus's letter informing him of Antiochus's death, news that prompts him to sail home with his pregnant queen. Unlike the opening, which designates information relayed by sight as misleading, these central acts present epistolary information as both accurate and trustworthy.

In the play's latter acts, however, the tension set up between visual (deceptive) and verbal or linguistic (veracious) becomes inflected with a kind of interpretive ethos in which sound and spoken language contain the ability to transform individuals as well as events. Set in a world of thickly sedimented corruption, acts 4 and 5 feature a sixteen-year-old virgin who becomes a chastening force in a world overrun by excessive male heterosexual desire. Unlike the Jacobean sex tragedy *telos*, where a superabundance of desire converts to jealousy and vengeance, *Pericles* rechannels this energy via the figure of Marina, who transforms male desire into chaste devotion via her use of highly polished rhetoric and vigorous logic. In addition to giving Marina metanoic abilities, the play seeks to protect her from the erotic gaze: despite the enormous sexual pressure exerted on her within its narrative,

Pericles attempts to circumvent Marina's physical appearance. Whereas others of Shakespeare's romance heroines, such as Imogen and Hermione, are subject to both real and imagined acts of voyeurism, Marina seems largely to resist the objectifying gaze both intra- and extradiegetically. She enters life and play in primal darkness ("A terrible childbed hast thou had, my dear / No light, no fire" [3.1.56–57]), and her father leaves her to be raised by surrogates, a decision that keeps him from recognizing her sixteen years later, as, in a sense, he has never seen her. In a divergence from both Gower's and Twine's earlier versions of *Pericles*, the brothel keepers do not parade Marina through the streets in an act of live advertisement; instead, Bolt cries her description through the market, saying he has "drawn her picture with my voice" (4.2.92).[51] Even the most vivid physical description of her (given by Pericles in the act 5 reunion scene) is rendered not through flesh-and-blood terms, but through a comparison to her mother:

> My dearest wife was like this maid, and such a one
> My daughter might have been. My queen's square brows,
> Her stature to an inch, as wand-like straight,
> As silver-voiced, her eyes as jewel-like
> And cased as richly, in pace another Juno. (5.1.98–102)

Rather than conveying an individualized image of the young woman, Pericles's mediated description sounds an idolatrous tone. Instead of seeing his daughter for the first time, he re-creates her as a funerary monument to his dead wife, even echoing some of the language that Cerimon used to describe Thaisa in the act 3 revival scene: "Her eyelids, cases to those heavenly jewels / Which Pericles has lost, begin to part / Their fringes of bright gold" (3.2.98–100). Just as the play's opening impedes spectatorial pleasure by merging moments of potential narrative and visual gratification with contradictory ones, here Marina's presence is eclipsed by the comparison to and absence of the original—her mother. Framed as a simulacrum, Marina's beauty activates only memory and mourning in her father, thereby demonstrating a chastened, benign version of the perverse desire aroused by another father's appreciation of his daughter's charms seen earlier in the play. This invocation and revision of the opening scene at Antioch offers an alternative to the corrupted and ultimately cataclysmic visual pleasure with which *Pericles* begins, thus suggesting a mode of looking that finds its terminus in imaginative and associative satisfaction rather than in the physical realm.

In *Pericles*, the recuperation of female beauty as a positive site of specta-torial engagement can only be achieved, however, by positing it through rhetoric that abates physical presence (such as the example above, where her father describes her as an effigy) or by rendering certain scenes through oral description. The play's dramatic mass conversion scene, where Marina trans-forms potential johns into chaste devotees, is narrated by two nameless wit-nesses in flashback:

> 1 GENTLEMAN: Did you ever hear the like?
> 2 GENTLEMAN: No, nor never shall do in such a place as this, she once being gone.
> 1 GENTLEMAN: But to have divinity preached there—did you ever dream of such a thing?
> 2 GENTLEMAN: No, no. Come, I am for no more bawdy houses. Shall's go hear the vestals sing?
> 1 GENTLEMAN: I'll do anything now that is virtuous, but I am out of the road of rutting for ever. (4.5.1–9)[52]

Many critics have noted Marina's near divinity,[53] but there is an important difference between this rendition of the miraculous and those told in most hagiographies, where the holy figure's presence is not only diegetically, but visually, central to the narrative.[54] Here, however, the audience receives it as a third-person, eyewitness account related via the individual experiences of two rehabilitated bystanders. While the two proselytes successfully convey a sense of Marina's potent reformative abilities, they describe almost nothing physical about the scene; instead, they focus on descriptions of language and sound. The first gentleman asks his counterpart if he has *heard* rather than seen "the like," and afterward they decide to buttress their newfound righ-teousness via an audial route—by going to hear the vestals sing. Even the first gentleman's mention of dreams—usually associated more with images than with sound—is preceded by a phrase that emphasizes listening rather than looking: "But to have divinity *preached* there—did you ever dream of such a thing?" (my italics). Despite Marina's successful conversion of male lust, the play cautiously keeps both her and the transformation scene out of the audience's sight lines.

While *Pericles* largely avoids scenes that would place Marina as the object of the masses' scrutiny, it dramatizes two instances where Marina is the object of a singular desiring male gaze. In both cases, Marina serves as an instrument of spectatorial discipline. Like the play itself, Marina impels her onlookers toward another, more complex way of interpreting what they see by redirecting their focus through language. And, while Shakespeare's *Pericles* stays true to its source material in portraying Marina as an unassailable presence, the play depicts her as an agent of change rather than an empathic representation of female helplessness. Whereas in Gower's and Twine's accounts, Marina appeals to her would-be assailants through more traditionally "feminine" methods (such as tears, self-abasement, and entreaties for mercy), Shakespeare's heroine forcefully turns their attention away from her and toward themselves, a dynamic that ultimately results in a form of masculine self-disciplining. Consider the heroine's plea to Lysimachus as told in Twine's *Patterne of Painfulle Adventures:*

> When shee was come thither, Athanagoras the Prince
> disguising his head and face, because hee woulde not be knowne,
> came first in unto her, whom when Tharsia sawe, she threw her
> selfe downe at his féete, and saide unto him: for the love of God,
> Gentleman, take pitty on me, and by the name of God I adjure you
> and charge you, that you do no violence unto me. . . . With these
> or such like wordes declared shée her heavie fortune, eftsoones sob-
> bing and bursting out into streames of tears, that for extreme griefe
> she could scarsly speake.[55]

Here, Tharsia declares the whole of her history, revealing herself completely to Athanagoras, who has come to "gather the floure of her virginitie." Luckily, her vulnerability suffices to move the prince, who "let fall a few tears, and departed." Marina, however, makes no such appeal; she commands Lysimachus with an authority that belies the precariousness of her situation: "If you were born to honor, show it now; / If put upon you, make the judgment good / That thought you worthy of it" (4.5.96–98). Rather than appealing to his sympathy through the spectacle of her grief, Marina redirects Lysimachus's attention toward his own actions, aristocratic honor, and masculine reputation.

Gower's Tharsia (Marina's analogue in the *Confessio*) similarly exhibits submissive behavior when confronted with her keeper, who has been commanded to take her maidenhood: "And thus sche kepte hirself fro schame, / And kneleth doun to therthe and preide / Unto this man."[56] By reminding her keeper of the power he has over her, Tharsia succeeds in inspiring his pity. Marina, on the other hand, takes Bolt to task in no uncertain terms when he comes to deflower her:

> Thou hold'st a place for which the pained'st fiend
> Of hell would not in reputation change.
> Thou art the damned doorkeeper to every
> Coistrel that comes enquiring for his Tib.
> To the choleric fisting of every rogue
> Thy ear is liable. Thy food is such
> As hath been belched on by infected lungs. (4.6.148–54)

While Marina's tirade seems an unlikely gambit, it works. Putting Bolt on the defensive (he responds with "What would you have me do?"), Marina once again removes herself as the object of his attention, offering an alternative that brings his self-degradation into sharp focus: "Do anything but this thou dost. Empty / Old receptacles or common sew'rs of filth. Serve by indenture to the public hangman—/ Any of these are yet better than this" (4.6.159–62). In deflecting Bolt's assault and assumption of sexual privilege, Marina reverses this power dynamic by turning the master's gaze on himself.

While this disparity between Marina and her earlier incarnations could be seen as an idiosyncrasy among Shakespeare's plays, this is not so. Another character written by the playwright several years earlier shares both Marina's unrelenting chastity and her experience of being the object of intense and unwanted sexual attention: Isabella in *Measure for Measure*. Unlike her romance counterpart, Isabella proves less successful in diverting the erotic pressure placed on her. When her pursuer (Angelo) makes it clear that the only way for her to save her brother's life is to yield to him sexually, her answer is as decisive as Marina's but couched in different terms:

> Were I under terms of death,
> The impression of keen whips I'd wear as rubies,
> And strip myself to death as to a bed,
> That longing have been sick for, ere I'd yield
> My body up to shame. (2.4.98–102)

Instead of displacing Angelo's focus onto himself, Isabella intensifies its concentration on her; although trying to illustrate her dedication to chastity, she fills her denunciation with corporeal imagery. Ostensibly she intends to

invoke images of physical self-discipline in order to cool Angelo's lust; however, she conflates the martyred body with that of her actual (and proximate)
one, thereby fanning the flames of his fantasy. The play's insistence on Isabella's physical-sensual body persists throughout this scene; she claims that
women are as frail "as the glasses where they *view* themselves" (122, my italics)
and "as soft as our complexions are / And credulous to falseprints" (127).
Unsurprisingly, Angelo fails to see the error of his ways, experiencing remorse
only once he has slaked his lust.

Marina's ability to transform the indiscriminate spectatorial gaze into
one that is self-reflexive and self-governing is part and parcel of *Pericles*'s
impulse to instruct its spectators with guidelines for "right looking." Unlike
Barbara Freedman's concept of "right spectatorship"[57] in which the comedic
spectator is inevitably sutured to particular viewing positions and (gendered)
identificatory positions, right looking suggests that while myriad spectatorial
positions, cathexes, and foci are possible for any given spectator, some are
more profitable (for play, playwright, and individual viewer) than others.
With regard to playwrights and theater companies, the sort of "profitability"
right looking offered could entail either material or reputational success or,
as Steven Mullaney has suggested, a way for them to insist on drama as art
rather than business. Countering Fredric Jameson's claim that Shakespearean
romance seeks to distance itself from "the bustling commercial activity at
work all around it,"[58] Mullaney cites *Pericles* as a significant exception: "In
the bawdyhouse at Mytilene, *Pericles* does allow the marketplace and the
trade of merchandise to be brought onstage."[59] Rather than arguing that the
play narratively embraces its commercial entertainment roots, Mullaney
claims *Pericles* grapples with the uneasy merger of art and commerce by subli-
mating the energies of the marketplace to those of a more empyrean nature.
Comparing Tharsia, the heroine of Twine's *Patterne of Painfulle Adventures*,
to her dramatic avatar, Marina, Mullaney finds them to be generically
inverted: "[Tharsia is] not merely a figure born to the popular stage, she is a
figure *of* the popular stage. . . . The theatrical impulse that Tharsia turns
to the profit of herself and her audience is suppressed in Marina's chaste
performance" (original italics).[60] Mullaney chalks up the difference between
Twine's and Shakespeare's heroines to "Shakespeare's systematic effort to dis-
sociate his art from the marginal contexts and affiliations that had formerly
served as the grounds of its possibility";[61] however, it is equally plausible that
this generic miscegenation derives from the density found in romance's warp
and woof, one woven from both textual and dramatic filaments. Seen thusly,

Tharsia's theatricality and Marina's didacticism become a characterological manifestation of early modern intertextuality: they suggest that the boundaries between printed and performed word were less absolute than our contemporary taxonomic understanding imagines them to be, in both the commercial and artistic realms. *Pericles*'s so-called "unwillingness to represent the highly theatrical transaction between an actor and an audience,"[62] may be as readily understood as the play's desire *to* represent the way that drama can circulate energies other than (or in addition to) the theatrical. Unlike the searing affective lash the theater was often cited as delivering—Gosson's "gunshotte of affection"[63]—*Pericles* imagines a communicative modality that entails more of a slow burn than immolation. Addressing spectators' faculty for reason (rather than passion) and their existence as individual and discerning witnesses (rather than as a fickle and capricious mob), right looking bears more than a passing resemblance to Erasmus's concept of "right reading," a practice in which readers "choose good books [and] develop active reading habits."[64] In fact, the term *right looking* appears (albeit infrequently) during the period; when used, it references devotional reading, such as Roger Fenton's 1611 treatise on usury: "But for matter of equitie and charitie among brethren, God did use more toleration and connivencie towards [the Jews] then he doth toward Christians, of right looking for more fruite at our hands then theirs, in regard of that Gospell of grace which we doe enjoy."[65] At other times, it appears as part of the widely circulated trope of the mirror as self-reflexive space: "This is the right *Looking-Glasse* of Man; before this Court of Justice for the Malefactours the Spirit inviteth and citeth all men to stand, as before a Looking-Glasse, wherein they may see themselves, and what the *hidden Secret Sin* is" (original italics).[66] While in this case, "right" signifies "true" and is used as an adjective to describe the "looking-glass" as opposed to a compound noun, the conjunction of the two terms in both examples suggests a kind of interpretive ethos concerned with cultivating moral righteousness in the viewer through self-reflexivity.

Like *Pericles, Cymbeline* is concerned with right looking and interpretive discipline; it also displays a greater number and variety of texts onstage and dramatizes both silent and audial reading. Spectatorial fashioning, however, occurs through less overt channels. The disciplinary structures scaffolded by Gower's guidance and Marina's ability to convert the sexualized gaze into a more self-reflexive one are largely absent in *Cymbeline*, a difference suggested by the plays' respective heroines. While Imogen and Marina share certain characteristics (chastity, acute judgment, and impressive resilience), Imogen comes under intense visual scrutiny; most ominously, she is voyeuristically preyed on in the dead of night by a virtual stranger while asleep. Rather than attempting to regulate the spectator's viewing practices through direct instruction and delimiting (or discouraging) facile visual pleasure, *Cymbeline* dramatizes both productive and destructive spectatorship and their respective rewards and consequences.[67] Dramatized largely through Posthumus, destructive spectatorship is yoked to hypercathexis, the emotionally excessive spectatorial identification often cited in antitheatricalist laments. Productive spectatorship, on the other hand, models cautious and analytical engagement: it suggests that right looking entails astute observation of (rather than enthrallment to) theatrical performance. While several of *Cymbeline*'s characters model right looking, the play offers its most fully fledged paradigm via Imogen, whose perspicacity and incisiveness as an exegete of character and motivation is unparalleled in the play. Notably, Imogen is also the character most frequently associated with reading; as Eve Rachelle Sanders points out, "Shakespeare entices belief that . . . he has given the audience access to Imogen's inner consciousness . . . in a series of scenes that show her in the process of deciphering words."[68] As Sanders also demonstrates, women's reading was by no means always affiliated with edification but was frequently imagined and represented as a subversive activity, one that could, like the theater itself, corrupt virtuous women by providing them with access to "scenes" of feverish desire and unadulterated lust, and offer tutelage in deception and intrigue (particularly against their husbands). Imogen's most focal scene of reading suggests this very doubleness: she is immersed in Ovid's tale of Tereus just before she is preyed on by Iachimo. As Wall-Randell perceives, "the suggestion is that Imogen has somehow opened her private space to sexual invaders by reading—by going to bed with—such a salacious book as Ovid."[69] Rather than construct a corollary between reading and moral edification (or degradation), *Cymbeline* replaces the moral self with the interpretive one; that is, the play associates the act of reading written texts with the ability to engage in discriminating spectatorship.

"Read and Declare the Meaning": Reading and Right Looking in *Cymbeline*

Cymbeline abounds with reading materials. Letters, books, catalogues, and tablets all take center stage during the play's many scenes of reading, most of which occur at pivotal diegetic moments.[70] Literary culture also gets a fair amount of play: *Cymbeline* borrows heavily from its two fictional sources (Boccaccio's *The Decameron* and the early sixteenth-century English prose narrative *Frederyke of Jennen*)[71] and presents Ovid's *Metamorphoses* as both prop and reference. This sort of intertextual detail permeates even smaller levels of signification; for example, Iachimo adapts (and perhaps parodies) one of the most aphoristic lines from Ovid's *Amores*: "Swift, swift, you dragons of the night" (2.2.48).[72] Finally, *Cymbeline* contains eleven instances of the word *read*, the most of any of Shakespeare's plays.[73]

While other Shakespearean plays eclipse *Cymbeline*'s use of variants of *read* (such as *reading* and *reads*), these alternative forms tend to reference the act of deciphering writing. For example, the three plays with the most instances of *read* (*All's Well That Ends Well*, [10], *Love's Labour's Lost*, and [17], and *Twelfth Night* [12]) use the term solely as a stage direction to indicate a character's action.[74] In *Cymbeline*, however, "to read" signifies "to interpret" as frequently as the act of examining writing. When discussing Imogen's choice of Posthumus for her husband despite his inferior status, one gentleman remarks, "By her election may be truly read / What kind of man he is" (1.1.53–54). Warning his restless foster sons about the caprices and iniquities of court life, Belarius uses himself as metaphor for their corrosive potential: "O boys, this story / The world may read in me" (3.3.55–56). On learning of his late queen's treachery, Cymbeline cryptically remarks, "Who is't can read a woman?" (5.5.48). And, in the play's final scene, the Roman commander orders his soothsayer to "read and declare the meaning" of Jupiter's tablet (5.5.435). At this moment, reading as physical act becomes fully integrated with its resonance as interpretive practice, a signifying trajectory that echoes the play's salvific *telos* toward reunion and resolution.

As these examples suggest, reading in *Cymbeline* does not always imply perusing or interpreting texts; three of the four instances cited above describe reading individuals as texts or, more accurately, close reading them. In fact, *Cymbeline*'s investment in delineating right and wrong interpretations of various characters and their motives can be clearly seen in the amount of time the play spends on dramatizing certain characters' assessment (or reading) of individual performances designed to procure a particular response. As Cynthia Lewis notes, "Perhaps [no other play] is so preoccupied with characters' misperceptions than is *Cymbeline*."[75] For the most part, characters' responses fall into one of two camps: overly invested and erratic or critically observant and acute. Only a select few (Imogen, Pisanio, and Cornelius, the physician), see through the nameless queen's façade to her ruthless ambition, and most of Cloten's scenes involve two courtiers whose divergent responses to their master play like a secular, farcical version of the good and bad angels in *Faustus*.[76] The primary structure through which the play elucidates right and wrong looking, however, is the triangulated relationship between Posthumus, Imogen, and Iachimo. A consummate (if at times overzealous) actor, Iachimo "plays" for both Posthumus and Imogen, but his efforts are met with radically different responses. Posthumus becomes completely consumed by Iachimo's narrative, allowing it to overwrite his experiential template with the one his rival suggests, the very sort of spectatorial immersion that Stephen Gosson terms "ravishment."[77] Imogen, however, takes in Iachimo's theatrics with a critical eye, retaining a sense of self even at those moments when he touches upon her most emotionally vulnerable points. The play does not, however, construct Imogen as a dispassionate observer: she is fully capable of narrative's immersive pleasure, such as seen at 2.2, where she stays up reading Ovid until midnight like the proverbial child under the covers with her flashlight. But whereas Imogen's Ovidian enthrallment does not appear to cloud her judgment (particularly with regard to reading others), Posthumus's overinvested engagement with performance alters not only his narrative about Imogen but how he sees the world. In consistently yoking reading and right looking, *Cymbeline* suggests that immersive reading facilitates productive and balanced spectatorship, while immersive spectatorship, on its own, leads to misprision, overidentification, and, finally, subjective alteration and ruin.

Of course, all of Shakespeare's plays dramatize instances of individual response to various characters' words and actions. *Cymbeline,* however, is unique in that it presents a character that embodies not performativity—the ability to don or doff certain ways of being and speaking that play a role in articulating subjectivity—but *performance*. That is, Iachimo occupies a near-allegorical position in the play, a kind of representation of theatrical presentation or "acting." Of course, a number of Shakespeare's plays feature a charismatic antagonist possessed of tremendous mimetic skill, but within *Cymbeline*'s structure, Iachimo functions rather differently than do his tragic precursors. Rather than plotting and accomplishing the downfall of the main characters (à la Iago or Edmund), all of Iachimo's energy is channeled into the act of performance itself. Consider the language that each uses when first framing his intentions:

IAGO: How? let's see:
  After some time to abuse Othello's ear
  That [Cassio] is too familiar with his wife.
  He hath a person and a smooth dispose
  To be suspected, framed to make women false.
  The Moor is of a free and open nature
  That thinks men honest that but seem so,
  And will as tenderly be led by th' nose
  As asses are.
  I have't, it is engendered! Hell and night
  Must bring this monstrous birth to the world's light. (*Othello*,
    1.3.393–403)

EDMUND: Well, then.
  Legitimate Edgar, I must have your land.
  Our father's love is to the bastard Edmund
  As to th' legitimate. Fine word, "legitimate".
  Well, my legitimate, if this letter speed
  And my invention thrive, Edmund the base
  Shall top th' legitimate. I grow, I prosper.
  Now gods, stand up for bastards! (*King Lear*, 1.2.15–22)

IACHIMO: If I bring you no sufficient testimony that I have enjoy'd
  the dearest bodily part of your mistress, my ten thousand ducats
  are yours, so is your diamond too: if I come off, and leave her in
  such honor as you have trust in, she your jewel, this your jewel,
  and my gold are yours, provided I have your commendation for
  my more free entertainment. (*Cymbeline*, 1.4.131–37)

Style, form, and content all underscore the differences between the first two
passages and the last. Iago's and Edmund's speeches are written in blank verse
and as soliloquies that highlight their dramatic heft and deadly intent behind
their words. Iachimo's declaration, however, is written in prose and spoken
at an impromptu homosocial gathering, giving it a more casual tone. More
telling is the way these characters articulate different understandings of their
various subjectivities. Iago and Edmund use the language of selfhood and
self-engendering; each sees himself as the agent of a new reality, one that will
swing the balance of social and sexual power in his favor. Iachimo, however,

draws on the language of commodity and exchange; his own self-image seems less at stake (or is at least constructed quite differently than Edmund's or Iago's). In focusing on the end (what he will get) rather than the means (how he will go about getting it), Iachimo's interests appear to reside primarily in what he can gain materially, sexually, and egotistically rather than in altering the world he knows or in imagining the effects of accomplishing such a change on his sense of self. However, while Iachimo foregrounds his potential profit in this passage, he does reveal a crucial facet of his self-image and hence his character in that he imagines himself as an illusionist. He never states what he will *do*, only what he will attempt—"*if* I bring you no sufficient testimony"—and then promises nothing more than to return with a good story, one that if well-delivered as a form of "entertainment" will ensure his success. Unlike Iago and Edmund, who must take on both acting and action in order to prosper, Iachimo needs only to give a convincing performance in order to get what he wants.

In addition to emphasizing Iachimo as an empty signifier, the play also spends a significant amount of time depicting alternative responses to his posturing via the lovers. Although Iachimo performs different roles for Posthumus and Imogen, he plays on a singular theme: infidelity. First encountering Iachimo during his exile in Italy, Posthumus unwisely boasts of his lady's unassailable virtue and, via her as synecdoche, the superior virtue of English-women over their continental counterparts. Irked, presumably by Posthumus's smugness, Iachimo proceeds to bait him with Imogen's chastity, finally getting Posthumus to agree to put it to the test. Whereas both missteps derive from an excess of pride and confidence, the latter is exacerbated by Posthumus's blunted intepretive skills in that he takes Iachimo literally: he reacts to rather than interprets Iachimo's words. This chain of misinterpretation begins early in the play. Although Iachimo leads Posthumus to believe that the wager between them is actually over the strength of Imogen's virtue, his true interests lie elsewhere:

> You may wear her in title yours: but you know strange fowl light
> upon neighboring ponds. Your ring may be stolen too: so your brace
> of unprizable estimations, the one is but frail and the other casual; a
> cunning thief, or a (that way) accomplished courtier, would hazard
> the winning both of first and last. (1.4.76–81)

In shifting the focus from Imogen's chastity to Posthumus's claims about it, Iachimo subtly redirects the course of the dispute. Imogen's importance wanes here (she is merely a titular possession in this passage), suggesting that Iachimo's stakes in the matter have far more to do with taking Posthumus down a peg than compromising his wife's integrity.[78] Refashioning the ring analogy he earlier used to make a point about Imogen's purported physical and spiritual perfection—"If she went before others I have seen, as that diamond of yours outlustres many I have beheld, I could not believe she excelled many" (1.4.62–64)—Iachimo now pairs it instead with Posthumus's "brace of unprizable estimations," a substitution that becomes especially significant at the end of the passage. While his statement that either thief or courtier "would hazard the winning of both" appears to refer to Posthumus's diamond and his wife, Iachimo actually pairs Posthumus's ring with his pride. His reference to the courtier invokes a figure who wields exquisite skill with both women and words—one who is an adept performer. In playing to Posthumus's tedious display of hubris, Iachimo seems to sense that the key to winning the wager lies not in seducing Imogen but in delivering a convincing performance of having done so.

Caught up in his own display of superiority at this moment, Posthumus does not catch Iachimo's shift in terms but sticks resolutely to the original tenure of their argument: "Your Italy contains none so accomplished a courtier to convince the honor of my mistress" (1.4.82–83). In failing to attend to the particulars of Iachimo's language, Posthumus makes a fatal mistake: he concerns himself with Imogen's vulnerability rather than realizing his own. On proposing the challenge, Iachimo clearly states that it is made "rather against your confidence than her reputation" (96–97), but Posthumus only perceives a further threat to Imogen's honor: "You are a great deal abus'd in too bold a persuasion, and I doubt not you sustain what you're worthy of by your attempt . . . a repulse" (99–101; 103) and when Iachimo finally lays the wager, he does so using evasive language that does more to prey on Posthumus's anxieties than actually seal the bargain:

> By the gods, it is one. If I bring you no sufficient testimony that I
> have enjoy'd the dearest bodily part of your mistress, my ten thou-
> sand ducats are yours, so is your diamond too: if I come off, and
> leave her in such honor as you have trust in, she your jewel, this
> your jewel, and my gold are yours: provided I have your commenda-
> tion for my more free entertainment. (1.4.131–37)

Cited earlier, this ambiguous passage is variously glossed in different editions of the play and purposefully obscure.[79] Iachimo never actually claims he will seduce Imogen or even make the attempt. Instead, he bases the wager on the strength of his "sufficient *testimony*," something that while ostensibly based in fact, hinges on how persuasively it is delivered. Even when he describes what would constitute a victory on his part, he does so through equivocations, saying only that if he "comes off" and "leaves her in such honor as you have trust in," he wins. Although "come off" carries all the resonances of a classic Shakespearean pun, the remainder of the clause is, I would argue, less ironic. As Iachimo has realized, winning the wager does not necessitate Imogen's corruption: he can indeed "leave her in such honor" as Posthumus trusts in because ultimately the wager is not a test of Imogen's honor but of Iachimo's abilities as a performer.

In the rivals' post-wager encounter, Posthumus initially displays a healthy skepticism toward his rival's claims of success, suggesting he will engage more cautiously with Iachimo's claims this time around. However, as the latter warms to his subject, finally producing the prop of Imogen's bracelet, Posthumus allows himself to become subsumed by Iachimo's narrative. Although Posthumus resists the connection that Iachimo attempts to forge between his knowledge of Imogen's chamber and knowledge of Imogen herself, these descriptions pave the way for Iachimo's later *coup de théâtre*. By spending so much time on the details of her bedroom, Iachimo leads his rival's imagination there, so that when he presents his more censorious proofs he has Posthumus exactly where he wants him:

> The chimney
> Is south the chamber, and the chimney-piece,
> Chaste Dian, bathing: never saw I figures
> So likely to report themselves; the cutter
> Was as another nature, dumb; outwent her,
> Motion and breath left out. (2.4.80–84)

Iachimo takes special pains to emphasize the power of representation here. While the tension between nature and art thematically links all of Shakespeare's romances, it here reinscribes a tension unique to *Cymbeline*. Iachimo's privileging of the artisan's craft and product over nature serves as an analogy for his own performative power in this scene: he too can create something that convinces as well as (or better than) the real thing. However, Shakespeare pairs this assertion of dramatic potency with an image that warns against passively accepting Iachimo's terms by raising the specter of undisciplined spectatorship—that of Diana bathing. Oddly absent, however, is any direct mention of Actaeon, an omission that leaves a noticeable lacuna in the tableau. Jonathan Bate has suggested that Iachimo's intra- and extradiegetic audiences occupy this absence, as they are asked to imaginatively see what Iachimo describes.[80] Taking this reading further than Bate's interpretation (who sees this moment as "effect[ing] in the audience's mind what *The Winter's Tale* feigns to deliver in performance: the metamorphosis of art into life"),[81] it is worth remembering that Actaeon's moment of visual gratification is dearly bought: occupying his spectatorial position, even imaginatively, is a risky business. By invoking this myth at this moment, the play again suggests the hazards of destructive spectatorship.[82]

If this reference escapes notice, however, there is always the negative example of Posthumus from which to learn. He tragically misreads Iachimo's intentions, believing that Iachimo offers his extravagant descriptions as proof rather than as setting. By the time Iachimo presents his evidentiary trump cards (the bracelet and the mole), Posthumus is too far gone to retreat to the higher ground of objectivity. Though warned by Philario not to jump to conclusions—"Sir, be patient: / This is not strong enough to be believed / Of one persuaded well of" (2.4.130–32)—Posthumus cannot stop his mind from following the avenue down which Iachimo has led it. By the time Iachimo gets to the corporeal "proof" of Imogen's birthmark, it is not even necessary, as Posthumus has already arrived at the scene of the purported crime:

> This yellow Iachimo, in an hour, was't not?
> Or less at first?
> Perchance he spoke not, but
> Like a full-acorned boar, a German one,
> Cried "O"! and mounted. (2.5.1–17)

And, while he is not, like Actaeon, physically rent asunder in punishment for his imaginative indulgence, its consequences will emotionally eviscerate him.

Situated between these two episodes is Imogen's initial encounter with Iachimo. Whereas Posthumus's sparrings with Iachimo occur before a group of other men, Imogen receives Posthumus alone in her chambers. Such divergent settings help exacerbate certain tensions that underpin these scenes: the male collective escalates the intensity of the masculine *agon* in 1.5 and 2.4, while Imogen's solitude in 1.7 emphasizes her vulnerability. It is, however, worth pointing out that Posthumus is positioned as a member of an *actual* audience whereas Imogen is in a private, solitary space; in other words, their respective placements mirror their interpretive identities and tendencies as spectator and reader. Other details add to this framing as well, particularly the presence of letters in 1.7: Imogen actually *is* a reader during the first part of her encounter with Iachimo. Significantly, she does not turn her attention to Iachimo until she has read most of Posthumus's letter, an ordering that further connects the act of reading with productive interpretive practice.

Perhaps Imogen's readiness to immerse herself in the written word unhinges Iachimo, for, uncharacteristically, he seems ready to give up his cause even before he begins. Addressing the audience in an aside, Iachimo shows little of the dexterous linguistic control seen earlier. Instead, he sounds bombastic and strained, even desperate:

> [*Aside*] All of her that is out of doors most rich!
> If she be furnished with a mind so rare,
> She alone is th' Arabian bird; and I
> Have lost the wager. Boldness be my friend!
> Arm me, Audacity, from head to foot,
> Or like the Parthian, I shall flying fight,
> Rather directly fly. (1.6.15–21)

Rather than provide the audience with any insight into his state of mind or ironic commentary about the situation in which he finds himself (two common types of Shakespearean asides), Iachimo here creates an entirely different setting and context for himself. His extended metaphor shifts the locale from Imogen's chambers to epic battlefields where empires (rather than individuals) clash and refashions himself as a highly mobile and elusive Parthian warrior.[83] Such imaginative self-fashioning suggests that before Iachimo can attempt his seduction of Imogen, he has to "plume up his will" by creating a grandiose setting for himself from which to stage his conquest. Unlike Iago, who shores up his confidence by conceiving of and enacting the "double knavery" of setting up Roderigo and Othello, Iachimo must instead create a degree of remove from his situation and intended actions; that is, he must return this encounter to the sphere of performance. Only after he has reimagined the scene as a fiction in which he plays a role is he able to push ahead with his plans.

Unfortunately, this particular performance is not among Iachimo's best. All of the topical maneuvering and sinewy phrasing that successfully ensnared Posthumus earlier is absent; instead, Iachimo's presentation resembles an overdone version of Herod. Breaking awkwardly into posturing almost immediately after Imogen greets him, he unleashes a metaphoric maelstrom on his captive audience:

> What! are men mad? Hath nature given them eyes
> To see this vaulted arch, and the rich crop
> Of sea and land, which can distinguish 'twixt
> The fiery orbs above and the twinned stones
> Upon the numbered beach, and can we not
> Partition make with spectacles so precious
> 'Twixt fair and foul? (1.6.31–38)

This odd amalgam of heroic language and underhanded intent pushes this moment toward the edge of parody, a shift in delivery Imogen notes immediately. Her initial reaction to his euphuistic advances is a sort of bemused astonishment: "What, dear sir, / Thus raps you? Are you well?" (1.6.49–50). Even when, after pursuing his theme further, he manages to instill doubt in her mind, she refuses to give in to her emotions, maintaining a degree of objectivity in the face of what she most fears: "My lord I fear / Has forgot Britain" (112). Her restraint finds linguistic emphasis in her metonymical self-designation: she does not say, "My lord has forgotten me" or even "his lady," but instead refers to herself as "Britain," indicating that even at her most emotionally vulnerable moment, she assesses Iachimo's story at a degree of remove. On seeing her waver, Iachimo attempts to push his advantage, but rather than allow him any further opportunity, Imogen closes the gateway to her imagination: "Let me hear no more" (117). When Iachimo finally proffers himself as the means to avenge Posthumus's infidelity, "I dedicate myself to your sweet pleasure, / More noble than that runagate to your bed, / And will continue fast to your affection" (1.6.136–38), she responds with imperious disdain:

> Away, I do condemn mine ears, that have
> So long attended thee. If thou wert honorable,
> Though wouldst have told this tale for virtue, not
> For such an end as thou seek'st, as base, as strange. (140–43)

Her interpretive accuracy forces Iachimo's hand, and he gives up his original gambit by making a quick retreat via the rhetoric of apology and panegyric: "Blessed you live long! A lady to the worthiest sir that ever / Country called his; and you, his mistress only / For the most worthiest fit. Give me your pardon" (158–61).

Iachimo makes one further attempt on Imogen; tellingly, this occurs once he risks no further exposure to her scrutiny—in the middle of the night when she is fast asleep. While the bedroom scene in *Cymbeline* contains echoes of related and more tenebrous episodes found in other, earlier Shakespearean narratives, the power dynamic between Iachimo and Imogen is different than those that exist between subject and object in *Lucrece* or *Othello*. Although each sequence begins with the looking, active male subject gazing on the female body in repose—the reduction of woman to the status of object—*Cymbeline* is not the inevitable outcome of a victim-perpetrator dynamic that has been looming for some time. After all, the first time Iachimo appears in Imogen's chamber, he is the one on display, a role reversal that inverts the more familiar positioning of male subject-female object. In addition, Imogen does not merely observe Iachimo; she sees through his pretext by reading his subtext, thereby gaining control over both him and the situation in which he places her. By the time he enters Imogen's chamber the second time, Iachimo's potency has been severely compromised—a position underscored by his entrance. Rather than stealthily entering her chamber, Iachimo crawls out from a trunk he earlier asked Imogen to place in her room for "safe stowage" (1.6.191), a moment that Alexander Leggatt claims is frequently met with modern audiences' laughter.[84] Whether a seventeenth-century audience would have found Iachimo's entry humorous is unclear, but, as Leggatt mentions, this moment could invoke an image culled from the tradition of the morality play—that of a devil emerging from the depths of hell. A ludic rather than macabre figure, the devil's entrance often signals a moment of comic relief, even as it provides the dramatic ingredients of temptation and deception essential to the psychomachic plot.[85] In morality plays, this figure operates within the limits of a dualistic universe; he must eventually give way to the *telos* of Christian salvation mandated by divine will. A medieval audience would have understood this instinctively since they knew the end even as they watched the beginning. For them, dramatic intrigue would have existed in the details of the narrative journey rather than its destination. And, although *Cymbeline* does not, finally, fall into the category of the miracle play, many critics have convincingly demonstrated its debt to the genre.[86] The play's reference, then, to this particular branch of *Cymbeline*'s lineage could have aroused certain interpretive associations for an early seventeenth-century audience still fluent in the symbolic language of the morality tradition. Iachimo's uncharacteristic entrance would have referenced not only the humor associated with the devil but also his ultimate powerlessness.

If, as Leggatt argues, this scene makes a metareference to its theatrical genealogy, it also invokes its literary antecedents. Besides opening with Imogen reading Ovid in her bed, Iachimo's entry from the trunk appears in only one of the play's possible sources—*The Decameron*. Melissa Walters argues that Boccaccio may be inscribed in this scene visually as well as narratively:

> Iachimo's lie that the trunk contains objects belonging to her husband may be metaphorically true. Iachimo is in the trunk because of misogynistic homosocial competition with Posthumus. The claim also inverts the function of Italian marriage *cassoni*, which were supposed to be involved with the joining of the couple. At least one such chest, dating from 1420–25, features [Boccaccio's] story of Bernabò and Zinevra (2.9), a key source for Shakespeare's play.[87]

Walters makes this point in service to her larger argument about the possibility of a material intertextuality that connects early modern drama to the Italian novella—a kind of ligature that trades on a symbolic and visual rhetoric as well as narrative tropes and plot points. This type of thickly sedimented metatextuality finds its crucible in the chest trick. Stepping into the imaginative space of Imogen's reading and emerging from Boccaccio's tale narratively and visually, Iachimo becomes indelibly inscribed *as* text, as something that not only should but must be read in order to be understood. Rather than distinguishing readers from spectators here, the play offers multiple referential templates—theatrical, material, and textual—that encourage interpretation rather than immersion. In offering access to interpretive (rather than visual) pleasure, an epistemological *jouissance* that proleptically suggests the Joycean secular epiphany, *Cymbeline* imagines a viewing public in which *all* spectators are readers.[88]

The conversional dynamic suggested in 2.2 becomes writ large in the play's final scene, where the multiple performed revelations, recognitions, and reunions only become fully legible once Philarmonus reads and explicates Jupiter's tablet. If, as J. M. Nosworthy suggests, *Cymbeline*'s conclusion enacts "a vision of perfect tranquility . . . in which Imogen, Iachimo, atone-ment, the national ideal have all ceased to have separate identity or individual meaning,"[89] the dissolution of the spectator-reader binary may seem merely a function of the play's trajectory toward homogeneity—the prerequisite con-dition of most utopian fantasies. However, two of the characters' immersion into this "perfect tranquility" occurs through augmentation rather than par-ing away. In an oddly recursive dramatic moment (in that it occurs after all the disclosures have already taken place), Posthumus remembers Jupiter's tablet and, displaying the heuristic dullness we have come to expect, calls for the soothsayer's assistance in deciphering it. Tellingly, the two individuals this prophecy most concerns are the characters who consistently misread peo-ple and situations in the play—Cymbeline and Posthumus. Even more tell-ing, however, is that they are also the only ones the soothsayer directly addresses in his exegesis, as if sensing they are the ones most in need of interpretive guidance:

> Thou, Leonatus, art the lion's whelp,
> The fit and apt construction of thy name,
> Being Leo-natus, doth impart so much:
> [*To Cymbeline*] The piece of tender air, thy virtuous daughter,
> Which we call *mollis aer*, and *mollis aer*
> We term it *mulier*: which *mulier* I divine
> Is this most constant wife. (5.5.443–49)

To the twenty-first-century bourgeois playgoer or literary critic, this moment verges on a parody of dramatic exposition and close reading; for a seventeenth-century spectator, it may have offered other interpretive and didactic possibilities. Most obviously, Philarmonus's patient work with lin-guistic detail models a kind of analysis that calls for slowing down one's response time in order to consider the details before rushing to partial comprehension, a mode of judgment to which bystanders call upon Post-humus to enact three times in the proof scene at 2.4. Equally significant, however, is that this *explicacion de texte* follows (rather than precedes) the enacted revelations, suggesting that reading functions as Derridean supple-ment to performance. Serving as both performance's addition and its replacement, the tablet augments and solidifies meaning for the spectators: so profound is its effect on Cymbeline that in the play's final speech, he

imagines himself not as a victorious ruler or loving father but as a composi-
tor who rules over a kingdom of readers: "Publish we this peace / To all
our subjects" (5.5.476–77).

Besides facilitating a kind of reflexivity in the spectators (both in terms
of considering the events that have passed and their own roles in them),
the tablet serves as a material marker of the performance's existence and the
experience(s) of those who witnessed it. If *Cymbeline* begins by connecting
reading with right looking, it ends by connecting textual and individual
inscription at both the narrative and metaphysical levels. Like most pro-
phetic communications, Jupiter's message is rendered primarily through a
metaphorical lexicon: except for the one direct reference to Posthumus,
it contains all the ambiguity that any self-respecting augury could want.
Structured thusly, it offers a kind of openness that makes it potentially
relevant to *any* interpretation, an opacity that the soothsayer arguably turns
to his advantage. But, possible chicanery aside, this interpretive example
amply demonstrates the reader's role in shaping or tailoring meaning so
that it speaks more directly, more intimately, to the individual subject—a
reading praxis that echoes Reformation ideas about the advantage, even
necessity, of cultivating a relationship between man and Scripture: "If any
man thirst for the truth and read the scripture by himself desiring God to
open the door of knowledge unto him God for truth's sake will and must
teach him."[90] Patrick Cheney has argued that because *Cymbeline* is Shakespeare's most self-citational play, his authorial presence permeates it more
than any of his other works.[91] Alongside the specter of Shakespeare-the-
author, however, *Cymbeline* casts another, more ill-defined shadow, that of
the (potential) reader. However, much as the lay scriptural reader occupied
a fraught position in the English cultural imaginary,[92] so too does the reading spectator in early modern spectatorial discourse, an incarnation I further explore via a brief reading of *The Winter's Tale*.

Great Creating Spectators

In her study *Reading Popular Romance in Early Modern England*, Lori Humphrey Newcomb challenges the abiding critical claim that *The Winter's Tale*
offers a paradigmatic example of Shakespeare's elevation of his source material (in this case, Robert Greene's prose romance *Pandosto*).[93] Setting up an
alternative paradigm for understanding the relationship of Shakespeare's

plays to their sources, particularly versions that circulated alongside them, Newcomb proffers the term *re-commodification*.[94] A market-driven form of intertextuality, re-commodification entails "the retelling and retailing of a textual commodity that already exists in some form. Re-commodification markets a given narrative to new audiences by (more or less) free deployment of highly visible features in print, for instance, title, format, length, and signals of authorship and genre affiliate a text with other known print commodities."[95] By default, re-commodification also requires territory marking, demarcations between where one author's creation ends and another's begins. While *The Winter's Tale* distinguishes itself via multiple channels (most notably through Shakespeare's completely new and hyper-theatrical ending), Newcomb suggests that the play sets itself "above" its prose source by "transforming the buying and reading of books into performances of social denigration."[96] This anxiety of influence seeps into both the personal and professional realms: Newcomb notes that Autolycus can be read as a send-up of Greene or, more specifically, "a demonized author of fictions who is exorcised to make Shakespeare's theatrical magic lawful."[97] In making her case, Newcomb further argues that *The Winter's Tale* sets up the book trade and the public theater as antithetical: the first is merely a "scene of consumption,"[98] whereas the second is a site of lawful magic.

In closing, I want to suggest that the anxieties clustered around reading in *The Winter's Tale* extend further than distinguishing between "elite" and "nonelite" readers and the ever-attenuating perimeter dividing art and commodity. Although imbricated with cultural apprehensions about authorship, interpreters, and interpretation, these concerns manifest in the play via the concepts of right and wrong looking. The play's most extended scene of consumption is not set in the marketplace but in the distorted, disorienting theater of Leontes's psyche. Unlike *Pericles* and *Cymbeline,* which provide various kinds of interpretive guidance, *The Winter's Tale* takes destructive spectatorship to its limits, recasting attentive watching and active interpretation as dangerously procreant acts. Unlike the destructive spectator posited by antitheatrical discourse, who has new realities created for him or her via what she or he sees portrayed onstage, or the belligerent consumer-spectator who attempts to shape entertainment commodity into what she or he wants to see, Leontes seems to create his new reality *ex nihilo.* Neither mimetic nor consumerist, this model of spectatorship suggests an interpretive agency so excessively and dangerously fecund that even Leontes himself is unable to imagine it as entirely self-generated:

> Affection! thy intention stabs the centre:
> Thou dost make possible things not so held,
> Communicat'st with dreams;—how can this be?—
> With what's unreal thou coactive art
> And fellow'st nothing; then 'tis very credent
> Thou may'st co-join with something; and that thou dost,
> (And that beyond commission) and I find it,
> (And that to the infection of my brains
> And hardening of my brows). (1.2.138–46)

Glossed in the Arden 2 edition of the play as "one of the obscurest passages in Shakespeare,"[99] Leontes's rant mimics logical analysis in its attempt to parse the imaginative processes that forge an individual's perception of his world. While it follows a diagnostic path, Leontes's disquisition fails to lead anywhere because he begins in the wrong place. Instead of recognizing the origins of "affection" as parthenogenetic, he addresses it directly, as though it were acting on him rather than generated by him. His break into apostrophe suggests the poet's call to his muse just before divesting himself of his creative burden,[100] but whereas the poet plays an active role in the vatic process, Leontes severs himself from the creative act he describes. Affection (rather than he) communicates with dreams to forge visions that coact with "what's unreal" and "co-join with something." Toward the end of the passage, Leontes envisions himself finding the progeny of affection and "something," which in turn infect his brains and harden his brows. In this vague-yet-causal scenario, Leontes plays the role of victim—a helpless bystander who witnesses the birth of his own misery.

Paradoxically, Leontes's tremendous expenditure of energy in animating and advancing a vision of himself as passive victim ends up demonstrating his active role in creating his own misery. He imagines himself as a virtual lodestone that draws people's attention—"They're here with me already; whisp'ring, rounding" (1.2.217)—and subsequently demands that Camillo accept his accusations against Hermione as truth: "My wife's a hobby-horse, deserves a name / As rank as any flax-wench that puts to / Before her troth-plight: say't and justify't!" (1.2.276–78). When Camillo refuses to give him the validation he longs for, Leontes responds with desperation:

Is whispering nothing?
Is leaning cheek to cheek? Is meeting noses?
Kissing with inside lip? stopping the career
Of laughter with a sigh (a note infallible
Of breaking honesty)? horsing foot on foot?
Skulking in corners? wishing clocks more swift?
Hours, minutes? noon, midnight? and all eyes
Blind with the pin and web, but theirs; theirs only
That would unseen be wicked? is this nothing?
Why then the world, and all that's in't is nothing,
The covering of the sky is nothing, Bohemia nothing,
My wife is nothing, nor nothing have these nothings,
If this be nothing. (1.2.284–96)

What begins as a catalogue of circumstantial evidence ends in a denunciation of everything—family, world, existence. Yet it is also the first intentionally generative act Leontes performs in the play. Whereas earlier he imagines himself as stumbling upon the image of Hermione and Polixenes betraying him, he now willfully inscribes it on the world. In order to do this, however, he must first undo the existence he knows: hence his first act of making is one of unmaking. In an inversion of the Genesis narrative where God creates the world in seven days, Leontes dismantles the very framework on which his life is based. This annihilation is emphasized by his repetition of "nothing" seven times; even the conditional "if" in the final clause does little to mitigate the effect of his pronouncement.[101] The chaos and instability hinted at by Leontes's earlier, volatile anger now become focused and fully realized: the passive recipient of possibility becomes the creator of a new reality; the reader becomes the author.

Although articulated through an extreme perspective in *The Winter's Tale*, the figure of the (over)writing spectator is consistent with Shakespearean tragicomedies' exploration of when, where, and how individual spectators' patterns of assessment and response can be encouraged, cultivated, and finally controlled. When Leontes comes to arrest Hermione, he interrupts a scene of storytelling: his young son has just begun whispering a story in his mother's ear. The "sad tale best for winter" presages and becomes *The Winter's Tale* but only after the creative force of Mamillius's story collides with that of his father's imagination—a sort of Newtonian version of the kinetics of drama. Although this fission results in a very sad tale indeed, when considered metadramatically (as opposed to narratively), it reimagines the relationship between play-text and spectator-reader as a symbiotic rather than an antagonistic or a didactic one. The essential interdependency between spectator and play can be read metaphorically through two pivotal events in which Leontes's actions play a principal role: his son's death and wife's resurrection. Leontes is the primary agent of his son's destruction in that he invalidates and ultimately obliterates the world his son occupies both materially and psychically. Like the winter's tale begun for pleasure, Mamillius's life is a unique and ephemeral moment in the play, one that cannot withstand the force of Leontes's violent revisions. Because Leontes does not recognize that his imaginative creation and his bodily issue cannot coexist, he destroys that which he should nurture and preserve—his progeny. In the case of Hermione, however, although Leontes causes her suffering and "death" in the play's first half, by the end he has reformed his interpretive ways. Rather than blindly imposing his own (mis)interpretation on what he sees, Leontes allows himself to share in Paulina's imaginative creation while still retaining an active role in its realization. Certainly, the success of the scene (for both the on- and offstage audiences) requires Leontes's participation; it is not until he expresses desire to witness, and hence believe, in Paulina's magic that Hermione is reawakened: "What you can make her do / I am content to look on, what to speak / I am content to hear. . . . Proceed. No foot shall stir" (5.3.91–93; 97–98). After plumbing the representational depths of the spectator's destructive potential, the play concludes with an affirmation of the reader-spectator's irreducible role in bringing *any* given work into commercial and artistic existence and circulation, and turning any given individual into an author or a playwright.

If *The Winter's Tale* attempts to include the spectator in its final vision of marital, familial, and artistic unity, it eludes one seventeenth-century playgoer who recorded his experience. Penned by Simon Forman, a London astrologer, physician, and avid theatergoer, the description omits any reference to the play's transcendent conclusion:

> In *The Winter's Tale* at the Globe 1611 on the 15 of May Wednesday, observe there how Leontes the King of Sicilia was overcome with jealousy of his wife with the King of Bohemia, his friend that came to see him, and how he contrived his death and would have had his cup-bearer to have poisoned, who gave the King of Bohemia warning thereof and fled with him to Bohemia. Remember also how he

sent to the oracle of Apollo, and the answer of Apollo, that she was
guiltless and that the King was jealous, etc., and how except the
child was found again that was lost the King should die without
issue, for the child was carried into Bohemia and there laid in a
forest and brought up by a shepherd. And the King of Bohemia his
son married that wench, and how they fled into Sicilia to Leontes,
and the shepherd having showed the letter of the nobleman by
whom Leontes sent away that child, and the jewels found about her,
she was known to be Leontes' daughter, and was then sixteen years
old.

  Remember also the rogue that came in all tattered like colt-
pixie, and how he feigned him sick and to have been robbed of all
that he had, and how he cozened the poor man of all his money,
and after came to the sheep-shear with a pedlar's pack and there
cozened them again of all their money, and how he changed apparel
with the King of Bohemia his son, and then how he turned courtier,
etc. Beware of trusting feigned beggars or fawning fellows.[102]

Forman certainly seems to have paid attention: he remembers many of the
play's details and reads Autolycus with moral, if not theatrical, accuracy. As he
also wrote an account of *Cymbeline,* perhaps he took that play's spectatorial
dictum of careful attentiveness to heart. Still, his version is rather different than
Shakespeare's (or at least the one that survived in the Folio), as Forman neither
mentions the play's ending nor its resemblance to Greene's romance. In eliding
both of these aspects of the play—aspects that have been deemed by critics as
among its most significant[103]—Forman eludes both the seventeenth-century
discursive networks emplaced to play upon him as a consumer of popular
entertainment and the twenty-first-century ones designed to pin him down as
an object of study. Despite attempts to fashion him as a reader and to read
him as a text, the material early modern spectator, in all his glorious idiosyncrasy, remains highly inscrutable, existing alongside his discursively constructed
avatar.

CHAPTER 4

The Language of Looking

Making Senses Speak in Jonsonian Masque

Before commencing the celebratory masque Prospero has orchestrated for his daughter's betrothal, he calls for a particular kind of attentiveness: "No tongue, all eyes. Be silent!" (4.1.59).[1] His injunction may seem like the early modern equivalent of the cell-phone announcement preceding present-day theatrical performances, but it functions as more than a reminder of spectatorial etiquette. Prospero does not merely tell the audience to be quiet; he attunes their perceptive apparatus to the visual register, siphoning all sensory channels toward seeing. His phrase "all eyes" is bracketed by dismissals of sound ("no tongue . . . Be silent!"), a paratactic command that completely bypasses listening as a mode of attentiveness. Although the heavily spondaic line makes it difficult to stress any particular word, "all eyes" hovers in its center—the position of privilege and authority, the vanishing point that in masque form, is the spectacle and from which the spectacle can best be seen, the "I" that sees all, embodied in the person of the king. And yet Prospero's command, issued verbally, demands audial reception (if not attentiveness), suggesting that these two forms of sensory engagement cannot be so cleanly severed.[2]

Jacobean masques, of course, were not entirely visual events, and *The Tempest*'s, containing some sixty-two lines of dialogue, an epithalamial song, music, and dancing, suggests that one cannot "attend" a masque only with one's eyes. When, at an earlier point, Prospero reminds Miranda of their shared past, he does so by admonishing her (and arguably those in the theater) to "ope thine ear. / Obey and be attentive" (1.2.37–38) and by repeatedly insisting that she hear his tale.[3] However, just as masque is not a solely visual experience, Prospero's narrative is not a wholly audial one. Shot through with graphic details, the experience of retelling their experiences becomes visceral, causing him to slip syntactically between past and present:

> In few, they hurried us aboard a bark,
> Bore us some leagues to sea, where they prepared
> A rotten carcass of a butt, not rigged,
> Nor tackle, sail nor mast—the very rats
> Instinctively have quit it. (1.2.144–48)

His temporal confusion suggests the trauma victim's familiar phrase: "It's as though it's happening again right before my eyes." Even before Prospero embarks on his narrative, he asks Miranda to try and remember their life before they came to the island, a request that hinges on her ability to access her eidetic past: "What *seest* thou else in the dark backward and abysm of time?" (1.2.49–50, my italics). Despite the fact it is being told (just as the masque is something that is shown), Prospero's narrative does not, *cannot*, engage only a single sense. Rather, once received by the ear, it enters the complex matrix of the imagination—a mechanism via which, as early modern commentators on the theater understood, the senses could become imaginative catalysts for one another, thereby producing a type of interpretive synaesthesia.

Prospero occupies a dual role in these scenes. Most obviously, he authorizes them in both senses of the word: he lends them authority (as father-sorcerer and witness), and he creates them (as epithalamial entertainment and familial history). This authority, however, is undercut by Prospero's desire to control *how* his audience experiences the fruits of his creative labor, as in each instance he seems intent on guiding his audience along certain sensory paths. In doing so, he takes on another role—that of impresario—one that resembles another author-emcee hybrid featured in Shakespearean romance: Gower in *Pericles*. But whereas Gower consistently encourages listening over looking,[4] Prospero's sensory privileging seems tied to genre: a masque must be looked at but a story, heard. However, as his narrative demonstrates, this perceptive taxonomy falls short: audial description bleeds into the visual and tactile realms, creating a sensory continuum. A tension arises between the desire to delimit sensory boundaries and the descriptive impracticality, even impossibility, of doing so. This discord, I believe, mirrors a shift occurring in seventeenth-century discourse about how the spectator "takes in" or processes different sorts of theatrical events. That such division in *The Tempest* revolves around these two particular sorts of entertainments—one narrative, one spectacular—is not surprising. It reflects an interpretive division severing sight from sound—a schism most pellucidly legible in the arena where masque (and, arguably, creative anxiety) would achieve its apotheosis: the Stuart court. *The Tempest*'s masque (and similar attempt to regulate sensory boundaries) might testify to its origins as a play written for James I's court or suggest a desire to capitalize on Jacobean masque's novelty—its seductive imbrication of royal celebrity, spectacular stage effects, and an exclusive (and exclusionary) sort of visual pleasure.[5] But I wish to offer another possibility: that the fault lines emerging between sight and sound in *The Tempest* reflect an alteration to the descriptive lexicon of the senses, changes most fully artic-ulated in the theatrical product generated by the yoking together of Ben Jonson's and Inigo Jones's creative powers.

That collaboration—and conflict—is well-trod critical ground: tradition views Jones as the visual innovator and Jonson as the verbal one, Jones as the scenic visionary whose stagecraft changed both how theater was produced and experienced and Jonson as the underappreciated poet who, throughout his career, fought against the tyranny of spectacle.[6] However accurate these claims, that division may not be the best, or only, way to comprehend the gradual shift toward the spectacular in seventeenth-century entertainment culture—what might be called a visual turn. As Stephen Orgel notes, "[Paint-ing and carpentry] were about to become the soul of drama too."[7] Andrew Gurr sees audience preference (rather than the Stuart court's taste for specta-cle) as the catalyst for the theater's move toward spectacularity. Claiming that amphitheater audiences tended toward "a debased preference for stage spectacle rather than the poetic 'soul' of the play," he sees this preference being solidified through Jones's innovations in set design.[8] However, Jones's major innovations—the introduction of the proscenium arch and stage machinery such as the *machina versatilis* and the *scena ductilis* that allowed for sets to move without visible assistance—were, until the Restoration, seen primarily by small, elite audiences rather than larger public ones.[9] More recently, Tiffany Stern has noted the ways in which the King's Men's move to the Blackfriars in 1608 altered the creative template of those playwrights writing for this company. Focused particularly on Shakespeare, Stern notes that "the atmosphere of the theater and the very look of the audience . . . were 'part' of the performance and affected the plays written for them."[10] Stern provides a compelling cultural materialist perspective on G. E. Bent-ley's claim that the Blackfriars clientele strongly influenced Shakespeare's last plays, citing details such as the visual effects of candlelight glistening on expensive embroidery, jewels, and feathers worn by spectators; the scent of tobacco; and the audience's physical proximity to the stage. While Stern's argument productively complicates Bentley's, it relies on an assumption that playwrights' crafting of their plays *follows* technological innovations (in this case, sartorial, narcotic, and spatial) rather than playing a role in their creation and emphasis. In addition, Stern imagines the pressure exerted on playwrights by the Blackfriars' constituency as an entirely welcome force; however, as I suggest in Chapter 2, there is ample evidence to suggest otherwise.[11] As Gower's and Prospero's inclination to articulate the boundaries between looking and listening suggests, new opportunities offered new challenges for playwrights, who were increasingly interested in distinguishing their creative terrain.

To focus exclusively on Jones's "painting and carpentry," the masque's spectacularity more generally, or the coterie audiences' tastes in fashion, staging, and genre as largely responsible for the seventeenth century's gradual emphasis on the eye over the ear in theatrical practices is to downplay the importance of shifts occurring in the language used to describe spectatorship.[12] Not only do those shifts occur alongside the new technologies of spectacle, but the wider cultural circulation of "the spectacular" (at least in terms of masque) occurs first through discourse and only later through staging technologies.[13] And, although court masque exerted significant influence on the public stage, its influence was *both* scenic and lexical; that is, literary and descriptive conventions drawn from masque were taken up by those writing for and about the early modern stage and its audiences. Rather than assuming that masque is best understood as an archive for elitist taste and razzle-dazzle entertainment practice, I am interested in interrogating masque's role in articulating and shaping the ways in which seventeenth-century England imagined (or reimagined) and represented spectatorship.[14] In particular, I want to trace the developing tendency to represent sight and hearing as separate, even oppositional, interpretive activities via the Jonson-Jones collaboration and consider how this alteration, in turn, helped alter the language of spectatorship.

Most broadly, my inquiry here considers how spectatorial discourses (those about playgoers and their perceptual, affective, and interpretive processes) influence and help produce both "real" spectators and spectatorial practices. As I argued in Chapter 3, when playwrights begin to conceive of their work as having two potential incarnations—theatrical and textual—they also imagine writing for two different "audiences"—playgoers and readers. Such alterations to conventions of address and the language of theatrical affect (particularly that associated with the senses) not only helps produce changes to the discursive spectator but plays a role in shaping spectatorial tastes and practices. Whereas this project's earlier chapters look at how (and what) the rise of early modern England's professional theater contributed to the discursive spectator's history, this chapter offers a model for the way in which discourse plays a significant role in shaping "real" or embodied viewers and their interpretive habits. Jonsonian masque offers a rich example of *how* such changes could occur first through representation and later become manifest in practice, given Jonson's interest (in multiple senses of the word) in "preserving" these performance ephemera for posterity and publication.[15] My argument engages with recent work on the early modern senses, especially with work that challenges sight's place at the top of the early modern sensory hierarchy.[16] My primary interest, however, lies in discerning how the senses were represented in popular discourse about and in masque and by tracing changes to the language used to describe and invoke the senses in court masque over a sixty-year period, offering an example of how epistemologies of sense perception can be created and circulated through discourse.

But how might such discursive transmissions work? Even if most Londoners could not actually see a masque designed by Jones, they would have had secondhand forms of access, such as those discussed in Chapter 2.[17] As the masque in *The Tempest* shows, the form itself was circulating, both representationally and metatopically, in the medium of popular drama. In addition, the very ephemerality of the court masque made it a noteworthy occasion. Usually performed only once to mark a major holiday or rite of passage for Jacobean England's version of the glitterati (the royal family and high-ranking nobles), court masques would have generated a certain amount of buzz. For example, in reporting epistolarily on Thomas Campion's 1613 *The Lord's Masque,* John Chamberlain (a personage defined by the *Oxford Dictionary of National Biography* as an "inveterate 'Paul's walker' ")[18] writes, "That night was the Lord's maske whereof I hear no great commendation save only for riches, theyre devises beeing long and tedious and more like a play then a maske."[19] When Chamberlain derogates *The Lord's Masque,* he does so based on secondhand information, or word of mouth, a form of knowledge revealed in his statement that he has *heard* no great commendation of it. Chamberlain's claim suggests that Londoners from various circles were discussing the *Lord's Masque* performance, not just those who had been in attendance. James Shirley dramatizes just such a moment of discursive transmission in his play *Love's Cruelty*, as Hippolit describes the experience of seeing a masque to one of the uninitiated:

> HIPPOLIT: A scene to take your eye with wonder, now to see a forest
> move, and the pride of summer brought into a walking wood; in
> the instant, as if the sea had swallowed up the earth, to see waves
> capering about tall ships. . . . In the height of this rapture, a
> tempest so artificial and sudden in the clouds, with a general
> darkness and thunder, so seeming made to threaten, that you
> would cry out with the mariners in the work, you cannot escape
> drowning, in the turning of an eye, these waters ravish into a
> heaven, glorious and angelicall shapes presented, the stars
> distinctly with their motion and music so enchanting you. . . .
> EUBELLA: Fine painted blessings! (2.2.19–33)[20]

Masques could be "broadcast" through such channels as conversation, gossip, and news; they could be (re)presented on the public stage by playwrights who drew upon their images, settings, and language.

It was not solely images from and language about the masque that permeated the seventeenth-century performance lexicon, however. In the above quote, Shirley dramatizes the experience of seeing the masque as something that happens *to* the spectator. The scene "takes" his eye with wonder, and the whole experience produces a vertiginous sort of sensory "rapture." The spectator cries out to the actors that they cannot escape drowning, but this response is generated by more than an empathic identification with their plight. He himself is drowning in the deluge of images pouring over him; he is lost somewhere in the fissures between reality and fiction that performance can expose. As the preeminent masque writer of the late Caroline period, Shirley may be doing a bit of self-promotion here, but his claims are not new ones. As I argued in Chapter 1, the theater's ability to ravish the spectator is what made it so dangerous, and Shirley's description here recalls the invective found in late sixteenth- and early seventeenth-century antitheatricalist polemic. There is, however, a notable difference. While the antitheatricalists describe spectatorial intoxication as an experience that involves all of the senses, Shirley's focuses only on sight. In *Love's Cruelty*, the organ of intake has become aligned with the spectator's experience of the performance: ravishment is equated with seeing. This formulation resembles the earlier one from *The Tempest*, where certain types of performance (as well as the specta-tor's experience of them) become yoked to particular senses, but thirty years separate the two plays. In 1631, Shirley may have written *Love's Cruelty* with a mind toward promoting rather than simply representing Jones's stagecraft, but in 1611 it is unlikely that Shakespeare would have done so.[21] Before Jones's spectacular devices became conventionalized as part of the staging practices of the professional stage, changes were occurring within the representational lexicon used to describe the spectator's experience, changes that played a significant and overlooked role in shaping viewing practices in the later seven-teenth century.

Early Masque and the Synaesthetic Mode

Before tracking the changes to how masque writers portray sensory engagement with spectacle over a half-century in court masque, I want to clarify briefly what I mean by the synaesthetic mode. My use of the term aligns with C. M. Woolgar's definition of *synaesthetic* as "words used in common for more than one sense and that imply no primary division of the ideas relating to these senses in the general consciousness."[22] Employed equally by playwrights and antitheatricalists, the synaesthetic mode could be used to describe an experience or sensation that defied linguistic representation, such as Bottom's dream or Orsino's description of music that begins *Twelfth Night*: "If music be the food of love, play on / Give me excess of it, that surfeiting, / The appetite may sicken and so die" (1.1.1–3), or, in the case of antitheatrical writings, to describe the disturbingly transformative effects of theatergoing. Whether this descriptive mode was merely a literary-dramatic convention or a genuine expression of how early modern subjects experienced certain kinds of sensory stimuli is diffi-cult to assess; however, as a literary convention, the synaesthetic mode is equally significant as an indicator of the cultural discourse surrounding sensory phe-nomenology and spectatorship. While it is unlikely that most of England's population consisted mostly of synaesthetes, the early modern cultural specta-torial lexicon did not articulate clear-cut sensory taxonomies. Consequently, the synaesthetic mode dominated sensory descriptions throughout the Elizabethan period, not only in drama and antitheatrical treatises but in other forms of entertainment and writings about them as well.

While both early and later masque engaged the synaesthetic mode, early masque demonstrates a pronounced disinclination toward heavy description of its scenic effects. Among the earliest surviving printed masques is an entertainment devised for Elizabeth's 1575 summer visit to Kenilworth Castle. Published in the following year by its author, George Gascoigne, the text demonstrates certain descriptive conventions similarly found in Jacobean masque, such as interspersing extradiegetic or eyewitness-type description with masque-text in the printed version. A major difference, however, is what Gascoigne describes in these asides. Unlike the Stuart masque writers, who use these intertextual additions to provide detailed accounts of setting and costume, Gascoigne spends little time on Kenilworth's *mise-en-scène*. In his initial description of the event, he pays only the most perfunctory attention to visual detail:

> Her Majesty passing on to the first gate, there stode in the Leades and Battlements therof, sixe Trumpetters hugelie advanced, much exceeding the common stature of men in this age, who had likewise huge and monstrous Trumpettes, counterfetted, wherein they seemed to sound. . . . And when her majestie entered the gate, there stoode *Hercules* for Porter, who seemed to be amazed at such a presence, upon such a sodain, proffered to stay with them. And yet, at last being overcome by viewe of the rare beutie and princelie countenance of her Majestie, yeelded himself and his charge, presenting the keyes unto her highness with these words.[23]

Gascoigne paints this opening tableau through broad strokes. Aside from scale (the size of the trumpeters), and Elizabeth's celestial beauty, there is little visual specificity. Color, costume, patterns are all glossed over, a stark contrast to the tendency of Jacobean masque writers to obsess over the details, such as the sheen of a certain type of pearl: "And for the front, ear, neck and wrist, the ornament was of the most choice and orient pearl, best setting off from the black."[24] Gascoigne's later descriptions similarly gloss over the visual accoutrements of the Kenilworth pageantry. A "Savage man," who opens part of an entertainment by surprising the queen as she returns from a hunt, is described only as "all clad in Ivie."[25] The subsequent "Ladie of the Lake" episode, which includes the appearance of multiple deities and special effects where people seemed to "go upon the water," contains only a slightly more exacting description: "*Protheus* appeared, sitting on a *Dolphyns* backe. And the *Dolphyn* was conveied upon a boate, so that the Owers seemed to bee his Fynnes."[26]

This disinclination in regard to the visual register when describing performance is not unique to Gascoigne. In a letter to Mr. Humfrey Martin, Robert Laneham, a minor court official and London mercer (or according to David Scott, William Patten, Teller of the Exchequer)[27] penned what reads as blow-by-blow account of the Kenilworth entertainments. While he provides rather more visual detail than Gascoigne—noting that Proteus's dolphin was "from hed to tayl waz . . . four & twenty foot long"—he spends far more time describing the musical interlude via the synaesthetic mode:

> July 18. Music from the Dolphin. Knights made a delectabl ditty of a song . . . compoounded of six severall instruments al coovert, casting soound from the Dolphin's belly within; Arion, the seauenth, sitting thus singing (az I say) withoout. Noow syr, the ditty in miter so aptly endlighted to the matter, and after by voys so delicioously deliverd: the song by a skilful artist intoo hiz parts so sweetly sorted: each part in hiz instrument so clean & sharpely toouched, every instrument again in hiz kind so excellently tunabl: and this in the eevening of the day, resoounding from the callm waters: whear prezens of her Maiesty, & longing too listen, had vtterly damped all noyz & dyn; the hole armony conueyd in tyme, tune, & temper, thus incomparably melodious: with what pleazure (Master Martin), with what sharpnes of conceyt, with what lyuely delighte, this moought pears into the heerers harts, I pray ye imagin yoor self az ye may; for, so God iudge me, by all the wit & cunning I haue, I cannot express, I promis yoo. . . . As for me, surely I was lulld in such liking, & so loth too leaue of, that mooch a doo, a good while after, had I, to fynde me whear I waz.[28]

Laneham's description of the masque's music may seem to support Gurr's claim, seconded by Bruce Smith, that unlike modern spectators, early modern audiences were more attuned to the audial than the visual.[29] More telling, however, are the terms Laneham uses to represent the effect music had on him. Rather than relying on terms that privilege a particular sense, Laneham's account evokes multiple imaginative, sensory, and sensual possibilities. A listener with a palate as well as an ear, Laneham hears voices "delicioously deliverd" and sounds "sweetly sorted." He also describes the instrumentals as "sharpely touched," suggesting a kind of intersubjective synaesthesia: as the musician touches his instrument to make music, the sounds "sharpely" touch the ear of the listener. Equally synaesthetically inclined is Laneham's use of "clean," a sensation in which *all* of the senses can participate. Toward the end of the passage, Laneham describes the music as peering into the very heart of the auditor, as though attempting to describe a sensory ravishment that a single perceptual mode could never encompass. Not articulated as separate and distinct phenomena, Laneham imagines the senses as imbricated and fungible components of a larger, more complex one.

The synaesthetic mode similarly permeates the masque-text itself.[30] In the "Savage Man" episode referenced earlier, Gascoigne uses it to underscore the wonder kindled by Elizabeth's presence. At times, he invokes the multisensory through metaphor, as when the Savage Man pairs the visual experience of seeing the queen and her ladies with the palpable one of heat:

> And since I see such sights,
> I meane such glorious Dames,
> As kindle might in frozen brestes,
> A furnace full of flames.[31]

At others, Gascoigne uses it in a less structured fashion. Toward the end of his monologue, the Savage Man strings together a series of variously appointed sensory illuminants, calling on the ears to help him decipher a visual query and receiving audial information through tactile mechanisms:

> What shall I do,
> what sunne shal lend me light?
> Wel Eccho, where art thou
> could I but Eccho finde,
> She would returne me answere yet
> By blast of every winde.[32]

The source of authority on which the Savage Man calls is an odd one. Besides the fact that he calls upon Echo (voice) to be the "sun" that "lends him light," she cannot provide him with answers; she can only repeat what she hears. The Savage Man's call to Echo, then, emphasizes sound *itself* rather than language, a detail that complicates the metaphor. Rather than creating a strictly figurative parallel where the "sunne/light" and "Eccho" stand in for visual and audial epistemologies, the metaphor posits an actual sensory exchange where sound is called upon to provide an answer to what began as a visual problem (the identity of the "glorious Dames").[33] Finally, the Savage Man imagines receiving Echo's answers "by blast of every winde," a phrase that invokes the harsh tactility of a blow as much as sound. Here, the synaesthetic mode functions less as a self-conscious rhetorical strategy than as an organic expression of how sense perception is experienced—not as disparate sensations but as a fluid continuum where barriers between sound, sight, and touch seem hardly to exist.[34]

Sidney's 1578 masque *The Lady of May* also exhibits these variations of the synaesthetic mode. Written as an outdoor entertainment for the queen, the masque presents an abbreviated version of a nuptial comedy. Pursued by two suitors, the Lady of May cannot bring herself to choose between them, so the quandary is delivered up to Elizabeth's wisdom. The masque begins as the girl's mother, begging the queen for help, describes the experience of Elizabeth's presence as a veritable banquet of the senses: "So dare I wretch my bashfull feare subdue, / And feede mine eares, mine eyes, my hart in you."[35] Later, once the conflict is resolved, the Lady praises her royal benefactor in lines that suggest a more organic form of sensory interpenetration:

Thus joyfully in chosen tunes rejoice,
That such a one is witnesse of my hart,
Whose cleerest eyes I blisse, and sweetest voyce,
That see my good and judgeth my desert.[36]

While these lines can be read as promoting proper sensory alignment (it is Elizabeth's eyes that see the Lady's "good" and her voice that pronounces judgment), the syntax challenges such a linear reading. By ending the second line with "voyce" and beginning the next with "that see," sense organ and sensory function are rendered ambiguous. Additionally, the singular form of the verb "see," while in agreement with "cleerest eyes," also offers the possibility of including "voyce" as part of its subject; both eyes and voice are represented as equal collaborators in the acts of seeing and judging.

The distinction between metaphorical and more "literal" uses of the synaesthetic mode illustrates a fine difference in the way it functioned in the latter part of the sixteenth century. Writers employed it to describe the ineffable or overwhelming, but they also used it to describe the *effect* of such transcendent encounters on the spectator-listener. Laneham wants to describe music but also to convey how it works on the hearer; Gascoigne and Sidney attempt to represent both the queen's presence and their experience of being in her presence. Able to signify this duality—both what is immanent in the admired object and in one's experience of it—the synaesthetic mode is a particularly apt form of expression for the masque. Designed for and around the monarch, the masque directs its action toward its most important specta-tor but, in doing so, places her at the heart of the spectacle. It must represent (through laudatory description) and present (through encomial address) the monarch; it must illustrate her celestial qualities and highlight the potency of her presence.

Seventeen years later, the multisensory mode still serves this intricate function but with a noticeable turn toward sensory parsing. Francis Davison's 1595 Shrovetide Gray's Inn entertainment, *The Masque of Proteus*, tells the story of Proteus's capture by the Prince of Purpoole. To obtain his freedom, Proteus must deliver the Adamantine Rock (a giant lodestone set under the Arctic pole) so that Purpoole can control the seas. But there is a catch: Pro-teus will relinquish the rock only if the prince shows him "a power, / Which in attractive virtue should surpas / The wondrous force of his Ir'ne drawing rock."[37] This "force superior" is, of course, Elizabeth. As in the earlier exam-ples, *Proteus* spends considerable time on the queen. Using synaesthetic superlatives, Davison articulates Elizabeth's physical presence as physical con-tact, saying that it "truly touches" the hearts of men, and rendering her virtue as a visual object, the "shining sunne" that banishes "shadowes."[38] The synaesthetic as experience, however, largely disappears. Instead, *Proteus* exhibits a nascent inclination that directs the audience's senses toward their "proper" targets: sights are seen and sounds are heard. The tale is both intro-duced and interrupted by requests from one of the characters to "tell" the story they so "long to heer," and when the Prince's squire prepares Proteus for the experience of the greater magnetism of Elizabeth, he tells him to "calme awhile your overweening vaunts / Prepare beleefe & doe but *use your eyes*" (81, my italics). Whereas in the Kenilworth entertainment and *The Lady of May*, a single sense seemed incapable of encompassing the "experience" of Elizabeth, *Proteus* suggests that vision is the preeminent sensory channel through which to know her.

Although nowhere near the fantastical setting of the Stuart masque, *Pro-teus*, with its "special effects" and raised platform stage, suggests the sort of stagecraft that later comes to dominate such court entertainments.[39] This tendency to separate audial and visual in *Proteus* may be part of a representa-tional attempt to "show" or showcase some of the masque's innovations in staging.[40] As masques became more visually elaborate, they correspondingly became more difficult to record and preserve. Unlike plays, where each performance might be ephemeral but was nonetheless repeated (though with probable variations), masques were conceived as one-time events. As such, their writers often expressed anxiety about redeeming them from the "common evil" of oblivion.[41] The masque that was prepared for publication demanded both authorial and archival labor. Simply transcribing the text will not do; the entire multivalent event must be "shown" in order to undertake any sort of conservation of the whole. Aligning sense and stimuli on the page constitutes one way that masque authors could communicate the sensory multiplicity of the masque-event with accuracy. By clearly delineating the visual, the vocal, the musical, and the kinetic, masque authors could both display the sensory multiplicity of the event and provide an organizational schema for representing the masque experience.

In the case of the most prolific of the Jacobean masque writers, however, an additional motive existed. Jonson's need to impose control over his work needs little rehearsal[42] and has been largely characterized in terms of understanding Jonson's relationship to changing ideas about the figure of the author, the concept of drama as literature, and his vexed relationship with his audiences.[43] William N. West's rich, nuanced study of the contested, often oppositional, meanings of the term *understander* suggests Jonson's significance in terms of fashioning an early modern lexicon of theatrical experience: "The use of *understander* as a technical term of theater in the first fifteen years of the seventeenth century can virtually be traced back to the works of Ben Jonson, the sharpest critic of the audience of his time."[44] However, Jonson played an equally vital role in refashioning the language used to describe sensory and spectatorial processes. As several critics note, one of the ways Jonson constructs a sense of authorial control in the masque text is by imagining and representing it as a homogenous *literary* entity, in that he begins to conceive of the masque as a text as much as a performance event.[45] Whereas early Jonsonian masques exhibit descriptive and formal tensions, later ones feel holistic, hermetic, complete—at least in terms of their textual life. For in order to create the literary masque, Jonson must find a way to exact representational control over the profuse (and, at times, chaotic) energies generated by the performed one. Whereas earlier masque writers used the synaesthetic mode to depict experiential excess and linguistic insufficiency, Jonson views language's moments of inarticulateness as something to be feared rather than celebrated. Part of the project of gaining control—over the text, the masque-spectacle, and Jones himself—is to convey the masque experience *as* precisely

controlled, ordered, intelligible, and representable. The intrinsic abundance
of the synaesthetic mode becomes problematic for, even antagonistic to, Jonson's authorial enterprise and ultimately cannot be a part of it.

Jonson's development of a language that allows him to "authorize" the
masque is a polymorphic process occurring over the thirty years he occupies the post of court poet. In terms of the synaesthetic mode, however,
a clear shift occurs within the first decade of his collaboration with Jones.
Rather than articulating the spectator's interaction with what is seen as
something that can (and often does) involve multiple senses simultaneously, Jonson depicts the spectator's senses as responding to their "logical"
determinants. Pairing descriptions of sets and costumes with injunctions
to the reader-spectator to "look" or "see," and emphasizing song and music
through references to the ear, Jonson carves out a more ordered sensory
universe. For earlier masque writers, the synaesthetic mode had offered
multiple experiential possibilities: sound can be like taste; sight can be felt.
But in the sensory palate that Jonson puts forth in his texts, looking is
looking and hearing is hearing—a demarcation that not only emphasizes
the singularity of each experiential mode but also, finally, their incompat-
ibility.

Jonson's "Invention": The Language of Looking

Jonson's early work for the Stuart court illustrates that initially he followed
in his predecessors' footsteps in his use of the synaesthetic mode, as it plays a
significant role in the two celebratory pageants he penned for the royal family's arrival in London and in the various instatement rituals surrounding
James's accession. The first of these, entitled "Part of King James's Entertainment in Passing to His Coronation," was performed as part of the king's
civic processional en route to his coronation. While related, civic pageantry
and court entertainments were not the same. The streets of London were a
far cry from the country estates of the nobility; therefore, space and design
possibilities were limited. Court entertainments contained long intervals of
music and dance, but civic pageants had little if any. Dialogue in the latter
tended toward lengthy encomial orations directed to the monarch rather than
providing a narrative framework for the event, and, perhaps most important,
the audience for civic pageants was larger and far more diverse. Certain elements nonetheless testify to a kinship between masque and civic pageantry,

particularly those of address, rhetoric, and dominant representational modes. In civic as well as court entertainments, the monarch is the primary addressee, the convergence of the entertainment's subject and its reason for being. While there are occasional comic interludes that might be spoken in dialect (and by hired actors), rhetoric tends toward the formal and ceremonial. For the most part, representation occurs through analogy rather than verisimilitude: allegory and emblem are central to the transmission of meaning in both forms. And, although the audience for civic entertainments was larger and more heterogeneous, Jonson did not make concessions to the masses: "[These shews . . . are] to be so presented, as upon the view, they might, without cloud or obscurity, declare themselves to the sharp and learned: and for the multitude, no doubt but their grounded judgments did gaze, said it was fine, and were satisfied."[46]

The models on which Jonson would have drawn, then, were those set down by his Elizabethan predecessors. Like them, Jonson makes use of the synaesthetic mode, particularly when addressing the king:

> Let thronging joy, love and amazement meet.
> Cleave all the air with shouts, and let the cry,
> Strike through as long, and universally,
> As thunder; for thou now art blissed to see
> That sight for which thou didst begin to be,
> When Brutus' plough first gave thee infant bounds,
> And I, thy Genius, walked auspicious rounds,
> In every furrow then did I forelook,
> And saw this day marked white in Clotho's book.
> The several circles both of change and sway,
> Within this *Isle*, there also figured lay;
> Of which the greatest, perfectest and last
> Was this, whose present happiness we taste. (281–93)

As was the case in *Proteus*, the text tends to align the experience of the monarch primarily with visual reception. However, the passage also contains numerous examples of synaesthetic expression: voices cleave and strike the air; England tastes the happiness of the arrival of both James and the nation's foretold destiny. Other examples appear in Jonson's early representations for and of England's new king and royal family. Written to commemorate

James's first parliamentary session, Jonson's *Panegyre* also uses the synaesthetic mode to communicate the effect of the king's presence on his people:

> With these he passed, and with his people's hearts
> Breathed in his way; and souls, their better parts
> Hasting to follow forth in shouts and cries,
> Upon his face all threw their covetous eyes. (31–34)

And in *The Entertainment at Althorpe*, performed in honor of Anne and
Henry's entry into England, Jonson addresses Henry as his "dear lord, on
whom my covetous eye / Doth feed itself, but cannot satisfy" (305–6).[47]

In 1605, Jonson embarked on what was his most significant royal commission to date: *The Masque of Blackness* for the court's Twelfth Night celebration. A watershed moment for Jonson and the masque form, it marks the
point where Anne, James's queen, and Jones begin to exert their influence on
both. For the masque, it meant a blossoming of the form's popularity and
expressive capabilities; for Jonson, it meant collaboration, or shared creative
control. In the civic and outdoor entertainments that precede his major
works for the court, Jonson exhibits confidence in his role as "inventor."
Although the civic pageants for James's coronation were orchestrated by Stephen Harrison (Dekker names him "the Chief Joiner" in his account of the
pageants), Jonson never mentions him.[48] Nor does he spend much time
describing Harrison's scenic work: "Thus far the complemental part of the
first; wherein was not only labored the expression of state and magnificence,
(as proper to a triumphal Arch) but the very site, fabric, strength, policy,
dignity and affections of the City were all laid down to life" (243–47). Jonson's early masques, however, strike a different tone. Often mentioning Anne
and especially Jones, Jonson carves up the masque text as though it were
Lear's map, staking out his creative territory as distinct from that of others.
The published text of *Blackness* (1608) begins with a statement about Jonson's
ingenuity in negotiating the queen's input: "Hence, because it was her majesty's will to have [herself and her ladies] as blackamores at first, the invention
was derived by me, and presented thus" (20–22). Following this claim, a
fifty-eight-line description of Jones's sets and costume is a far cry from his
concise description of the *mise-en-scène* in *The King's Entertainment*.

Equally striking in these early masques, however, are the changes to Jonson's narrative persona. Rather than the commanding, impersonal voice that

dominated his early Stuart entertainments, here the narrator seems split, shifting between what we might call a narrator persona and an eyewitness:[49]

> First, for the scene, was drawn a Landtschap consisting of small woods, and here and there a void place filled with huntings; which falling, an artificial sea was seen to shoot forth, as if it flowed to the land, raised with waves which seemed to move, and in some places the billow to break, as imitating that orderly disorder which is common in nature. In front of this sea were placed six tritons in moving and sprightly actions, their upper parts human, save that their hairs were blue, as partaking of the sea color, their denisent parts fish, mounted above their heads, and all varied in disposition. From their backs were borne out certain light pieces of taffeta as if carried by the wind, and their music made out of wreathed shells. Behind these a pair of sea-maids, for song, were as conspicuously seated; between which two great sea-horses, as big as the life, put forth themselves, the one mounting aloft and writhing his head from the other, which seemed to sink forward (so intended for variation, and that the figure behind might come off better); upon their backs Oceanus and Niger were advanced. (23–39)

Initially, the narrator persona is foremost. Speaking with an authoritative voice, the narrator does not subjectively recount the effect of the spectacle on him (the first thing I perceived . . .) but dictates the manner in which it will be experienced: "First, for the scene." He concludes the description of the "Landtschap" with an interpretation of its symbolism, "as imitating that orderly disorder which is common in nature," a move that suggests the privileging of the interpretive gaze over the phenomenological one.

Soon after, however, the narrator persona gradually shifts toward the stance of an eyewitness. The next sentence consists mostly of straightforward reportage. Perhaps there is a hint of interpretation in the phrase "as partaking of the sea color," which punctuates the previously mentioned color of the tritons' hair, but it is otherwise unadorned by subjective interjections. The subsequent description, "From their backs were borne out certain light pieces of taffeta as if carried by the wind, and their music made out of wreathed shells," has an element of fancy, even wonder, to it: the movement of gauzy fabrics evokes the elements themselves, and shells seem to make music. Finally, the description reaches a visual crescendo and interpretation goes by the wayside, bowled over, it seems, by theatrical spectacle: "Two great sea-horses, as big as the life, put forth themselves, the one mounting aloft and writhing his head from the other, which seemed to sink forward." The descriptive control exhibited in the earlier part of the passage here slips from the narrator's grasp. There is a touch of the breathless in clauses like "as big as the life" and the somewhat awkward rendering of the sea-horses' maneuvers, a sense of immediacy compounded by the fact that these lines are the only ones written in active voice. It is almost as if this authorial persona, overwhelmed by *Blackness*'s visuals, attempts to mimic the rapidity with which visual stimuli can communicate with the spectator. Even the parenthetical addendum (which, for a moment, seems as though it will turn toward interpretation rather than looking) ends up interpreting the spectacle through its own visual terms rather than through the symbolic ones used earlier: "the one mounting aloft and writhing his head from the other . . . (so intended for variation, *and that the figure behind might come off better*)" (my emphasis). The authority of the narrator persona gives way to the wonder of the eyewitness; the astute commentator becomes the astonished viewer.

Alongside this narrational split in *Blackness*, another division appears: the tendency to register the spectator's experience through disparate sensory channels. *Blackness*'s narrator seems initially to want to shrug off the importance of the masque's visuals: "So much for the bodily part, which was of Master Inigo Jones his design and act" (78–79). The following fifty-nine lines, however, consist of an elaborate description of *Blackness*'s sets and read like an obsessive meditation on their visual impact: "These thus presented, the scene behind seemed a vast sea, and united with this that followed forth from the termination or horizon of which (being the level of the state, which was placed in the upper end of the hall) was drawn, by the lines of perspective, the whole work shooting downwards from the eye; which decorum made it more conspicuous, and caught the eye afar off with a wandering beauty. To which was added an obscure and cloudy night-piece that made the whole set off" (65–71). Here, the narrator underscores the visual on several levels. Most obvious is the barrage of optical language: the description abounds with references to perspective, lines, horizon, presentation, trajectory, and contrast. Homophones, such as "scene" and "sea," stress this fixation on the visual, an emphasis further accentuated by repeated references to the organ of sight itself. While the interchangeability of "I" and "eye" is a popular early modern trope, there is little in this passage of the subjective *jouissance* usually suggested by such wordplay. Instead of simply standing in for the viewing subject, the "eye" seems to engulf all traces of it, situated, as it is here, in a world of geometry and composition rather than one of interpretation and meaning.

While the narrator situates Jones's contribution squarely in the visual realm, he establishes Jonson's firmly in the audial. After finishing his account of the *mise-en-scéne*, the narrator turns abruptly to describing the subsequent part of *Blackness* primarily through sound: "By this, one of the tritons, with two sea-maids, began to sing to the others' loud music, their voices being a tenor and two trebles." Engaging a sonic lexicon of volume and tone, the narrator forges an associative connection between his poetry and the ear, a dynamic reinforced by *Blackness*'s first spoken lines: "Sound, sound aloud / The welcome of the orient flood / Into the west" (76–78). He introduces two other songs using similar descriptive emphases, "They were again accited to the sea with a song of two trebles, whose cadences were iterated by a double echo" (276–77), as well as mentioning the organ of reception in the song itself: "If you do not stop your ear / We shall have more cause to fear / Sirens of the land" (271–73).

The move to distinguish Jonson's artistic product from Jones's via a sensory armature that divides sight from sound is inchoate in *Blackness*. A more coherent expression appears in Jonson's next masque for the Stuarts. Performed in 1606 as part of the festivities celebrating the marriage of the young earl of Essex, Robert Devereux, to Frances Howard, daughter of the earl of Suffolk, *Hymenai* trumped Jones's previous effects: "Ben Jonson turned the globe of the earth standing behind the altar, and within the Concave sate the 8. men-maskers."[50] As if in response to the wondrous spectacularity of Jones's staging, Jonson prefaces his printed version of the masque with an elaborate and personalized defense of poesy:

> This it is hath made the most royal princes and greatest persons,
> who are commonly the personators of these actions, not only studi-
> ous of riches and magnificence, in the outward celebration or show,
> which rightly becomes them, but curious after the most high and
> hearty inventions to furnish the inward parts, and those grounded
> upon antiquity and solid learning; which though their voice be
> taught to sound to present occasions, their sense or doth or should
> always lay hold on more removed mysteries. And howsoever some
> may squeamishly cry out that all endeavor of learning and sharpness
> in these transitory devices, especially where it steps beyond their

little or (let me not wrong 'em) no brain at all, is superfluous, I am
contented that these fastidious stomachs leave my full tables and
enjoy at home their clean empty trenchers, fittest for such airy tastes,
where perhaps a few Italian herbs picked up and made into a salad
may find sweeter acceptance than all the most nourishing and sound
meats of the world. For these men's palates let me not answer, O
muses. It is not my fault if I fill them out nectar and they run to
metheglin. (9–27)

Jonson's self-justification appeals to multiple sensory registers. Addressing
the visual first, he points to the "riches and magnificence" in the "outward
celebration and show" of the masque. He then moves to audial description,
articulating the masque's poetry as both the "voice" that "sounds to present
occasion" and that which can reveal "more removed mysteries." Following a
brief nod to the tactile by mentioning the "sharpness" of the masques'
"devices," Jonson turns toward his extended metaphor on taste, in which he
imagines his detractors as gastronomic gulls seduced by "airy" foreign flavors
that provide little sustenance. Moving easily between sight, sound, touch,
and taste, Jonson calls on almost the entire sensorium to plume up his work.
In doing so, Jonson champions it doubly: the synaesthetic mode tends to
connote an experience that surpasses representation. Choosing it here suggests he wants to lend his work an empyrean status, to claim for it a sublimity
that cannot be captured through mere prose. But his use of the synaesthetic
mode here contains a notable difference from earlier examples. Whereas usually that mode expresses an intermingling of the senses, here they appear
sequentially and relatively discrete. Indeed, the whole passage seems driven
by a desire to taxonomize experience, for in addition to disarticulating the
senses, Jonson parses experiential modalities as well: "It is a notable and just
advantage that things subjected to understanding have of those which are
objected to sense; that the one sort are but momentary and merely taking;
the other impressing and lasting. . . . So short are the bodies of all things, in
comparison of their souls" (1, 4–5). Just as he imagines the masque as composed of various sensory parts rather than as the sum of them, here he anato-
mizes its communicative apparatus through binaries: subjected and objected,
understanding and sense, lasting and momentary, and finally, soul and body.
    Jonson's dissection of the masque in *Hymenai* may reflect a desire for
individual recognition in a form that resembles a work of tapestry: each
thread (set, music, choreography, and language) means little without the

others. But the linguistic strategies he adopts herald a change in the language of sensory experience that extends beyond the purview of Jonson's artistic self-fashioning. Even the monarch himself—the entity most often described via the synaesthetic mode in masque—is representationally altered. Jonson refers only briefly to James I in *Blackness*: "This sun is temperate and refines / All things on which his beauty shines" (242–43); however, his opening description of the masque's *mise-en-scène* invokes the king via its frequent mention of the metonymized "eye" that is "caught" by the set's "wandering beauty" (76). In court entertainments, the "eye" does not represent the viewpoint of just any spectator but that of the monarch's. In part, this association comes from the fact that all court masques are for and about the ruler as their ideal spectator, but here the connection is especially close. *Blackness* was the first court masque held at Whitehall, and the Banqueting House was spatially organized to facilitate the king's perspective.[51] Correspondingly, Jones's set was intended to cater to the best seat in the house, and it was from this perspective that his designs were imagined and carried out.[52] The "eye" from which "the whole work shoots downwards" is James's eye; synechdocally, however, it is also James himself. That Jonson should make such a connection is not extraordinary: as God's agent on earth, James was often portrayed as omnipresent and all-seeing.[53] But in the context of how masque had tended to represent the monarch, it marks a noticeable shift. Whereas earlier entertainments articulated the monarch's presence as transcendent and ineffable and described its effect on the spectators through the synaesthetic mode, *Blackness* only indirectly refers to the king by suggesting that the eye, by itself, is a sufficient representational reliquary for the monarch's person and presence.

If *Blackness* symbolizes the monarch as an eye, *The Masque of Beauty* (1608) and *The Haddington Masque* (1608) make him the object of the eyes of many. In *Beauty*, we find James poised somewhere between looking subject and looked-at object:

> BOREAS: Which among these is Albion, Neptune's son?
> JANUARIUS: What ignorance dares make that question?
>   Would any ask who Mars were in the wars?
>   Or which is Hesperus among the stars?
>   Of the bright planets, which is Sol? Or can
>   A doubt arise 'mong creatures, who is man?
>   Behold whose eyes do dart Promethan fire

> Throughout this all; whose precepts do inspire
> The rest with duty; yet commanding, cheer;
> And are obeyed more with love than fear. (20–29)

Among Jonson's masques, *Beauty* is unique in opening with the encomial address to the king rather than (as was typical) building *toward* this moment. As both the symbol for and realization of order and beneficence, the "natural" place to draw attention to the king follows the resolution of conflict with which Jacobean masque usually begins.[54] *Beauty,* however, places James at the center of the spectacle: in performance, these words would have been the first ones spoken, directing the spectators' gaze on him.[55] On the page, this passage directly follows Jonson's extradiegetic description of setting and costumes, a placement that allows for an elision between scene and king, rendering both as spectacle. In each case, the masque-text reinforces such connections. Boreas's request to identify the king is answered through analogue, a representational form that partially subscribes to the convention of depicting the sovereign as inexpressible. However, by presenting each component of the epic simile as a test of visual identification (could you pick out the brightness of Hesperus among the stars or discern a human form among animals?), Jonson crafts the entire metaphor using sight as the connective tissue. Finally, when Januarius discloses the sought-after presence, he does so with a command to look: "Behold whose eyes do dart Promethan fire." This revelation is not, finally, an overt objectification of James; after all, his are the eyes that "dart Promethan fire" at the beholder. But it is a rendition of the king constructed almost wholly through the visual imaginary. Jonson's subsequent masque, *Haddington,* contains a similar image of the king, which draws attention to the visual symbols of his earthly power: "Look on this state, and if you yet not know / What crown there shines, whose scepter here does grow" (180–81).

Rather than imagining and articulating the king wholly through the visual register, Jonson's 1611 *Oberon, The Fairy Prince,* revisits the multisensory mode to portray James and the effect of his presence:

> Melt earth to sea, sea flow to air,
> And air fly into fire,
> Whilst we in turn to Arthur's chair
> Bear Oberon's desire,
> Than which there nothing can be higher,

Save James, to whom it flies:
But he the wonder is of tongues, of ears, of eyes.
Who hath not heard, who hath not seen,
        Who hath not sung his name?
The soul that hath not, hath not been
        But is the very same
With buried sloth, and knows not fame,
Which doth him best comprise:
For he the wonder is of tongues, of ears, of eyes. (220–33)

A revisiting but not a return: although this description of James engages three senses, their borders are clearly demarcated.[56] Orgel claims that *Oberon* marks the moment where the Jonson-Jones collaboration attains "a new sort of unity," demonstrating the artists' "increasing ability to think in each other's terms."[57] Noting the ways in which Jones begins to "devise settings that could serve as the media for action of some complexity," Orgel focuses primarily on the evidence for Jones's adapting to the poet's vision.[58] However, Jonson's alteration of the multisensory mode in *Oberon* suggests Jones's imprint on the author's imagination and descriptive lexicon. Whereas Elizabethan and earlier Jacobean descriptions of the sovereign imagine a confluence of the senses, *Oberon*'s enumerates them, forcing them apart. No longer imagined as an entity that simultaneously occupies the observer's every perceptual channel, the sovereign's presence becomes instead an ordered and sequential experience. And, while *Oberon*'s encomium invokes three senses (rather than only vision), "eyes" provides the anchor for the rhyme royale's concluding couplets, underscoring sight's preeminence both for readers and auditors.

In that subsequent entertainments bear an unmistakable similarity to it in terms of structure and narrative tendencies, *Oberon* set a standard for Jonsonian masque.[59] Paradoxically, the new unity Orgel sees as attained by poet and architect[60] was achieved partly through division: *Oberon*'s sensory fault lines are drawn more deeply than in Jonson's earlier masques. Besides presenting looking and hearing as separate experiences, *Oberon* contains multiple sensory imperatives, not unlike those found in *The Tempest*. For the most part, these are commands to look rather than to listen. Silenus (the satyr's leader) three times orders his followers to "see" or "look." Each time, the order precedes a particularly spectacular event: the scene changes from sylvan grove to "glorious palace" (100–9) and the entrance of the "nation of fays" (the dancers) and Oberon in his chariot (213–18).[61] *Oberon* is also the first of Jonson's masque to cut extradiegetic description to a minimum—four lines as opposed to the nineteen found in its predecessor, the 1609 *Masque of Queens*. In place of the elaborate recitation on Jones's sets are dialogic injunctions to "see and "look"—a sort of shorthand encapsulation of the wonder formerly captured by the eyewitness-persona. But while this alteration may deemphasize Jones's contributions in the printed masque, the intradiegetic sensory commands underscore them in the masque's performance. Such imperatives cannot help but direct the spectators' attention toward Jones's devices, which produce wonder primarily through visual spectacle.

It is, finally, the alteration to the descriptive lexicon of wonder that heralds one of the greatest changes to the early modern discourse on spectatorship. Like Jonson's compression of his descriptions of Jones's stagecraft, his renditions of the king suggest a transformation in representations of the ineffable. Jonson's 1621 *The Gypsies Metamorphosed* displays a more fully fledged version of the monarchical encomium found in Oberon: "Let us alone; bless the sovereign and his senses. / We'll take 'em in order, as they have being; and first of seeing" (1234–36). The verse goes on to enumerate and "bless" all five of the monarch's senses, a division textually emphasized by Jonson's numbering of them on the page—the only time he uses such a strategy in all of his printed masques. And, while *Gypsies* is unique to the Jonsonian masque corpus in several ways (subject matter, exhibition, and number of performances),[62] it demonstrates its genealogical connection to *Oberon* via this panegyric constructed through a rendition of sensory experience as disparate, self-contained, and systematic. But a greater change, perhaps, is one explicitly expressed by Wonder herself in Jonson's aptly named *The Vision of Delight* (1617). Reacting to her first sight of the bower of Zephyrus, Wonder manages to express the inexpressible:

> Wonder must speak or break: what is this? Grows
> the wealth of nature here, or art? . . .
> I have not seen the place could more surprise;
> It looks methinks like one of Nature's eyes,
> Or her whole body set in art. Behold! (132–33, 150–52)

While there are brief mentions of other sensory stimuli in the twenty-four-line passage, it is largely a one-dimensional ekphrasis, constructed almost wholly through visuality.[63]

The Language of Looking and Spectatorial Practice

Late in his career, Inigo Jones famously stated that masques were "nothing but pictures with Light and Motion."[64] He makes no mention of poetry or song. By 1640, the year in which Jones designed his last court entertainments, he may have been right. One of his final collaborations (this time with William Davenant), *Salmacida Spolia* (1639), has 496 lines: only 72 are dialogue. Jones is not alone, however, in making such claims. While dismissing masques as "toys" and stating that dancing, one of the masque's principal components, is a "Meane and Vulgar Thing," Francis Bacon waxes rhapsodic in describing what he sees as their principal virtue: "Let the *Scenes* abound with *Light*, specially *Coloured* and *Varied*: And let the Masquers, or any other, that are to come down from the *Scene*, have some Motions upon the *Scene* it selfe, before their Comming down: For it drawes the Eye strangely, and makes it with great pleasure, to desire to see that, it cannot perfectly discerne" (original italics).[65] Something of the synaesthetic metaphor lingers here—the stagecraft "feed[s] and relieve[s] the eye"—but overall the visual register dominates Bacon's descriptive lexicon. Analogous to Prospero's parsing of sight from sound that precedes *The Tempest*'s nuptial masque, Bacon's sole mention of the audial in this passage is to mark it as that which distracts from the spectacle: "The alteration of scenes, *so it be quietly and without noise,* are things of great beauty and pleasure"[66] (my italics).

But while Bacon privileges the masque's visual offerings (particularly its stagecraft) as its most commendable offering, he does not wholly dismiss its other sensory libations. Much like Jonson's treatment of the senses in *Oberon* and *The Gypsies Metamorphosed,* Bacon taxonomizes the masque's sensory appeals, designating them as almost wholly independent experiences. Immediately following his praise of visual spectacle, Bacon follows with a commendatory catalogue for the ideal masque:

Let the *Songs* be *Loud*, and *Cheerefull*, and not *Chirpings*, or *Pulings*. Let the *Musike* likewise, be *Sharpe*, and *Loud*, and *Well Placed*. The *Colours*, that shew best by Candlelight, are White, Carnation, and a Kinde of Sea-Water-Greene; And *Oes* or *Spangs* as they are of no great Cost, so they are of most Glory. As for *Rich Embroidery*, it is lost, and not Discerned. Let the *Sutes* of the *Masquers*, be Gracefull, and as such as become the Person, when the Vizars are off: Not after Examples of Knowne Attires; Turks, Soldiers, Mariners and the like.

> . . . Some *Sweet Odours*, suddenly comming forth, without any drops
> falling, are, in such a Company, as there is Steame and Heate,
> Things of great Pleasure; and Refreshment. . . . But All is Nothing,
> except the *Roome* be kept Cleare, and Neat.[67]

Again, remnants of multisensory metaphor can perhaps be discerned in
Bacon's demand that the music be "sharpe" and "well-placed," but these
adjectives have little of the sensual richness and sensory play found in Laneham's earlier articulation of "sharpely touched" instruments. Equally revelatory, however, is Bacon's seeming inability to keep the visual from
encroaching on all aspects of his description. His brief advice about the
masque's musical components backtracks into a further extended meditation
on its visual allurements, addressing issues of light, color, and costume. While
he does address scent (an experience rarely recorded in printed masques), he
concludes with a spatial injunction that reorients the reader squarely in the
visual imaginary: "But All is Nothing, except the *Roome* be kept Cleare, and
Neat."

    If Jonson's linguistic fashioning for the masque permanently influenced
the form, a more challenging question remains: what role did these alterations
to the language of looking play in shaping ideas about spectatorship in the
period? While it would be overstating the case to say that Jonson's representational innovations determined the shape that discourses about spectators and
spectatorship were to take, his language did more than reflect them. Near the
end of Jonson's masque-writing career, Peter Hausted (one of the so-called
Sons of Ben) staged an adaptation of *Epicoene* at Cambridge in 1632. In
defending his choice to keep scenery to a minimum, he writes: "I doe confesse
we did not goe such quainte ways as we might have done; we had none
of those *Sea-artes*, knew not how, or else scorn'd to plant our *Canvas* so
advantageously to *catch* the *wayward breath* of the *Spectatours*; but freely and
ingenuously labourd rather to *merit* rather than *ravish* an *Applause* from the
Theater" (original italics).[68] That Hausted demeans the scenic aspect of drama
is predictable: as one of Jonson's poetic disciples, he likely shared his mentor's
opinions on the theater's increasing reliance on spectacular stagecraft. More
telling are the terms through which Hausted imagines the theatrical experience. In claiming that he and his fellows "labourd rather to *merit* rather than
ravish" applause, he aligns the linguistic-poetic with reason or judgment and
the visual with an overwhelming sort of passion, a forgetting of the self. In
this case, the visual and verbal have been fully severed; rather than imagining

theater as an entity that produces wonder by creating an illusion that evokes all the senses in the spectator, here only the visual generates the marvelous.

I offer Jonson's contribution to the parlance of sensory engagement as an example of how a given culture's "language of looking" plays a role in shaping spectatorial practice. Doubtless the critical tendency in early modern studies to downplay this influence is due largely to the difficulty of tracing such discursive residuum via historical spectators: records of developments in stagecraft and pageantry are more readily available and seem, at first glance, more legible. However, this bias may also be an effect of (scholarly) discourse. Orgel uses Antony à Wood's account of William Strode's 1636 play, *The Floating Island,* to support his claim that by the 1630s, stagecraft would become "the soul" of drama too:

> It was acted on a goodly stage reaching from the upper end of the
> Hall almost to the hearth place, and had on it three or four openings
> on each side thereof, and partitions between them, much resembling
> the desks or studies in a Library, out of which the Actors issued
> forth. The said partitions they could draw in and out at their plea-
> sure upon a sudden, and thrust out new in their places according to
> the nature of the Screen, whereon were represented Churches,
> Dwelling houses, Palaces, etc. which for its variety bred very great
> admiration. Over all was delicate painting, resembling the Sky,
> Clouds, etc. At the upper end a great fair shut [shutter] of two leaves
> that opened and shut without any visible help. Within which was
> set forth the emblem of the whole Play in a mysterious manner,
> Therein was the perfect resemblance of the billows of the Sea rolling,
> and an artificial Island, with Churches and Houses waving up and
> down and floating, as also rocks, trees and hills. Many other fine
> pieces of work and Landscapes did also appear at sundry openings
> thereof, and a Chair was also seen to come gliding on the Stage
> without any visible help. All these representations, being the first . . .
> that were used on the English stage.[69]

As Orgel posits, Wood's account suggests that spectators were learning to associate the magic of the theater with what we would now call special effects. Highly attuned to visual detail, eloquent and extremely thorough, this summary of *The Floating Island* does not even mention the play text, focusing instead on particulars of staging and set. But whereas Orgel takes Wood at his word, assuming that his sketch is a literal rendering of his experience, I would caution that we cannot really know how *The Floating Island* engaged with Wood's affective and imaginative faculties, nor should we necessarily infer that he seeks to express his own sensory and subjective response. His chronicling of *The Floating Island* recalls *Blackness*'s prefatory material, suggesting an account based on descriptive precedent rather than phenomenological experience. Indeed, Wood's descriptive fluency belies the novelty referenced in its final line: "All these representations being the first . . . that were used on the English stage." Such ease of expression does not necessarily testify to Wood's wealth of experience in viewing stage spectacle; rather, it demonstrates his knowledge of and facility in using its descriptive conventions. Given the purported scarcity of such machinations on the public stage up until the mid-1630s, Wood's "experience" with such spectacles may have as readily come from accounts of them (such as those provided by Jonson in his printed masques) as from firsthand experience. Of Wood's account, Orgel remarks, "Jonson might have observed, vindictively, that Wood scarcely sees the play for the scenery."[70] It is less likely, I think, that the poet would have imagined the importance of his own role in shaping a spectator like Wood's viewing practices and the language through which he articulated them.

The Discursive Spectator and
the Question of History

Around the same time Jonson begins rendering the practices of looking and hearing as separate interpretive modalities in his masques, he makes a related move in one of his stage comedies. *Bartholomew Fair*'s "induction" (a lengthy, multicharacter prologue) separates those who have come to see the play into lookers and hearers. Setting forth an "Articles of Agreement," a contract stipulating what the audience can expect from the play and what the author requests from them in return, the induction parodies the consumerist nature of the public theater as Jonson perceives it: "It shall be lawful for any man to judge his six pen'worth, his twelve pen'worth, so to his eighteen pence, two shillings, half a crown, to the value of his place" (78–81).[1] While the Stage-Keeper, who begins the induction, initially addresses the audience collectively as "gentlemen" (lines 1 and 27), the Articles of Agreement, read by the Book-Holder and Scrivener, divide those who come to view Jonson's play into "spectators" and "hearers" (lines 58–59, 66, and 121). The first time the audience is addressed, Jonson uses the interchangeable "or" ("the said spectators or hearers"), suggesting that any given audience member could participate in either interpretive group or perhaps that they might move between these categories at different times during the play's duration. The other two instances of these conjoined terms connect them with "and" instead of "or," which creates a more collective entity: either every audience member is *both* a spectator and a hearer, or these two "types" of interpreters intermingle indiscriminately in the theater, a kind of sensory amalgamation that recalls the synaesthetic metaphor.

Despite these traces of commingled senses and communal experiences, a pronounced tendency to parse, even partition, sensory experience and spectators persists. Even with *Bartholomew Fair*'s more prevalent use of "and" to move between spectators and hearers on a continuum, the Articles still seem drawn toward taxonomizing their present and future audiences into categories, ones yoked to certain Jonsonian biases: "It is covenanted and agreed, by and between the parties abovesaid, that the said spectators and hearers, as well as the curious and envious as the favoring and judicious" (66–67). One syntactical interpretation of this line suggests a parallelism between "spectators" and those who are "curious and envious"[2] and pairs hearers with the "favoring and judicious," a spectatorial taxonomy underscored by the play's portrayal of the foolish puritan Busy as one who speciously critiques the theater as if it were solely a series of images: "I will remove Dagon [the puppet] there, I say, that idol, that heathenish idol, that . . . beam in the eye" (5.5.4, 7). Finally, in the play's epilogue, Jonson depicts the king as the true arbiter of the play's merit because he will judge it as much by what he has heard as opposed to privileging what he has seen:

> Your Majesty has seen the Play, and you
> Can best allow it from your Ear and View
> You know the Scope of Writers, and what store
> Of Leave is given them, if they take not more,
> And turn it into Licence: you can tell,
> If we have us'd that Leave you gave us, well:
> Or whether we to Rage, or Licence break,
> Or be prophane, or make prophane Men speak?
> This is your Power to judge (Great Sir) and not
> The Envy of a few. Which if we have got,
> We value less what their dislike can bring,
> If it so happy be t' have pleas'd the King. (Epilogue, 1–12)

While Jonson's concluding salvo begins with the king having "seen" the play, the subsequent line privileges the sovereign's ear, again suggesting that theatrical experience involves sight and hearing equally. As the passage continues, however, Jonson refers to his play (and perhaps all plays) as an entity primarily composed of the spoken word: "or make prophane men *speak*," a distinction that heralds his later dissection of poetry from spectacle. But despite this

slight privileging of the audial realm, sight and audition still orbit a synaesthetic cynosure in the epilogue, in which both function as parts of a larger
sensory and interpretive universe.

Seventeen years later, Jonson places the intertitle "To Make the Spectators Understanders" beneath the title of his masque *Love's Triumph Through
Callipolis*. In doing so, he signals a clear alignment of understanding with
something other than the kind of "base" and visually oriented spectatorship
that dominates his discourse about the public theater. Although William N.
West argues that the concept of "understanders" is a fraught one throughout
the sixteenth and seventeenth centuries, he concedes that many playwrights
"followed Jonson in his interest in print and authorial property [who] also
refer to their understanders, usually picking up . . . that cognitive understanding is what is most desirable in an audience."[3] West here traces a similar
alteration in the discursive spectator's makeup (although he does not name
this figure), focusing on the ways in which "understanding" shifts from an
embodied and corporeally integrated epistemology to one more confined to
cognition. But while he notes that such "cognitive understanding" becomes
progressively more aligned with the (seemingly) antipodal interpretive mechanisms of audition and reading (even aligning, at one point, embodied
knowledge with synaesthetic perception),[4] he is less interested in the corresponding sensory division between visual and audial perception, a demarcation that cuts deep fissures into spectatorial discourse then as well as now.
When John Webster plaintively laments in the prologue to *The White Devil*
(1612) that his play "wanted a full and understanding Auditory," he suggests
a discourse in which "understanders" is becoming sutured to "hearers."[5]
While it is difficult to gauge Webster's accuracy in assessing trends in spectatorial practice, early modern playwrights' representation of looking and listening as disparate, even antithetical, activities plays a significant role in the
long history of conceptualizing the spectator as a visually oriented and passive
entity swept along by spectacle rather than engaging in the rigors of intellectual interpretation.

Such distinctions are given a moral cast in John Milton's 1634 masque,
Comus, which narrates the rabble-rousing god of festivity's attempt to seduce
a young and virtuous maiden. Comus endeavors to "charm" the Lady by
whisking her off to a palace of sensuality, where he encourages her to "see
. . . all the pleasures / That fancy can beget on youthful thoughts" (668–69).[6]
The Lady's ability to preserve her chastity is directly related to her ability to
resist visual temptation; she tells Comus that he "canst not touch the freedom

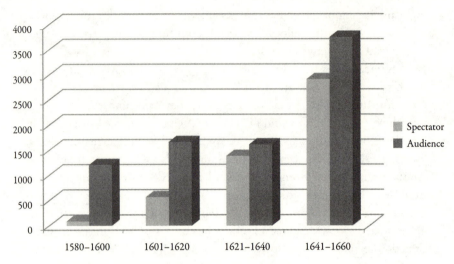

FIGURE 1. Use of the Terms *Spectator* and *Audience*
in *Early English Books Online*, 1580–1660

of [her] mind" (663) because he cannot charm her judgment as he does her
eyes (758). It is, of course, ironic that the Lady crafts her critique of Comus
through these terms, given that she is a character in an event designed specifically to charm the eyes of the spectators. However, in constructing her
defense as a tacit critique of visual pleasure, Milton follows Jonson's concept
of the masque as a platform for encouraging, even molding, spectators into
understanders. In doing so, Milton also follows the Jonsonian assumption
that the spectator *needs* to be led away from passive (if pleasurable) looking
and toward active interpretation.

  In 1642, the English Civil War commenced. Charles I moved his court
to Oxford and had little time for masques, and London's theaters closed
for eighteen years. While there were no public theater audiences during
this period, the term *spectator* continued its lexical ascendency. A search in
the *Early English Books Online* (*EEBO*) database for the term between 1620
and 1640 reveals 1,383 instances of its use; between 1640 and 1660, this
number more than doubles to 2,913 (see Fig. 1). While the total number of
hits in *EEBO* for *audience* still exceeds those for *spectator* during the period
between 1641 and 1660, this period also shows the number of texts that
include the term *spectator* as exceeding those including *audience* for the first
time (see Fig. 2).[7]

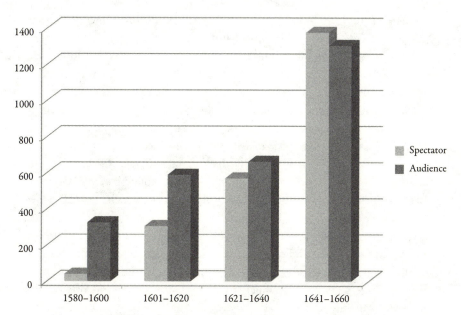

FIGURE 2. Number of Texts in *Early English Books Online* That Include
the Terms *Spectator* and *Audience*, 1580–1660

In addition to its continued proliferation in print, the meaning of *specta-tor* becomes rather more fixed during the years of the theaters' closing. Gone is the interplay between active and passive that Sidney evoked in his initial use of the term; instead, *spectator* is used regularly to denote an individual who passively looks on rather than actively engages, whether intellectually, physically, affectively, or eidetically. Peter Heylyn makes this distinction in his 1660 history of the English Church's reformation, saying that at Anne Boleyn's execution, "some few [were] permitted to be present, rather as witnesses than spectators of her final end."[8] Similarly, Richard Allestree's conduct manual *The Gentleman's Calling* uses *spectator* to denote an impotent onlooker: "If he have no power to assist him, is onely a spectator, not a reliever of his suffering."[9] Further enhancing the tendency to portray the spectator as submissive receptacle is mid-seventeenth-century writers' frequent use of the passive spectator as the inverse of the omniscient creator. Possibly coined as a response to the Calvinist doctrine of predestination, the "idle spectator" becomes a figurative antonym for God. In a sermon at Westminster Abbey in 1647, Nathaniel Hardy stated, "God is . . . not an idle spectator or bare permitter."[10] Anthony Burgess's treatise on original sin repeats this claim—"we do not make God an idle Spectator, as it were, of Adam's fall"[11]—as does Henry Hammond in his treatise on grace: "God is no helpless spectator."[12] While the metaphor of God-as-spectator was not new, in the early decades of the seventeenth century, it was more often presented as a metaphor of God's similitude with his mortal creation rather than contrast, such as in Robert Burton's *Anatomy of Melancholy*: "God is a Spectator of all thy miseries, he sees thy wrongs, woes and wants, and can helpe thee in an instant, when it seems to him good."[13] It is not only that the figuration of God changes in such invocations of spectatorship; in addition, the concept of the spectator metamorphoses from a potent figure of authority to a colorless, feeble shadow that is the antithesis of great creating nature itself.

This incarnation of the spectator is a far cry from Beaumont's fiery grocer or Shakespeare's acute and highly invested interpreters called upon to play a significant role in Hermione's awakening. Nor does the late seventeenth-century usage seem to have much to do with the varied and often vocal audiences who attended the early modern theater. Then again, they were no longer there. Whatever and whomever Tudor-Stuart spectators had been, they were, as a material presence, gone after 1642. During the period when the theaters were closed, the early modern theatrical spectator existed primarily *as* a discursive form—as memory (both individual and cultural) and in those few accounts that had been set down. This pallid, two-dimensional onlooker for which the term *spectator* comes to stand must, at least in part, be constructed from images and language generated during the prewar period—images and language that were, as I have argued, moving toward depicting the spectator as a more visually oriented and passively entertained figure. It is a figure that retains a powerful presence in critical discourse, for even West's thoughtful tracing of "understanding" as a measure of spectatorial engagement traffics in this deeply embedded narrative about the theatrical spectator, at least in terms of the active-passive binary: "Unlike modern theater, which with the edge of the stage divides passive audience from active player (a tendency which film exacerbates), early modern plays show the theater's whole circle, embracing both stage and pit, as set apart from the world outside it." That West does not acknowledge the fact that a great deal of modern theater seeks to trouble the audience-stage boundary and remind audiences of their active role (if not demand it) in creating theater aptly demonstrates the pervasiveness of the passive spectator as potent discursive presence.[14]

I do not wish to pin the sum total of changes that occur to ideas about spectators and spectatorship in the seventeenth century on the playwrights and masque writers of the period. It is, however, a widely held critical tenet that English theater audiences changed during this period; for example, Susan Bennett in *Theater Audiences* claims, "In the seventeenth century, however, there is a move towards . . . audiences becoming increasingly passive and increasingly bourgeois."[15] Of course, the language of representation alone cannot drive such change; as I have argued, cultural pressures such as shifts in staging conventions, exhibition practices, and class structures played large roles as well. But I emphasize language here because paradoxically it has been the silent partner in the construction of the spectator, both in the early modern period and in our own. That the discursive spectator should play a role in shaping the real one should not come as a surprise; as postmodern subjects, we have become accustomed to language's power in constructing the world we inhabit. This understanding is not limited to academia but extends more broadly across contemporary culture. My students know they are not supposed to call people deprecatory names based on their race, religion, class, or sexual orientation, even if many of them do not fully understand why. They have some vague sense, however, that it has something to do with what Foucault made explicit in his claim that power relations produce speaking, hence empowered, subjects, who are separated into who gets to name and who bears the burden of being named—that when they speak a name intended to shame or derogate they participate in what Pierre Bourdieu calls the "oracle effect," a situation in which "someone speaks in the name of something *which he brings into existence by his very discourse*" (my italics).[16]

Recently, the question of discourse's role in producing subjects has resurfaced in discussions over trigger warnings, a current manifestation of cultural concerns about representation's potency.[17] In a recent *Signs* article, Jack Halberstam alludes to trigger warnings *as* a discourse, one with the potential to shape affective and psychic experience: "The trigger warning . . . presumes and to a certain extent produces putative viewers or listeners who want to know what is to come in class or online because they fear their reaction to such material and wish either to mentally prepare to engage with it or to avoid it altogether. The trigger warning, in other words, believes in a student or viewer who is unstable and damaged and could at any time collapse into crisis."[18] While not making as explicit a connection between trigger warnings and subject formation as Halberstam, Greg Lukianoff (a constitutional lawyer and president of the Foundation for Individual Rights in Education) and

Jonathan Haidt (a social psychologist) outline a cause-and-effect process in which discourse acts as a catalyst for alterations in interpretive, affective, and institutional practices:

> The idea that words (or smells or any sensory input) can trigger searing memories of past trauma—and intense fear that it may be repeated—has been around at least since World War I, when psychiatrists began treating soldiers for what is now called post-traumatic stress disorder. But explicit trigger warnings are believed to have originated much more recently, on message boards in the early days of the Internet. Trigger warnings became particularly prevalent in self-help and feminist forums, where they allowed readers who had suffered from traumatic events like sexual assault to avoid graphic content that might trigger flashbacks or panic attacks. Search-engine trends indicate that the phrase broke into mainstream use online around 2011, spiked in 2014, and reached an all-time high in 2015. The use of trigger warnings on campus appears to have followed a similar trajectory; seemingly overnight, students at universities across the country have begun demanding that their professors issue warnings before covering material that might evoke a negative emotional response.[19]

Lukianoff and Haidt here imagine trigger warnings' genesis to follow a relatively standard gestational pattern: the phrase-concept comes into being to meet a lexical and taxonomic need: in this case, *trigger* becomes part of the psychoanalytic terminology used to describe a particular manifestation of trauma (that of World War I veterans' combat experience). After its inception, a period of stasis for the phrase ensues, one reignited by popularized cultural discourses as "self-help" and "feminism," and discursively transmitted and augmented by social media platforms and the Internet's all-encompassing reach. Eventually, the phrase passes into the mainstream realm of common parlance where it takes hold with a vengeance. In many ways, the trajectory Lukianoff and Haidt trace for the term *trigger warnings* resembles the one this study charts for the rise of *spectator*. The first term constitutes a discursive utterance—a warning—about representation's uncanny ability to cause the subject to experience narrative and imagery with all the force of an event that occurs in the material world. The second often stands in for those vulnerable to the particular perceptual and ontological disorientation articulated by moralists, playwrights, and media theorists (and now students) as a unique epiphenomenon of artistic representation, whether literary, theatrical, cinematic, or digital. Both terms constitute a linguistic response to cultural moments in which discourse about representation and those who engage with it becomes destabilized, moments in which interpretive practices surrounding representation and (or as) artistic, educational, and entertainment commodity accrue new resonances and wider networks.

Rather than offer a stance on whether to use trigger warnings in our classrooms (the ideological vortex into which many popular and scholarly discussions get pulled),[20] I want to conclude by demonstrating some of the hermeneutic advantages that come from placing the concept of trigger warnings as a point on a long-form discursive history. In part, this perspective allows for an emphasis on other, more submerged negotiations underlying the trigger warning debate, ones largely repressed by the "safe space" vs. "free speech" narrative. But it also allows for a demonstration of how the discursive spectator as historical presence might bring further insight on current debates about representation's effect on the viewer. Surprisingly, despite the fact that two fields besieged with calls for trigger warnings on syllabi—literature and film studies—remain dominated by historicist scholarship, analyses of trigger warnings focus myopically on their etiology in the present or the proximate past. Indeed, the overwhelming majority of scholars writing on the subject accept Lukianoff and Haidt's assertion that the concept of trigger warnings arrives sometime during the early twenty-first century. Alexa Lothian summarizes this tacit consensus, stating that "the ascendance of trigger-warning discourse is usually traced to feminist bloggers' use of the language of trauma and to the flowering of social justice discourse on Tumblr."[21] While Lothian offers an alternative to this genesis (via the fan fiction genre and the discourse generated by its respective "networks and communities"), she still places trigger warnings' point of origin in the late twentieth century.[22] Similarly, while Halberstam yokes trigger warnings to the modern U.S. film and television rating system, he traces this discourse only as far back as the 1930s Hays Code.[23] Perhaps because Halberstam's historical gaze extends no further than the twentieth century, he ends up relying somewhat tepidly on the Frankfurt-school bias that technology exerts the dominant influence in producing spectators: "The generational difference in pedagogical styles, in classroom technologies, in mediascapes, and in the relations between canons and experimental or alternative archives have all transformed the contemporary classroom into a wild zone where on any given day, in any given class, a student can be expected to be bombarded with material—not at the pace that culture generally dumps information, imagery, and news onto audiences but certainly at a pace that would have been unthinkable a few decades ago."[24] While Halberstam does cite a few nontechnological influences (or not necessarily media-drive ones), his description of the contemporary classroom eerily resembles Benjamin's analysis of cinema's effect on the spectator cited earlier in this study. Both conjure images of dehumanized combat zones in which film spectators or students fall victim to technology's speed and destructive capacity. As discussed in Chapter 2, however, Benjamin's use of such imagery is not novel: early modern antitheatricalists and playwrights engaged in similar combative metaphors to describe the theater's effect on the spectator with some frequency. Despite these similarities in descriptive conventions that extend *across* time, Halberstam never pauses to consider why, if the multimediated classroom is so new and so overwhelming, descriptive conventions used to discuss students who experience these forms of technological legerdemain display remarkable similarities to those used to describe sixteenth-century theater audiences and early twentieth-century filmgoers. More pointedly, why does Western culture return to certain discursive and representational conventions about the spectator when confronted with new media and exhibition practices?

An additional parallel exists between the descriptive conventions of early modern spectatorial discourse and those of contemporary trigger warnings discourse. Addressing the recent rise of trigger warning demands in Ireland, William Reville resurrects the language of pathology and contamination-infection: "A very unhealthy censorship of freedom of expression on university campus is spreading like a contagion across the UK, imported from the US, and is now starting to affect Ireland."[25] Reville here sounds a note similar to those playwrights who mourn their plays' poor reception by a few nasty, censorious spectators whose vociferous obloquy proceeds to "infect" the entire audience. Such naysayers feature prominently in *Bartholomew Fair*'s previously mentioned induction, which warns against "censure by contagion" (88), and Fletcher's dedicatory epistle to *The Faithful Shepherdess*:

Sir, I must ask your patience, and be true;
This play was never liked, unless by few
That brought their judgments with em, for of late
First the infection, then the common prate

Of common people, have such customs got
Either to silence plays, or like them not.[26] (1–6)

Like Fletcher, Reville imagines this "infection" as primarily caused by a wrongheaded interpretation. Fletcher's refractory spectators do not appreciate *The Faithful Shepherdess* because they are "common" and wallow shamelessly in their ability to "silence" plays they do not understand. Reville's dissident students are overcoddled children who do not understand that their unreasonable demands denigrate and erode the very foundations of liberal society.[27] Both writers understand these resistances as dangerous, even potentially fatal: Fletcher laments his play's and authorial reputation's fate, and Reville proclaims that scholarship (and by extension his profession) is under "grave threat."[28]

What might such moments of discursive recursivity signal? Despite his overarching dismissiveness toward trigger warnings, Reville senses they have something to do with shifts in higher education's loci of authority, control, and expertise: "[The culture of trigger warnings] assumes college students have extremely fragile psyches that must be protected, and anyone who interferes with that aim should be punished. A culture is created whereby everyone must constantly monitor what they say for fear they will be charged with insensitivity, aggression, or worse."[29] Although articulated via a scenario in which classroom culture transforms into a fascist regime, Reville's description draws attention to certain institutional and professional fault lines that have recently become newly destabilized. In particular, he testifies to a crisis of authority: the person in front of the class may have expertise in their field, but they hold none in any given student's emotional and psychic constitution. Rather than understanding this conflict as simply a generational or technological narrative,[30] however, we should also explore it as a historical-discursive one. As *Monster* endeavors to show, numerous factors contributed to early modern England's reinvigorated fascination with the entertainment spectator: rapid developments in and a widespread expansion of theatrical culture; the change from theater as a predominantly church- and guild-sponsored form to a for-profit, commercial one; Reformation iconoclasm; and the gradual transformation of feudal class structures. While under different sorts of pressures, the university is also undergoing relatively rapid alterations, including decreased public funding; ever-expanding administrative apparatuses; greater pressure on assessment, outcomes, and demonstration of the student-consumer's return on investment; a profound attenuation in tenure-line faculty positions; and higher, more varied workloads for all faculty. Significantly, despite their historical, cultural, and institutional differences, both arenas demonstrate a link between rapid transformation and an uptick in concerns about representation's powers of suggestion and influence.

Of course, both the early modern professional theater and the twenty-first-century university respond and are subject to other, more widespread cultural movements, ones that generate profound anxieties about changes in collective and individual power and control, both perceived and real. At such moments, the discursive spectator (whether articulated via the early modern theatergoer, the early twentieth-century film consumer, or twenty-first-century college student) comes into greater focus and play, as a field on which competing ideological positions contend. Unlike real individuals, which can be difficult to understand, predict, and control, the discursive spectator offers a more malleable surface onto which fears and fantasies can be projected. Early modern playwrights at the mercy of public opinion and the concomitant vicissitudes of economic viability siphon such anxieties into the fantasy of "disciplining" unruly, unlettered audiences impervious to sophistication and erudition. Twenty-first-century academics trying to salvage their sense of intellectual activism and, in some cases, social prestige, locate a primary source of such attenuations in their current generation of overprotected, narcissistic students rather than in the neoliberal university juggernaut, an entity that often seems far beyond contingent and permanent faculty members' ever-more-limited sphere of influence. Dennis Kennedy notes that a similar displacement mechanism (and disciplinary fantasy) undergirds both the entertainment and advertising industries:

A final point about the audience for electronic media: a number of commentators now assert that the standard notion of the TV audience as an observable phenomenon is a fiction made at the convenience of the television industry and too easily accepted by scholars. Related to judgements about the undominated [sic] uses of TV that viewers can make . . . writers such as Ien Ang (1991) assert that industry notions are completely detached from the actuality of the audience, that the industry lacks any interest in what spectators really think or do, instead presenting data to advertisers or state agencies that can convince them of the value of financial sponsorship.[31]

Although he does not explicitly articulate it as such, the "fiction" to which Kennedy refers is, finally, one of influence and power. Advertisers and television producers require network support and advertising money to exist, commercial entities to which they are subject. They, in turn, construct a discursive entity—a television viewer-consumer backed by a persuasive narrative told by the consumerist pillars of market research and data—that they *can* manipulate and use, perhaps, to influence those forces over which they have little control. Rather than a material manifestation of various cultural, commercial, and ideological struggles (a cartographic narrative legible from the rearview of temporal distance), the discursive spectator offers insights into a less stable, less linear terrain that offers alternative inroads on how such negotiations are undertaken, circumvented, and deferred.

Some may say that a study focused primarily on the discursive spectator is little more than smoke and mirrors; as a colleague and friend once said to me, "Oh, I get it. You're working on fake people." But considering the fact that the discursive spectator has lingered in the Western cultural imaginary for millennia and remains a force to be reckoned with in our own hypermediated cultural moment, I believe it is quite real indeed and has a great deal more to contribute to the fields of theater, film, and audience studies.

NOTES

INTRODUCTION

Notes to epigraphs: Plato, *The Dialogues of Plato,* vol. 1, trans. B. Jowett (Oxford, Oxford University Press, 1920), 651; Augustine, *Confessions,* trans. Henry Chadwick (Oxford, Oxford University Press, 1992), 101; *Selections from English Wycliffite Writings,* ed. Anne Hudson (Toronto, University of Toronto Press, 1997), 99; William Prynne, *Histrio-Mastix, The Players Scourge or Actors Tragedie* (London: Printed by E.A. and W. for Michael Sparke, 1633); Sigmund Freud, "Psychopathic Characters on the Stage," *Psychoanalytic Quarterly,* 11.4 (1942), 459–64; Richard Barry "The Moving-Picture Bubble," *Pearson's Magazine,* January 1911; Benedict Carey, "Shooting in the Dark," *New York Times,* February 11, 2013.

1. Dennis Kennedy, *The Spectator and the Spectacle: Audiences in Modernity and Post-modernity* (Cambridge: Cambridge University Press, 2009), 4.

2. This bias comes out of Frankfurt School theories of mass culture, such as those put forth by Theodor Adorno, Max Horkheimer, and Walter Benjamin, and has been perpetuated by film theory, particularly by apparatus theorists such as Christian Metz in *The Imaginary Signifier: Psychoanalysis and Cinema,* trans. Celia Britton, Annwyl Williams, Ben Brewster, and Alfred Guzzetti (Bloomington: Indiana University Press, 1982); and Laura Mulvey in "Visual Pleasure and Narrative Cinema," *Screen* 16 (1975), 6–18. However, scholars of the early modern theater often accept the idea that the spectator is a "modern" entity as well; see for example, Andrew Gurr's *Playgoing in Shakespeare's London,* 3rd ed. (Cambridge: Cambridge University Press, 2004) , 1.

3. Michelle Aaron, *Spectatorship: The Power of Looking On* (London: Wallflower, 2007), 3. Aaron claims that the spectator is the child of two parents: the political upheavals in France in May 1968 and the rise of structuralism in the academy.

4. Roberta E. Pearson and William Uricchio, for example, claimed that the "magic bullet theory," which holds that the spectator has no defenses against being imaginatively permeated by what she or he sees, was "first formulated in the early stages of mass-communications research in the 1940's." See " 'The Formative and Impressionable Stage': Discursive Constructions of the Nickelodeon's Child Audience," in *American Movie Audiences: From the Turn of the Century to the Early Sound Era,* ed. Melvyn Stokes and Richard Maltby (London: British Film Institute, 1999), 67. More often, however, this assumption is tacit rather than explicit; for example, Will Brooker and Deborah Jermyn's *The Audience Studies Reader* (London: Routledge, 2003) begins with writings from the 1950s onward.

5. Walter Benjamin, *Illuminations: Essays and Reflections,* ed. Hannah Arendt, trans. Harry Zohn (New York: Schocken, 2007), 240. Michael O'Connell makes a similar comparison in

his book *The Idolatrous Eye: Iconoclasm and Theater in Early-Modern England* (Oxford: Oxford University Press, 2000). Although his primary interest is in the link between the early modern iconoclastic tendencies and the rise of the professional theater, he compares the sixteenth and seventeenth centuries to our own, saying that "I want to propose that this tension [between word and image] becomes conflict when technologies of representation are in a state of transition, when we become acutely aware of, and correspondingly anxious about, the power of one in relation to the other" (5).

6. The bias that the spectator is the product of the twentieth century goes hand in hand with the concept that mass culture only becomes fully realized once it is disseminated by twentieth-century technology. For an alternative reading, see José Antonio Maravall's *The Culture of the Baroque,* trans. Terry Cochran (Minnesota: University of Minnesota Press, 1986).

7. Jonas Barish, *The Antitheatrical Prejudice* (Berkeley: University of California Press, 1981), 1. As its title suggests, Barish's study focuses on the transhistorical bias that the theater's influence presents a psychic danger to the spectator.

8. See David Bevington, *Medieval Drama* (Boston: Houghton Mifflin, 1975), 8.

9. I take 1576 as my starting date because it is the year the first amphitheater was built (James Burbage's Theater), which marks the beginning of the period when professional playing would become an early modern English cultural phenomenon, one that I see as a form of mass culture.

10. Jean-Christophe Agnew, *Worlds Apart: The Market and the Theater in Anglo-American Thought, 1550–1750* (Cambridge: Cambridge University Press, 1986), xi.

11. Ibid., 108.

12. Valerie Traub, "The New Unhistoricism in Queer Studies," *PMLA* 128.1 (2013), 21–39.

13. Eve Kosofsky Sedgwick, *The Epistemology of the Closet* (Berkeley: University of California Press, 1990), 47. Sedgwick here critiques genealogical narratives of sexual identity à la Foucault; this phrase refers to her critique of David Halperin's *One Hundred Years of Homosexuality and Other Essays on Greek Love* (New York: Routledge, 1990).

14. Annamarie Jagose, "Feminism's Queer Theory," *Feminism and Psychology* 19.2 (2009), 158. Quoted in Traub, "New Unhistoricism," 22.

15. Traub discusses some of the problems inherent in periodization, while offering a balanced and thoughtful rationale for why simply discarding it is equally problematic. See "Unhistoricism," 32.

16. I use "call-and-response" here rather than the more standard "dialectic" as the latter implies that when cultural pressures and discourses are formed in response to one another, they "produce" something new, a dynamic that tends toward a more teleological trajectory in that it emphasizes what is produced (the synthesis) rather than the interaction and instabilities in the interaction between discourses (or thesis and antithesis).

17. Traub, "Unhistoricism," 30.

18. Jeremy Lopez, *Theatrical Convention and Audience Response in Early Modern Drama* (Cambridge: Cambridge University Press, 2003), 17.

19. Alfred Harbage, *Shakespeare's Audience* (New York: Columbia University Press, 1941); E. K. Chambers, *The Elizabethan Stage* (Oxford: Clarendon, 1974), 4 vols.; Ann Jennalie Cook, *The Privileged Playgoers of Shakespeare's London, 1576–1642* (Princeton: Princeton University Press, 1981); and Gurr, *Playgoing.*

20. Also included in this category are Michael Neill's " 'Wit's Most Accomplished Senate': The Audience of the Caroline Private Theaters," *Studies in English Language* 18 (1978), 341–60; Richard Levin's "Women in the Renaissance Theater Audience," *Shakespeare Quarterly*

40 (1989), 165–74; William Ingram's *The Business of Playing: The Beginnings of the Adult Professional Theater in Elizabethan London* (Ithaca, NY: Cornell University Press, 1992); Mary A. Blackstone and Louis Cameron's "Towards 'A Full and Understanding Auditory': New Evidence of Playgoers at the First Globe Theater," *Modern Language Review* 90 (1995), 556–71; and Jean E. Howard's essay "Women as Spectators, Spectacles and Paying Customers," in *Readings in Renaissance Women's Drama: Criticism, History, and Performance, 1594–1998*, ed. S. P. Cerasano and Marion Wynne-Davies (London: Routledge, 1998), 81–86.

21. For example, two of the most heavily inflected psychoanalytic studies of early modern theatrical spectatorship, Thomas Cartelli's *Marlowe, Shakespeare, and the Economy of Theatrical Experience* (Philadelphia: University of Pennsylvania Press, 1991) and Barbara Freedman's *Staging the Gaze: Postmodernism, Psychoanalysis, and Shakespearean Comedy* (Ithaca, NY: Cornell University Press, 1991), were published in the same year.

22. It should be noted that the majority of these inquiries use an essentially hybrid approach in that they often use early modern historical evidence and primary texts and modern theoretical paradigms. However, few studies allow both possibilities equal air time. My own taxonomic method for organizing studies of early modern audiences, then, places them according to what I have understood to be their dominant methodological approach.

23. See, for example, Muriel Bradbrook, *Themes and Conventions of Elizabethan Tragedy* (Cambridge: Cambridge University Press, 1960); Alan C. Dessen, *Elizabethan Drama and the Viewer's Eye* (Chapel Hill: University of North Carolina Press, 1977) and *Elizabethan Stage Conventions and Modern Interpreters* (Cambridge: Cambridge University Press, 1984); Robert Weimann, *Shakespeare and the Popular Tradition in the Theater* (Baltimore: Johns Hopkins University Press, 1978); Michael Hattaway, *Elizabethan Popular Theater* (London: Routledge, 1982); Ralph Berry, *Shakespeare and the Awareness of the Audience* (London: Macmillan, 1985); Marion Lomax, *Stage Images and Traditions: Shakespeare to Ford* (Cambridge: Cambridge University Press, 1987); Bruce Smith, *The Acoustic World of Early Modern England: Attending to the O-Factor* (Chicago: University of Chicago Press, 1999); Anthony B. Dawson and Paul Yachnin, *The Culture of Playgoing in Shakespeare's England: A Collaborative Debate* (Cambridge: Cambridge University Press, 2001); Jonathan Gil-Harris and Natasha Korda, eds., *Staged Properties in Early Modern English Drama* (Cambridge: Cambridge University Press, 2002); Ruth Lunney, *Marlowe and the Popular Tradition: Innovation in the English Drama Before 1595* (Manchester: Manchester University Press, 2002); Jeremy Lopez, *Theatrical Convention*; Tanya Pollard, *Drugs and Theater in Early Modern England* (Oxford: Oxford University Press, 2005); Charles Whitney, *Early Responses to Renaissance Drama* (Cambridge: Cambridge University Press, 2006); Matthew Steggle, *Laughing and Weeping in Early Modern Theaters* (Aldershot, U.K.: Ashgate, 2007); and Alison Hobgood, *Passionate Playgoing in Early Modern England* (Cambridge: Cambridge University Press, 2014).

24. Freedman, *Staging the Gaze.*

25. Apparatus theory proposes an institutional model of spectatorship in which the spectator's viewing processes become shaped by technological apparatuses of film, such as camera angle and editing practices. It further argues that film is an ideal mechanism for disseminating and entrenching ideological positions because film so readily conceals its own constructedness, which allows it to immerse its viewers more fully in the illusion of real experience. Freedman discusses the theories of two of apparatus theory's most important proponents, Christian Metz and Laura Mulvey, to shape the theory of spectatorship she puts forth in her argument.

26. Freedman, *Staging the Gaze*, 9.

27. Ibid., 9–10. Freedman includes other representational forms (such as anamorphic painting and trick perspective images) among those cultural forms that facilitate this alternative way of looking.

28. For example, three recent studies of early modern audiences either do not mention Freedman (Lopez, *Theatrical Convention*) or include her in their bibliography but do not engage with or reference her work in any detail (Whitney, *Early Responses*, and Hobgood, *Passionate Playgoing*). Her departure from the academy sometime in the 1990s may have contributed to this lack of attention.

29. Stephen Greenblatt, *Learning to Curse: Essays in Early Modern Culture* (New York and London: Routledge, 1990), 190.

30. Freedman, *Staging the Gaze*, 16. In Freudian terms, the "split subject" refers primarily to the heterogeneous nature of the psyche (id, ego, superego). The Lacanian split subject is born out of the mirror-stage, where the infant recognizes his image in the mirror and perceives it as a more perfect and holistic version of the self. Freedman sees the Lacanian split subject as related to the way Shakespearean comedy deconstructs the spectatorial subject's perceived position of mastery through misrecognition (see pp. 52–66).

31. Freedman, *Staging the Gaze*, 49–51.

32. Carla Mazzio and Douglas Trevor, "Dreams of History: An Introduction," in *Historicism, Psychoanalysis and Early Modern Culture*, eds. Mazzio and Trevor (New York: Routledge, 2000), 2.

33. This tendency has been abated by a number of important studies on sound and film, such as Elizabeth Weis and John Belton, eds., *Film Sound: Theory and Practice* (New York: Columbia University Press, 1985); Rick Altman, *The American Film Musical* (Bloomington: Indiana University Press, 1987), *Sound Theory/Sound Practice* (New York: Routledge, 1992), and *Silent Film Sound* (New York: Columbia University Press, 2004); Sara Kozloff, *Invisible Storytellers: Voice-Over Narration in American Fiction Film* (Berkeley: University of California Press, 1988); Kaja Silverman, *The Acoustic Mirror: The Female Voice in Psychoanalysis and Cinema* (Bloomington: Indiana University Press, 1988); James Buhler, David Neumeyer, and Rob Deemer, eds., *Hearing the Movie: Music and Sound in Film History* (New York: Oxford University Press, 2001); Britta Sjogren, *Into the Vortex: Female Voice and Paradox in Film* (Urbana: University of Illinois Press, 2006); and Jay Beck and Tony Grajeda, eds., *Lowering the Boom: Critical Studies in Film Sound* (Urbana: University of Illinois Press, 2008).

34. See, for example, Smith, *Acoustic World*; Elizabeth D. Harvey, ed., *Sensible Flesh: On Touch in Early Modern Culture* (Philadelphia: University of Pennsylvania Press, 2003); Gina Bloom, *Voice in Motion: Shaping Sound in Early Modern England* (Philadelphia: University of Pennsylvania Press, 2007); Carla Mazzio, *The Inarticulate Renaissance: Language Troubles in an Age of Eloquence* (Philadelphia: University of Pennsylvania Press, 2009); and Holly Dugan, *The Ephemeral History of Perfume: Scent and Sense in Early Modern England* (Baltimore: Johns Hopkins University Press, 2011).

35. Lopez, *Theatrical Convention*, 14.

36. Ibid., 7, 14.

37. Lopez admits, "We do not have very much evidence about how audiences felt about specific plays or specific moments in specific plays" (*Theatrical Convention*, 19).

38. Ibid., 7.

39. Ibid., 8.

40. Lopez relies primarily on antitheatrical discourse in order to flesh out this audience in his first chapter.

41. Bruce Smith, *Phenomenal Shakespeare* (Malden, MA: Wiley-Blackwell, 2010), 28; and Pollard, *Drugs and Theater*; Whitney, *Early Responses*; Steggle, *Laughing and Weeping*; and Hobgood, *Passionate Playgoing*. Other studies that use a similar approach to early modern audiences studies include Jane Tylus's "'Par Accident': The Public Work of Early Modern Theater," in *Reading the Early Modern Passions: Essays in the Cultural History of Emotion*, ed. Gail Kern Pastern, Katherine Rowe, and Mary-Floyd Wilson (Philadelphia: University of Pennsylvania Press, 2004); Paul Menzer's "The Actor's Inhibition: Early Modern Acting and the Rhetoric of Restraint," *Renaissance Drama* 35 (2006), 83–112; Steven Mullaney, "Affective Technologies: Towards an Emotional Logic of the Early Modern Stage," in *Embodiment and Environment in Early Modern England*, ed. Mary Floyd-Wilson and Garrett A. Sullivan Jr. (Basingstoke, U.K.: Palgrave Macmillan, 2007), 71–89; and Katharine A. Craik and Tanya Pollard, eds., *Shakespearean Sensations: Experiencing Literature in Early Modern England* (Cambridge: Cambridge University Press, 2013).

42. Whitney, for example, cites a wide range of audience experience, much of which is culled from what he calls "allusions" or references to audience response found in drama and a variety of forms of cultural production produced by "those not professionally engaged in the theatre" (*Early Responses*, 2). Hobgood looks both at the inchoate terrain of "the incredibly porous periphery between the Renaissance stage and its audiences, and in the dynamic emotional interfaces that arise in the midst of this 'in-between-ness'" (*Passionate Playgoing*, 4) and at a more traditionally historicist archive that includes philosophical, medical, and moralist works on emotion.

43. For example, see Carol Chillington Rutter's *Enter the Body: Women and Representation on Shakespeare's Stage* (London: Routledge, 2001).

44. Hobgood, *Passionate Playgoing*, 8.

45. Smith, *Phenomenal Shakespeare*, 34.

46. Hobgood, *Passionate Playgoing*, 9.

47. Ibid.

48. Ibid., 10.

49. Cathy Caruth, *Unclaimed Experience: Trauma, Narrative, and History* (Baltimore: Johns Hopkins University Press, 1996), 4. While Caruth here speaks about traumatic experience, given Hobgood's characterization of the early modern theater as "an intensely corporeal, highly emotive activity characterized by risky, even outright dangerous bodily transformation," it provides an apt commentary on the kind of experience Hobgood claims theatergoing as engendering (*Passionate Playgoing*, 10).

50. Stephen Purcell, *Shakespeare and Audience in Practice* (Basingstoke, U.K.: Palgrave Macmillan, 2013), 147.

51. Mullaney, "Affective Technologies," 71.

52. Notably, an exception to this is Freedman's *Staging the Gaze*.

53. Numerous critics have pointed out this tendency. Lopez deals with it in some detail in *Theatrical Convention*, particularly in chap. 1.

54. Barish, *Antitheatrical Prejudice*, 92.

55. There is no clear consensus on when English professional theater began. In the introduction to *English Professional Theatre, 1530–1660* (Cambridge: Cambridge University Press, 2000), Glynne Wickham places it in the early part of the sixteenth century, "By 1530, it had become customary to commission talented poets . . . to write (or 'make') plays for these companies of professional actors" (2), but sees this trajectory towards stationary, professional theaters as stalled by Henry VIII's "decision to challenge the hitherto acknowledged right of the Pope

in Rome to regulate the Church in England" (ibid.). Herbert Berry claims that "Investors had decided by the 1560s and 1570s that permanent theaters in and around London could yield great profits, thought, presumably, players might come and go" (287). *The Cambridge Companion to English Renaissance Drama*, edited by A. R. Braunmuller and Michael Hattaway (Cambridge: Cambridge University Press, 1990), places it slightly earlier than Wickham, using 1497 as the start date for its chronological table.

56. Regarding the shift from royal patronage to commercial viability, see Suzanne Westfall, "The Useless Dearness of the Diamond: Theories of Patronage Theater" (13–42) and Alexander Leggatt, "The Audience as Patron: *The Knight of the Burning Pestle*" (295–315), both in *Shakespeare and Theatrical Patronage in Early Modern England*, ed. Paul Whitfield White and Suzanne R. Westfall (Cambridge: Cambridge University Press, 2002).

57. David Bevington and Milla Riggio, "'What Revels Are in Hand?' Marriage Celebrations and Patronage of the Arts in in Renaissance England," in *Shakespeare and Theatrical Patronage in Early Modern England*, ed. Paul Whitfield White and Suzanne R. Westfall (Cambridge: Cambridge University Press, 2002), 131.

58. Andrew Gurr states that while admission to the theater cost one penny, the minimum price at the Blackfriars was between threepence and sixpence. Boxes could cost five times as much in the hall playhouses as they did at the amphitheaters. See Gurr, *Playgoing*, 31.

59. Ibid., 185.

60. Philip Sidney, *The Countess of Pembroke's Arcadia* (London: Printed by William Ponsonbie, 1598).

61. Lukas Erne, *Shakespeare as Literary Dramatist*, 2nd ed. (Cambridge: Cambridge University Press, 2013), 1.

62. See, e.g., Gurr, *Playgoing*, 116.

63. Richard Dutton, *Ben Jonson: Authority: Criticism* (New York: St. Martin's, 1996), 109.

64. *Hymenai*, preface, line 18, in Stephen Orgel, ed., *Ben Jonson: The Complete Masques* (New Haven: Yale University Press, 1969), 76.

65. I reference the subtitle to *Love's Triumph Through Callipolis*, which was Jonson's final masque: "To Make the Spectators Understanders."

66. Herbert Blau, *The Audience* (Baltimore: Johns Hopkins University Press, 1990), 7.

67. Quoted in Blau, *The Audience*, 7.

68. "Spectator, n.," Oxford English Dictionary Online, September 2014, Oxford University Press, http://www.oed.com/view/Entry/186071 (accessed October 19, 2014).

69. "Spectre, n.," ibid.

70. This phrase occurs in book IX of Plato's *Republic*. Ian Munro has an extended and thoughtful reading of this expression's half-life in early modern England in *The Figure of the Crowd in Early Modern England: The City and Its Double* (Basingstoke, U.K.: Palgrave, 2005), 105–42.

CHAPTER 1

1. Maxim Gorky, untitled, in *In the Kingdom of the Shadows: A Companion to the Early Cinema*, ed. Colin Harding and Simon Popple (Madison, NJ: Fairleigh Dickinson University Press, 1996), 5.

2. Auguste and Louis Lumière were early innovators of film technology, particularly the use of perforated film as a means of "feeding" film through the camera and projector. Their version of the film camera/projector, called the *cinèmatographe*, was put on public exhibition in Paris in 1895; soon after, it was being widely exhibited throughout Europe.

3. Tom Gunning argues that early film audiences were eager to experience the technological "thrills" of modern life as a means of compensating for, even escaping, the monotonies imposed on the working class by industrial life. See "The Cinema of Attractions: Early Film, Its Spectator and the Avant-Garde," in *Early Cinema: Space, Frame, Narrative*, ed. Thomas Elsaesser (London: British Film Institute, 1990), 56–62.

4. Harding and Popple, *In the Kingdom of the Shadows*, 5.

5. Ibid.

6. Ibid.

7. William Shakespeare. "A Midsummer Night's Dream," *The Norton Shakespeare*, 3rd ed., eds. Stephen Greeblatt, Walter Cohen, Jean E. Howard, Katharine Eisaman Maus, Gordon McMullan, and Suzanne Gossett (New York: W.W. Norton & Company, 2015). All quotes from Shakespeare's plays taken from this edition.

8. Anthony Munday, *A Second and Third Blast of Retreat from Plaies and Theaters* (London: Henrie Denham, 1580), 105.

9. Ibid., 56.

10. Harding and Popple, *In the Kingdom of the Shadows*, 5.

11. Tiffany Stern, *Documents of Performance in Early Modern England* (Cambridge: Cambridge University Press, 2009), 2. Stern takes this term from the period itself but productively thinks through its resonances for better understanding how early modern plays were constructed.

12. Early modern inhabitants of London, whether native-born or migrant, had likely seen been some form of "pleying," as morality and miracle plays, interludes, and other forms of drama had been popular in England for hundreds of years.

13. Harding and Popple, *In the Kingdom of the Shadows*, 5. The full quote is, "Curses and ghosts, evil spirits that have cast whole cities into eternal sleep come to mind and you feel as though Merlin's vicious trick is being played out before you."

14. O. Winter, for example, notes the effect of "life stripped of colour and sound . . . the picture is subdued to a uniform and baffling grey . . . a spectacle that frightens rather than attracts" (Harding and Popple, *In the Kingdom of the Shadows*, 15–16). The *Punch* article, published two years later (this time on an American Biograph film) states, "My eyes! My head! and the whizzing and whirling and twittering of nerves and blinkings and winkings that it causes in not a few spectators . . . It is a night-mare!"

15. Harding and Popple, *In the Kingdom of the Shadows*, 1–2.

16. Jonas Barish and, more recently, Jeremy Lopez, have discussed the rhetorical and metaphorical redundancy of the antitheatricalists' prose. Barish points out that "they repeat themselves, and each other, without shame or scruple" (*The Antitheatrical Prejudice* [Berkeley: University of California Press, 1981], 88), and Lopez says that "because the antitheatricalists teneded to repeat and plagiarize each other's arguments, it can be difficult to take them seriously" (*Theatrical Convention and Audience Response in Early Modern Drama* [Cambridge: Cambridge University Press, 2003], 20). While it is clear that the antitheatricalists engaged in a good bit of "borrowing" from each other, this repetition suggests exactly the kind of discursive bloodlines of spectators and spectatorial practice, or what we might, in contemporary parlance, call bias. Like Lopez, I believe that what the antitheatricalists choose to repeat contains more

significance than the fact that they engage in "parroting." However, while Lopez looks at the ways these seeming redundancies testify to particular facets of early modern audiences' actual experience with and at the theater, I am interested in their role in constituting the discursive spectator.

17. Andrew Gurr, *Playgoing in Shakespeare's London,* 3rd ed. (Cambridge: Cambridge University Press, 2004), 1

18. Philip Sidney, *An Apologie for Poetrie* (London: Printed for Henry Olney, 1595).

19. See Appendices 1 and 2 of this book. Other scholars follow this singular (spectator)-collective (audience) association fairly closely; for example, Dennis Kennedy in *The Spectator and the Spectacle: Audiences in Modernity and Postmodernity* (Cambridge: Cambridge University Press, 2009), more or less accepts this distinction: "In general I use *audience* to refer to a group of observers of a performance, while *spectator* refers to an individual member of an audience" (5).

20. The *Oxford English Dictionary (OED)* gives the date 1584 for the *Arcadia;* most sources cite 1590 as the date of first publication.

21. Gurr, 102–3.

22. Ibid., 104. Gurr includes Heywood, Dekker, Marston, Beaumont, and Webster among those playwrights who shared (at least in part) Jonson's negative opinion of "spectators."

23. According to the *OED*, Spenser is the second author to use the term "spectator" in 1595, in Sonnet 44 of his *Amoretti*.

24. Gurr, *Playgoing* 109.

25. For example, Richard Huloet's 1572 English/Latin/French dictionary translates *spectator* as "beholder." See *Huloets dictionarie newelye corrected, amended, set in order and enlarged, vvith many names of men, tovvnes, beastes, foules, fishes, trees, shrubbes, herbes, fruites, places, instrumentes &c.*, ed. John Higgins (London: 1572).

26. *The Joyful and royal entertainment of the ryght high and mightie Prince, Frauncis the Frenche Kings only brother*, trans. Arthur Golding (London: Imprinted by Thomas Dawson for William Ponsonby, 1582).

27. Philip Sidney, *The Countess of Pembroke's Arcadia* (London: Printed by William Ponsonbie, 1590).

28. I refer here to the myth of Aristophanes that appears in Plato's *Symposium*. Aristophanes tells the story of the world's origin, when it was populated by three "sexes": male, female, and bisexual. Each had two sets of everything: faces, limbs, and genitals, and were therefore "complete" within themselves. However, they grew ambitious, and to prevent them from challenging the gods, Zeus split them in halves. This catastrophe is the origin of love, in that each of us goes through life searching for the individual (or half) that will again make us whole. See Plato, *Symposium,* trans. Alexander Nehamas and Paul Woodruff (Indianapolis: Hackett, 1989), 25–31.

29. Stephen Greenblatt, *Renaissance Self-Fashioning from More to Shakespeare* (Chicago: University of Chicago Press, 1980), 1.

30. Francis Rous, *Thule, or Vertue's History: To the honorable and vertuous Mistris Amy Audely. By F.R. The first booke,* (London: Printed by Felix Kingston for Humfrey Lownes, 1598), in *Early English Books Online,* http://ets.umdl.umich.edu/cgi/t/text/text-idx?c = eebo;idno = A11081.0001.001 (accessed November 12, 2007).

31. Samuel Daniel, *The Complete Works in Verse and Prose of Samuel Daniel,* ed. Alexander B. Grosart (New York: Russell & Russell, 1963), 78.

32. *The Complete Works,* ibid. While these writers used *spectator* to describe someone simultaneously engaged in both active and passive modes of interaction, others paired it with the locale the term would become most commonly associated with in the seventeenth century: the theater. This usage was not always literal. In Sonnet 44 of the *Amoretti,* Spenser introduces the term in his version of the recurrent metaphor of the world as theater: "My love like the Spectator idly sits / beholding me that all the pageants play." Often, such references contained adjudicatory supplications to patrons, such as Nicholas Breton's plea that opens his *Pasquils fooles-cap*: "I haue found you a kinde *Spectator* of my *Labours,* so let mee entreat you, at my hands to accept this treatise, with a foolish *title*" (original italics). Edmund Spenser, *The Yale Edition of the Shorter Poems of Edmund Spenser,* ed. William Oran, Einar Bjorvand, and Ronald Bond (New Haven: Yale University Press, 1989), 94; and Nicholas Breton, *Pasquils fooles-cap sent to such (to keepe their weake braines warme) as are not able to conceiue aright of his mad-cap* (London: Printed by R. Bradock for Thomas Johnes, 1600), http://eebo.chadwyck.com/search/full_rec?SOURCE = var_spell.cfg&ACTION = SINGLE&ID = 99899046&ECCO = &FILE = ../session/1499985402_2827&SEARCHSCREEN = CITATIONS&DISPLAY = AUTHOR &SUBSET = 64&ENTRIES = 145&HIGHLIGHT_KEYWORD = default (accessed November 24, 2007).

33. Charles Whitney, *Early Responses to Renaissance Drama* (Cambridge: Cambridge University Press, 2006), 198.

34. *Stationers' Register,* April 16, 1591. See *Records of the Court of the Stationers' Company, 1576 to 1602,* ed. W. W. Greg and E. Boswell (London: Bibliographical Society, 1930).

35. John Northbrooke, *Spiritus est vicarius Christi in terra. A treatise wherein dicing, dauncing, vaine playes or enterluds with other idle pastimes [et]c. commonly vsed on the Sabboth day, are reproued by the authoritie of the word of God and auntient writers* (London: Printed by H. Bynneman for George Bishop, 1577).

36. William Burton, *A sermon preached in the Cathedrall Church in Norwich, the xxi. day of December, 1589. By W. Burton, minister of the word of God there. And published for the satisfying of some which took offence thereat* (London: 1589). See also Burton, *The Rowsing of the Sluggard, in 7. Sermons Published at the request of divers godly and well affected* (London: Printed by the Widow Orwin for Thomas Man, 1595), where he states that "[the English] having put off the shoes of preparation for the Gospell, and put on the shoes of preparation for all kinde of vanitie, preferring playes before preachings, tables and cardes before the olde and new Te|stament, resoluing to be just of the Kings religion, and to stand to nothing for feare of alteration" (134).

37. For comparison, see Robert Edgeworth's *Sermons very fruitfull, godly, and learned, preached and sette foorth by Maister Roger Edgeworth* (London: Printed by Robert Cali, 1557); Thomas White's *A sermon preached at Pawles Crosse on Sunday the thirde of Nouember 1577* (London: Printed by Henry Bynneman for Francis Coldock, 1578); Arthur Dent's *A sermon of repentaunce a very godly and profitable sermon preached at Lee in Essex by Arthur Dent, Minister of God's word* (London: 1582); and Henry Smith's *The sermons of Maister Henrie Smith gathered into one volume. Printed according to his corrected copies in his life time* (London: Printed by Richard Field for Thomas Man, 1593).

38. Numbers 11:4–6. *The New Oxford Annotated Bible,* 3rd ed., ed. Michael D. Coogan (Oxford: Oxford University Press, 2001).

39. A similar device is, of course, used in the biblical passage I cite, where the Israelites actually *speak* as one, but this does not diminish the effect of communality that Northbrooke

creates through his rhetorical and conventional choices in *Spiritus est vicarius Christi in terra*; it is not, in other words, simply lazy and repetitious proselytizing.

40. Thomas Nashe, "Piers Penniless His Supplication to the Devil," in *Thomas Nashe: The Unfortunate Traveler and Other Works,* ed. J. B. Steane (London: Penguin, 1972), 113. Nashe's satire also contains the first instance I have found in which *spectator* is used to refer to literal theatergoers.

41. The account of the women's visit to Christ's tomb occurs in Matthew 28.1–2; Mark 16.1–4; Luke 24.1–3, and John 20.1. John differs from the synoptics in that only Mary Magdalen visits the tomb. See *New Oxford Annotated Bible,* 3rd ed.

42. David Bevington, ed., *Medieval Drama* (Boston: Houghton Mifflin, 1975), 36. This particular version of the *Visitatio Sepulchri* is from the twelfth-century St. Lambeth MS, but there are examples of this particular narrative dating back to the ninth century. As Bevington points out, liturgical drama had its roots in the Mass itself, and a definitive point of origin for some of the more extended dramatizations that often took place during Easter week is difficult to pin down.

43. Bevington notes that sometime between the twelfth and fourteenth centuries, liturgical drama began transitioning into the more populous cycle drama, but he also notes this was neither a smooth nor absolute change. Both likely coexisted during the Middle Ages, and many intermediate, even interdependent forms existed during this period. See *Medieval Drama,* 227–41.

44. Bevington, *Medieval Drama,* 7.

45. Steven Mullaney references this passage briefly in his exploration of early modern historical memory, particularly as it is posited and disseminated by the theater (in particular, Shakespeare's first tetralogy): "'The Talbot' is always a virtual and collective self as well as an individual and embodied one—or rather, he is an individual self because he is a virtual and collective self. . . ." Talbot "lives" virtually through the collective, affective memory the theater generates and sustains, and, as Mullaney argues, functions differently (although no less powerfully) than historical memory. It is this sort of embodied memory or reanimating faculty that I explore as a discourse rather than as affective phenomenon. See *The Reformation of Emotion in the Age of Shakespeare* (Chicago: University of Chicago Press, 2015), 122.

46. This argument has been most fully explored by Jonathan Dollimore, in *Radical Tragedy, Religion, Ideology and Power in the Drama of Shakespeare and His Contemporaries* (Brighton, U.K.: Harvester, 1984), and C. L. Barber, in his posthumously published *Creating Elizabethan Tragedy,* ed. Richard Wheeler (Chicago: University of Chicago Press, 1988).

47. See also Charles Whitney on the "pluralistic theatre" (*Early Responses,* 196–200). Whitney sees "pluralism" as the early modern theater's ability to foster "different interpretations and underwr[i]te different sides of social conflict" (197). My own argument focuses less on how the theater addressed different ideological viewpoints and more on how early modern theatrical discourse begins to articulate the theater as an individual experience.

48. Thomas Kyd, *The Spanish Tragedy,* ed. J. R. Mulryne (London: Methuen, 2007), 76.

49. Ibid., 75.

50. There has been a great deal of scholarly debate in the last thirty years over how much (if at all) Seneca influenced the genre of early modern revenge tragedy; however, most critics of *The Spanish Tragedy* agree that *Thyestes* has at least some influence on the play's structure and, to a lesser degree, its content. See, for example J. R. Mulryne's assessment of the play's

Senecan influences in the introduction to the most recent New Mermaids edition (Kyd, *Spanish Tragedy*).

51. Seneca, "Thyestes," in *Seneca, His Tenne Tragedies,* ed. Thomas Newton (New York: Knopf, 1927), 55.

52. Tantalus is punished in the underworld for having served the gods a banquet made from his son, Pelops, an act that resulted in the cursing of the House of Atreus.

53. Lopez argues that the presence of "at least one metaphor involving food" in the anti-theatricalists' shared parlance had a variety of resonances: "Eating, like playing, and especially eating excessively, is time spent indulging oneself when one could be serving or helping others; food, like the sumptuous variety of sensory experience at plays, provides the potential for surfeit, which is gluttony; eating, like playgoing, requires leisure time, which can lead to idleness; food nourishes the body as the word of God nourishes the soul, and as one destroys the body by feeding it improperly (or starving it), so one destroys the soul by indulging in things contrary to (or lacking) the word of God" (*Theatrical Convention*, 29). Underneath the surface critiques couched in the dietary metaphor, however, lies a tacit acknowledgment of the theater's sensory appeal, as my reading indicates.

54. Northbrooke, *Spiritus est vicarius Christi in terra*, 64.

55. Matthew 26:26. *New Oxford Annotated Bible*, 3rd ed.

56. Caroline Walker Bynum delineates the way in which devotional practice in medieval and early modern Europe understood the communal table as a celebration, both metaphoric and literal, of Christ's final meal with his disciples and subsequent sacrifice. See *Holy Feast and Holy Fast: The Religious Significance of Food to Medieval Women* (Berkeley: University of California Press, 1987).

57. For more on the history of the sensory hierarchy in Western culture, see, for example, John I. Beare's *Greek Theories of Elemental Cognition from Alcmaeon to Aristotle* (Oxford: Clarendon, 1906),; and David Summers's *The Judgment of Sense: Renaissance Naturalism and the Rise of Aesthetics* (Cambridge: Cambridge University Press, 1990).

58. Stephen Gosson, *The Schoole of Abuse* (London, 1579), 15.

59. Ibid., 17.

60. Carla Mazzio, "Acting with Tact: Touch and Theater in the Renaissance," in *Sensible Flesh: On Touch in Early Modern Culture,* ed. Elizabeth Harvey (Philadelphia: University of Pennsylvania Press, 2003). About the multisensory metaphor, Mazzio says that "it is actually the sense of touch that consistently informs both modes of sensory reception in antitheatrical treatises" (178). But whereas Mazzio argues that it is touch specifically that "disrupts the boundaries between the senses themselves," I would argue that there is something about the interaction between the spectator and the theatrical spectacle that causes the antitheatricalists to attempt such a linguistic figuration—one that implies the sort of contact Mazzio wants to emphasize in her essay.

61. Mazzio, "Acting with Tact," 179.

62. See Chapter 1, note 34.

63. Aristotle classified this type of metaphor as "species-species" in that it involved a comparison between two related entities (in this case the senses). Most critics would now classify this type of comparison as metonymy rather than metaphor.

64. Donald Davidson, "What Metaphors Mean," *Critical Inquiry* 5 (1978), 31–47.

65. Irving Massey, however, claims that there are numerous uses of synaesthesia found in eighteenth- and nineteenth-century French literature. He also avers that "the idea of synaesthe-

sia is of course very old." Like Heller-Roazen, he locates its origins in classical Greek philoso-phy. See Massey, "A Note on the History of Synaesthesia," *Modern Language Notes* 71.3 (1956), 203–6.

66. Daniel Heller-Roazen, *The Inner Touch: Archaeology of a Sensation* (New York: Zone, 2007), 81. Heller-Roazen goes on to trace a history of the term's usage through late antiquity.

67. Ibid.

68. Mullaney, *Reformation*, 150.

69. Shakespeare, *A Midsummer Night's Dream*, 4.1.199–207.

70. Jennifer Waldron, "'The Eye of Man Hath Not Heard': Shakespeare, Synaesthesia, and Post-Reformation Phenomenology," *Criticism* 54.3 (2012), 403–17. Waldron's argument centers on the way that theatrical phenomenology intersects with the entanglement of Protes-tant and Catholic ideas of embodiment.

71. *Stationers' Register,* February 25, 1592, in Greg and Boswell, *Records of the court.*

72. Munday, *Second and Third Blast,* 55–56.

73. Gosson, *Schoole of Abuse,* 41.

74. Thomas Lodge, *Protogenes can know Apelles by his line though he se him not and wise men can consider by the penn the aucthoritie of the writer thoughe they know him not* (London: 1579), in *Early English Books Online,* http://eebo.chadwyck.com/search/full_rec?SOURCE = var_spell.cfg&ACTION = ByID&ID = 99841491&ECCO = param(ECCO)&FILE = ../ses sion/1499988901_8480&SEARCHSCREEN = CITATIONS&DISPLAY = AUTHOR&HIGH LIGHT_KEYWORD = param(HIGHLIGHT_KEYWORD) (accessed February 23, 2016).

75. Sidney, *An Apologie for Poetrie,* 47.

76. Thomas Heywood, *An Apology for Actors* (London: Printed by Nicholas Okes, 1612).

77. George Gascoigne, "Supposes," in *Drama of the English Renaissance I: The Tudor Period,* ed. Russell A. Fraser and Norman Rabkin (New York: Macmillan, 1976), 102.

78. Shakespeare, *Henry V,* 1.0.17–20.

79. William Prynne, *Histrio-mastix: The Players Scourge* (London: Printed by E. A. and W. I. for Michael Sparke, 1633). Munday also references "real" scenes from the theater, but he is more concerned with women who attend and are naïvely seduced by "secret friends" than by specific social types. For a feminist-materialist reading of Munday's anxiety, see Jean Howard, "Women as Spectators, Spectacles, and Paying Customers," in *Readings in Renaissance Women's Drama: Criticism, History, and Performance, 1594–1998,* ed. S. P. Cerasano and Marion Wynne-Davies (London: Routledge, 1998), 81–86.

80. Ben Jonson, for example, playfully courts his varied audiences in the prologue to *Epicoene or the Silent Woman,* saying that his play holds something for "ladies: some for lords, knights, squires; Some for your waiting-wench and city wires; Some for your men, and daugh-ters of Whitefriars" (22–24). At the other extreme, Francis Beaumont's *The Knight of the Burn-ing Pestle* is an extended satire of a particular stereotype (the merchant-spectator), one that seems to have been unappreciated by actual early modern audiences, as the play was an unquali-fied commercial failure, according to the publisher's letter that appeared with the play's first printed edition in 1613. Jonson, *Epicoene or the Silent Woman,* ed. Richard Dutton (Manchester: Manchester University Press, 2008); Beaumont, *The Knight of the Burning Pestle,* ed. Sheldon P. Zitner (Manchester: Manchester University Press, 2004).

81. Munday, *Second and Third Blast.*

CHAPTER 2

Notes to epigraphs: William Shakespeare, *Hamlet,* 2.2.568–72, in *The Norton Shakespeare,* 3rd ed., ed. Stephen Greenblatt et al. (New York: W. W. Norton, 2016). Miguel de Cervantes, *Don Quixote,* trans. Walter Starkie (New York: New American Library, 1957), 58.

1. Geoffrey Bullough mentions both Plutarch's *Life of Pelopidas* (75 C.E.) and the anonymous *A Warning for Fair Women* (1599) as possible sources for Shakespeare's reference to the guilty spectator (Bullough skews more toward the latter). *Life of Pelopidas* includes a mention of Alexander of Pherae's walking out of a tragedy because he did not want his people to see him weeping—a narrative that Philip Sidney also cites in his *Apology.* See Bullough, *Narrative and Dramatic Sources,* vol. 7 (New York: Columbia University Press, 1966), 38. For further support of Plutarch as source, see Patricia S. Gourlay, "Guilty Creatures Sitting at a Play: A Note on Hamlet, Act II, Scene 2," *Renaissance Quarterly* 24.2 (1971), 221–25. However, the particular slant found in *Hamlet,* where the play actually incites a confession from the spectator, is also found in Thomas Heywood's *An Apology for Actors* (London: Printed by Nicholas Okes, 1612):

> At *Lin* in *Norfolke,* the then Earle of *Sussex* players acting the old History of Fryer
> *Francis,* & presenting a woman, who insatiately doting on a yong gentleman, had
> (the more securely to enioy his affection) mischieuously and seceretly murdered her
> husband, whose ghost haunted her, and at diuers times in her most solitary and
> priuate contemplations, in most horrid and fearefull shapes, appeared, and stood
> before her. As this was acted, a townes-woman (till then of good estimation and
> report) finding her conscience (at this presenment) extremely troubled, suddenly
> skritched and cryd out Oh my husband, my husband! I see the ghost of my husband
> fiercely threatning and menacing me.

While the *Apology* was written later than *Hamlet,* both accounts seem to reference either a contemporary theatrical anecdote or myth circulating in the early seventeenth century, which may suggest a more contemporary and idiosyncratic version of it that was circulating in England. See Sidney, *An Apologie for Poetrie* (London: Printed for Henrie Olney, 1595).

2. Vladimir Nabokov famously dismissed Cervantes's novel because of its "hideous cruelty" in his *Lectures on Don Quixote,* ed. Fredson Bowers (New York: Harcourt Brace, 1983). While Nabokov cited Cervantes's treatment of his hero as the satire's principal cruelty, satire is, in many ways, predicated on a kind of violence in its desire to hold a mirror up to someone or something and strip away the easing fictions of subjective and institutional ideology. More relevant for my purposes here is the way *Don Quixote* plays out (albeit satirically) the early modern anxiety that what the spectator-reader sees, she or he very well might do.

3. Shakespeare, *Hamlet,* 2.2.292.3–292.9. This passage is omitted in Hamlet's Second Quarto, in which Rosencrantz answers Hamlet's question with a single line: "I think their inhibition, comes by the means of the late innovasion" (1379–80). *The Tragicall Historie of Hamlet, Prince of Denmarke* (London: Printed by I.R. for N.L., 1605). No line numbers.

4. For example, the major anthologies *The Norton Shakespeare, The Riverside Shakespeare,* and the Royal Shakespeare Company's *William Shakespeare Complete Works* all concur that these lines reference "the new fashion for boy actors" (RSC). While fewer editions mention the

Poetomachia directly in conjunction with these lines (exceptions include the Arden 3 *Hamlet*, edited by Ann Thompson and Neil Taylor, and the Bedford *Hamlet*, edited by Suzanne Gossett), a number of scholars have made this connection. Roslyn Knutson offers an excellent history of this commentary in "Falconer to the Little Eyases: A New Date and Agenda for the 'Little Eyases' Passage in Hamlet," *Shakespeare Quarterly* 46.1 (1995), 1–31.

5. Although it remains unclear whether the Poetomachia resulted from a genuine and antagonistic *agon* between playwrights or was a publicity stunt generated by theatrical companies, in either case, the war offers insight into a period of hyperbolized audience response and the fiscal and artistic repercussions of such immediacy. Knutson suggests alternative possibilities to the rivalry narrative in "Falconer to the Little Eyases."

6. Michael Shapiro, *Children of the Revels: The Boy Companies of Shakespeare's Time and Their Plays* (New York: Columbia University Press, 1977), 76–77.

7. In *Don Quixote,* of course, the barber and the "giants" are separate entities. It is uncertain whether Beaumont had read *Don Quixote* before he wrote *Knight* (it was not translated into English until 1612), but it is very likely he had heard of it. See Lee Bliss, " 'Don Quixote in England: The Case for 'The Knight of the Burning Pestle,' *Viator* 18 (1987), 361–80; Valerie Wayne, "*Don Quixote* and Shakespeare's Collaborative Turn to Romance," in *The Quest for Cardenio: Shakespeare, Fletcher, Cervantes and the Lost Play,* ed. David Carnegie and Gary Taylor (Oxford: Oxford University Press, 2012), 217–38; and Roger Chartier, *Cardenio Between Cervantes and Shakespeare* (Cambridge: Polity, 2013), 15–17.

8. *The Knight of the Burning Pestle,* ed. Michael Hattaway, 2nd ed. (London: Methuen, 2002), vii–ix. All quotes from the play are taken from this edition.

9. Wayne, *Don Quixote.*

10. John Fletcher, *The Faithful Shepherdess,* ed. Florence Ada Kirk (New York: Garland, 1980), 7. Other examples (besides that of *Knight* itself) include John Webster's *The White Devil* (1612), where Webster references his play as an organism that the "uncapable multitude" is unable, despite their best efforts, to "poison" ("To The Reader," 22–23), and Thomas Middleton's dedicatory epistle to *The Witch* (1609–16), where he cites his play as having been made to "lie so long in an imprisoned obscurity" (Epistle, 7). See Webster, *The White Devil* and Middleton, "The Witch," in *Thomas Middleton: The Collected Works,* eds. Gary Taylor and John Lavagnino (Oxford: Clarendon Press, 2007).

11. Thomas Middleton, *The Family of Love* (London, 1608), in *Early English Books Online,* http://eebo.chadwyck.com/search/full_recSOURCE = pgimages.cfg&ACTION = ByID&ID = V12879 (accessed August, 16, 2013). Other examples include Thomas Dekker's *Old Fortunatus,* where Fortunatus claims that "shortly there will creep out in print some filthy book of the old hoary wandering knight, meaning me: would I were that book, for then I should be sure to creep out from hence"; Mamillius's telling of the "sad tale best for winter" that begins the tragic actions in *Winter's Tale* and, arguably, the ending of that play itself, where life and art are irrevocably imbricated. In addition, as both Katharine Eisaman Maus and Jeffrey Masten have pointed out, the paternal trope (where the play is figured as the author's/authors'/printer's progeny) is fairly widespread. See Maus, "A Womb of His Own: Male Renaissance Poets in the Female Body," in *Sexuality and Gender in Early Modern Europe: Institutions, Texts, Images,* ed. James Grantham Turner (Cambridge: Cambridge University Press, 1993), 266–88; and Masten, "My Two Dads: Collaboration and the Reproduction of Beaumont and Fletcher," in *Queering the Renaissance,* ed. Jonathan Goldberg (Durham, NC: Duke University Press, 1997), 280–309.

12. Theater historians especially have been interested in the question of "why" *Knight* failed in the theater. Because of its later success in the Restoration and beyond, most critics have concluded that its metatheatrical exploration of the nature and agency of the spectator was either "too advanced" for the audience in 1607 (the likely date of its first performance), or that the play, which satirizes a member of the citizen class and his wife, offended certain members of that demographic in attendance. See, for example, Alfred Harbage, *Shakespeare and the Rival Traditions* (New York: Macmillan, 1952); Shapiro, *Children of the Revels*; Lee Bliss, *Francis Beaumont* (Boston: Twayne, 1987); Alexander Leggatt, "The Audience as Patron: *The Knight of the Burning Pestle*," in *Shakespeare and Theatrical Patronage,* ed. Paul Whitfield White and Suzanne Westfall (Cambridge: Cambridge University Press, 2002), 295–314; Brent E. Whitted, "Staging Exchange: Why *The Knight of the Burning Pestle* Flopped at Blackfriars in 1607," *Early Theatre: A Journal Associated with the Records of Early English Drama,* 15.2 (2012), 111–30; and Andrew Gurr, *Playgoing in Shakespeare's London,* 3rd ed. (Cambridge: Cambridge University Press, 2004), 121–22.

13. Shapiro, *Children of the Revels,* 74, 100. Shapiro goes on to say that *Knight* likely failed because "some status-seeking spectators may have seen the grocer and his wife as insulting caricatures of themselves, while those who felt their status declining may have taken the intrusion as an unpleasant omen" (77).

14. Jeffrey Masten, *Textual Intercourse: Collaboration, Authorship, and Sexualities in Renaissance Drama* (Cambridge: Cambridge University Press, 1997), 23.

15. Leggatt, "Audience as Patron," 298–99.

16. Ibid., 300.

17. In mass culture theoretical parlance, this model has been called the "hypodermic model." See, for example, Will Brooker and Deborah Jermyn, eds., *The Audience Studies Reader* (London: Routledge, 2003), 5–6.

18. In the introduction to their collection *Imagining the Audience in Early Modern Drama* (New York: Palgrave Macmillan, 2011), Jennifer Low and Nova Myhill discuss two "types" of spectators often metadramatically represented by playwrights, the "judicious" and the "aberrant" spectator. The violent spectator could be understood as an offshoot of the "aberrant" spectator, one articulated in response to the vicissitudes of spectatorial tastes and responses. However, as I argue throughout this study, neither the judicious nor the aberrant spectator is entirely created by early modern dramatists but is developed from earlier spectatorial models. Rather than created by playwrights, they are adapted by them.

19. Tiffany Stern, "Taking Part: Actors and Audience on the Stage at the Blackfriars," in *Inside Shakespeare: Essays on the Blackfriars Stage,* ed. Paul Menzer (Selinsgrove, PA: Susquehanna University Press, 2006), 35–53.

20. John Day, *The Isle of Gulls* (London: Printed for William Sheares, 1633). In "Taking Part" (ibid.), Stern focuses on the King's Men's Blackfriars era; however, well before 1608, many playwrights wrote for both the adult and children's companies (or had ambitions to do so), and a variety of spectators frequented both amphitheater and hall performances. Playwrights, then, were grappling with this expanded and unstable spectatorial landscape well before the King's Men moved to the Blackfriars. Indeed, regardless of whether the War of the Theaters was real or feigned, it stands as a testament to experiments in theatrical convention, audience address, exhibition, staging, and publicity.

21. See Leggatt, "The Audience as Patron," 275.

22. Kathleen McLuskie, "Figuring the Consumer for Early Modern Drama," in *Rematerializing Shakespeare: Authority and Representation on the Early Modern Stage,* ed. Bryan Reynolds

and William N. West (Basingstoke, U.K.: Palgrave Macmillan, 2005), 190. Low and Myhill also point out that playwrights and others involved in the professional theater industry "knew the extent to which their audiences controlled them economically, and, as a result, aesthetically" (*Imagining the Audience,* 5).

23. Movement is central to Benjamin's slippery concept of aura. Mechanical reproduction diminishes aura in that the viewer no longer experiences the "original" artwork's presence in time and space (particularly in the space for which it was designed). Inherent in this theory is the fact that the work of art no longer has the potency to draw spectators to its location; rather the consumer-spectator can manipulate the object (or its reproduction) so that it comes to him or her. See Walter Benjamin, *Illuminations: Essays and Reflections,* ed. Hannah Arendt, trans. Harry Zohn (New York: Schocken, 1969).

24. Benjamin, *Illuminations,* 238.

25. Ellen Mackay, *Persecution, Plague, and Fire: Fugitive Histories of the Stage in Early Modern England* (Chicago: Chicago University Press, 2011).

26. Ibid., 8–9.

27. Benjamin, *Illuminations,* 241.

28. Paratextual apparatuses were not in and of themselves new in the seventeenth century. However, as David Bergeron points out, the early part of the seventeenth century saw them used to communicate new perspectives and concerns: "But in the first decade of the Jacobean era, playwrights had begun to usurp this prerogative [from printers and publishers] and to use this prefatory space for an expression of their ideas about the play, about the status of the theater, about any topic that concerned them" (458). See "Paratexts in Francis Beaumont's *The Knight of the Burning Pestle,*" *Studies in Philology* 106.4 (2009), 456–67.

29. Edward Sharpham, *Cupid's Whirligig* (London, 1607). Like *Knight, Cupid's Whirligig* was written in the early seventeenth century for the Children of the King's Revels.

30. Benedict Anderson, *Imagined Communities,* rev. ed. (London: Verson, 1991).

31. For example, Dekker's *The Gull's Hornbook* (c. 1609) contains an extended parody of a hall theater audience in the chapter "How a Gallant Should Behave Himself in a Playhouse." Other examples include Jonson's satire in *Bartholomew Fair* (1614) and Dekker's prologue to *If This Be Not a Good Play Then the Devil Is in It* (1611).

32. Masten, *Textual Intercourse,* 23.

33. John Willett, ed. and trans., *Brecht on Theatre* (New York: Hill and Wang, 1964).

34. Ibid., 91.

35. Ibid., 71.

36. For a thorough review of these studies, see Doc Rossi, "Brecht on Shakespeare: A Revaluation," *Comparative Drama* 30.2 (Summer 1996), 158–87.

37. While not yet associated with the theater, *alienation* was already part of the early modern lexicon of estrangement. Frequently used to connote man's separation from God, it encompassed several secular resonances as well. The *OED* cites "the action of estranging, or state of estrangement in feeling or affection" as the most common usage by the seventeenth century, but other variants included "the action of transferring the ownership of anything to another," "the taking of anything from another," and "the withdrawal, loss, or derangement of mental faculties; insanity." In each case, *alienation* describes a category of deprivation—loss of transcendent, originary self, affective loss, loss of property, loss of reason. Nathan Rotenstreitch has argued that early use of *alienation* in Western thought connoted a positive rather than

negative state of being, a state of self-estrangement that brought one closer to God. Rotenstreitch claims that the concept begins to metamorphose in the nineteenth century; however, according to the *OED*, alienation had taken on both negative and secular resonances by the fifteenth century. See Rotenstreitch, *Alienation: The Concept and Its Reception* (Leiden: E. J. Brill, 1989), 3–8.

38. Sigmund Freud, *Group Psychology and the Analysis of the Ego,* ed. and trans. James Strachey (New York: W. W. Norton, 1959), 50. J. Laplanche and J.-B. Pontalis similarly define identification as an essential component of subject-formation, "whereby the subject assimilates an aspect, property, or attribute of the other and is transformed, wholly or partially, after the model the other provides. It is by means of a series of identifications that the personality is constituted and specified." See *The Language of Psychoanalysis,* trans. Donald Nicholson-Smith (New York: W. W. Norton, 1973), 206.

39. Jacques Lacan, *Ecrits,* trans. Bruce Fink (New York: W. W. Norton, 2006).

40. Diana Fuss, *Identification Papers* (New York: Routledge, 1995), 34. Given that most early theories of film spectatorship derive directly from Lacan's mirror-stage concept, it may seem odd that I do not discuss them here. Such theories draw on the Lacanian model primarily because it imagines an apparatus (the mirror) as an essential component in the subject's creation of an idealized self-image, a mechanism that has been seen as an analogue of the camera for the film spectator. Such subjective and viewing technologies are not what I wish to emphasize in the sort of identification suggested by the Citizen in *Knight.* Rather, it is the desire to see a more ideal image of the self, an entity realized through an image (or in this case, a performance) *other than* the self that I see as related to Lacan's concept of identification.

41. Judith Butler, *Bodies That Matter: On the Discursive Limits of "Sex"* (New York: Routledge, 1993), 219.

42. José Esteban Muñoz, *Disidentification: Queers of Color and the Performance of Politics* (Minneapolis: University of Minnesota Press, 1999), 11.

43. Butler, *Bodies That Matter,* 219.

44. Leggatt, "Audience as Patron," 300.

45. "Consumer, n." OED Online, December 2013, Oxford University Press, http://www.oed.com/view/Entry/39978?redirectedFrom = consumer (accessed January 14, 2014).

46. The Citizen's representational self-construction here is reminiscent of Laplanche and Pontalis's analysis of the relationship between Freud's concept of the ego-ideal and identification: "The ego-ideal is composed of identifications with cultural ideals that are not necessarily harmonious." See Laplanche and Pontalis, *Language of Psychoanalysis,* 208. To place this idea in a historical context, the Citizen's ideal image of himself is constructed out of certain images gleaned from his profession (the pestle, for example) and those taken from the literary tradition of romance and (perhaps) those being culturally circulated through the chivalric revival initiated by Prince Henry.

47. Interestingly, the Citizen's identificatory process demonstrates the problem with binaristic models of identification, as his trajectory more resembles the transvestic model that Mary Ann Doane describes as an alternative for the female film spectator: she can either masochistically identify with her onscreen "passive" gendered counterpart or transvestically identify with the male protagonist. While the Grocer does not alter the gender of his constructed stage-surrogate, neither does he propose an exact copy of himself but one that enacts fantasies of class and professional mobility. See Mary Ann Doane, *The Desire to Desire: The Woman's Film of the 1940s* (Bloomington: Indiana University Press, 1987).

48. Elias Canetti, *Crowds and Power,* trans. Carol Stewart (New York: Viking, 1962), 22.

49. John Day, *Isle of Gulls.*

50. Leslie Thompson, "Who's In, Who's Out? *The Knight of the Burning Pestle* on the Blackfriars Stage," in *Inside Shakespeare: Essays on the Blackfriars Stage,* ed. Paul Menzer (Selinsgrove, PA: Susquehanna University Press, 2006), 64.

51. Stage sitting was a practice limited to the hall playhouses and constituted a complex display of spectatorial performativity, which could include drawing attention to oneself by occupying the physical space of the performers, wearing ostentatious clothing, and providing audial and gestural "commentary" on the play. This practice is satirized in Dekker's *The Gull's Hornbook;* for a historical analysis, see Gurr, *Playgoing,* 34–37.

52. On the masculine composition of stage sitters, see Gurr, *Playgoing,* 36, 46, and Leggatt, "Audience as Patron," 300. Historically speaking, the practice of stool sitting inherently involved multiple violations of the work being produced onstage. The first (and most benign) form was distraction: accounts of gallants "pulling focus" through exaggerated reactions to the play and ostentatious displays of fashion abound in the period. Even when not engaging in intentionally disruptive behavior, the stage spectators' bodily presence often interfered with the performance space, a problem to which Ben Jonson refers in *The Devil Is an Ass*:

> This tract
> Will never admit our vice because of yours
> Anon, who worse than you, the fault endures
> That you yourselves make? When you will thrust and spurn
> And knock us o' the elbows and bid, turn. (Prologue, 8–12)

53. Thompson, "Who's In, Who's Out?" 64.

54. The other moments in the play where the Citizen threatens violence are at 1.205–6; 2.14–16 and 273–74; Int. 2.5–8; and 4.15–20.

55. Regarding the representation of class mobility on the early modern English stage *as* fantasy (rather than realistic reflection of actual mobility), see David Scott Kastan's "Workshop and/as Playhouse: Comedy and Commerce in *The Shoemaker's Holiday,*" *Studies in Philology* 84 (1987), 324–37.

56. This other type of violence is, I believe, related to the sort that Leo Bersani describes as "psychic dislocation of mobile desire." The Citizen's desire to see himself represented in a certain way manifests most profoundly through representational violence (which Bersani calls "noncatastrophic violence") rather than real violence (the sort exhibited in his initial interruption of the play and later threats against the players) because representational violence allows for both the expression of his alienation and preservation of the experience of watching his surrogate self onstage. See Bersani, *The Freudian Body: Psychoanalysis and Art* (New York: Columbia University Press, 1996), 70–78.

57. Cynthia Marshall, *The Shattering of the Self: Violence, Subjectivity, and Early Modern Texts* (Baltimore: Johns Hopkins University Press, 2002), 2, 41.

58. Tammy Clewell, "Mourning Beyond Melancholia: Freud's Psychoanalysis of Loss," *Journal of the American Psychoanalytic Association* 52.1 (2004), 43–67.

59. Sigmund Freud, "Mourning and Melancholia," *Standard Edition of the Complete Psychological Works of Sigmund Freud,* vol. 14 (London: Hogarth, 1957), 249–50.

60. Ibid., 251.

61. According to the *Oxford English Dictionary,* the definition of "consumer" as "a person who uses up a commodity; a purchaser of goods or services, a customer," is in use by the end of the seventeenth century. See n. 44.

62. Leggatt, "Audience as Patron," 296.

63. See n. 8. Zachary Lesser has an astute reading of critics' widespread acceptance of Burre's claim that the play failed because the audience missed its "privy mark of irony." See *Renaissance Drama and the Politics of Publication* (Cambridge: Cambridge University Press, 2004), 226–30.

64. Thomas Dekker, *The Gull's Hornbook*, ed. R. B. McKerrow (New York: AMS, 1971), 52.

65. Jeffrey Masten, "Beaumont and/or Fletcher: Collaboration and the Interpretation of Renaissance Drama," *English Literary History* 59 (1992), 346–47. Masten cites the play's complex parentage (authors, publisher, theater manager, and audience) as a paradigmatic example of the essentially collaborative nature of early modern drama, but *Knight*, I would add, endures a particularly violent nativity.

66. See, for example, Maus, "A Womb of His Own," and Anne-Julia Zwierlein, "Male Pregnancies, Virgin Births, Monsters of the Mind: Early Modern Melancholia and (Cross-) Gendered Constructions of Creativity," in *The Literature of Melancholia: Early Modern to Postmodern*, ed. Martin Middeke and Christina Wald (Basingstoke, U.K.: Palgrave Macmillan, 2005), 35–49.

67. This image may have had particular currency in 1613 when *The Knight* was first printed owing to the chivalric revival initiated by Prince Henry. Regarding the issue of surrogation, this connection becomes even more pertinent. Historians have claimed that unlike his father, Henry enjoyed immense, almost iconic, popularity among his subjects, an affective bond James both envied and feared. In terms of my argument here, the relationship between Henry and his father evokes the sort of surrogacy with which I see *The Knight* engaging. Often referred to as "England's hope," Henry came to stand in for the sort of prince that England longed for but did not have in James. See Roy Strong, *Henry, Prince of Wales and England's Lost Renaissance* (London: Thames and Hudson, 1986), 14–15.

68. Interestingly, this division goes against the traditional patriarchal line of inheritance, in which the eldest is heir to the family estate and the younger sons must find alternative means of making their "name" in the world. Arguably, this alteration is facilitated by the fact that *Knight* here demonstrates a matrilineal inheritance model, as it is Mrs. Merrythought who has "laid up" for her younger son.

69. See, for example, Ind. 60–61 and 67–75; 1.277–78; 2. 129–30, 165–66, 201–5, 343–44; and 3.160–62, 336–37.

70. See the play's *dramatis personae*, which designates Rafe simply as "her man."

71. Laurie E. Osborne, "Female Audiences and Female Authority in *The Knight of the Burning Pestle*," *Exemplaria* 3.2 (1991), 517.

72. Osborne, "Female Audiences," 491–92. Regarding Jean Howard's and Stephen Orgel's claims about female audiences, see Howard, *The Stage and Social Struggle in Early Modern England* (London: Routledge, 1994), and Orgel, "Nobody's Perfect: Or Why Did the English Stage Take Boys for Women," *South Atlantic Quarterly* 88 (1989), 7–29.

73. Marion A. Taylor, "Lady Arbella Stuart and Beaumont and Fletcher," *Papers in Language and Literature* 8 (1972), 253, quoted in Osborne, "Female Audiences," 515–16. Taylor bases her claim on an excerpt from the *Calendar of State Papers* that states "in a certain comedy the playwright introduced an allusion to her person and the part played by the Prince of Moldavia. The play was suppressed." Osborne points out that Taylor's argument depends on dating the play at 1609 and that it does not refer to Jonson's *Epicoene,* which contains a similar reference.

74. This phrase is taken from the title of chapter 4 of Jean Howard's *Stage and Social Struggle*.

75. See Frances E. Dolan's *Marriage and Violence: The Early Modern Legacy* (Philadelphia: University of Pennsylvania Press, 2008).

76. In addition to these scholars, Natasha Korda has done important work on showing multiple ways in which women were involved with the early modern theater, particularly the way in which women's labor allowed the business of theater to exist. See Korda, *Labors Lost: Women's Work and the Early Modern English Stage* (Philadelphia: University of Pennsylvania Press, 2011).

77. For example, both Diana Henderson and Pamela Allen Brown read Nell as a clear attempt to demean women's participation in theater audiences, while critics such as Osborne and, more recently, Valerie Billings, see Nell as a figuration that reveals traces of women's subversion of patriarchal norms of both theatergoing and spectatorial desire. See Diana Henderson, "The Theater and Domestic Culture," in *A New History of Early English Drama*, ed. John D. Cox and David Scott Kastan (New York: Columbia University Press, 1997), 173–94; Pamela Allen Brown, *Better a Shrew Than a Sheep* (Ithaca, NY: Cornell University Press, 2003); Valerie Billings, "Female Spectators and the Erotics of the Diminutive in *Epicoene* and *The Knight of the Burning Pestle*," *Renaissance Drama* 42.1 (2014), 1–28; and Osborne, "Female Audiences."

78. Even studies that tread the line between representations of spectators and real audiences with care tend to elide these two realms with some ease. For example, Valerie Billings's recent work on female spectatorial desire uses Nell to illustrate the ways in which women's voyeuristic pleasures may have been ignited by the spectacle of the boy actor (or, indeed, any male) and states that the theater's fictional potency renders these figures "diminutive by their dependency or low social status" ("Female Spectators," 3). While Billings is careful to state that "this is not to say that all female spectators experienced boy company plays as erotic," her primary interest in Nell's responses is "interrogating female spectatorship at boy company performances at the beginning of the seventeenth century" (2), suggesting that one *can* unearth the *semina* of women's viewing practices (in this case both spectatorial and erotic) from their representations.

79. See Osborne, "Female Audiences," 497, 505. Osborne notes that Ronald Miller's reading of Nell is somewhat of an exception to this bias; however, as she points out, "Miller does not, on the whole, distinguish Nell from George in her powers over the production" (497).

80. Charles Whitney, *Early Responses to Renaissance Drama* (Cambridge: Cambridge University Press, 2006), 5. Tiffany Stern's recent work on playbills suggests that word of mouth would not have been the only means of publicity available to theater companies; however, she also acknowledges that oral transmission constituted one of the most significant forms of spreading the word: "At the end of each performance, an announcement would be made asking the audience to sanction a particular choice of play for the following afternoon." See Stern, "Taking Part," 36.

81. Paul Yachnin, "Performing Publicity," *Shakespeare Bulletin* 28.2 (2010), 211.

82. See Brown, *Better a Shrew*, 60–67, for a brief history of the term and its resonances in early modern England.

83. Karen Newman, "City Talk: Women and Commodification," in *Staging the Renaissance: Reinterpretations of Elizabethan and Jacobean Drama*, ed. David Scott Kastan and Peter Stallybrass (New York: Routledge, 1991), 184. See also Keith Botelho, *Renaissance Earwitnesses:*

Rumor and Early Modern Masculinity (Basingstoke, U.K.: Palgrave Macmillan, 2009), who makes the case that "gossip" tended to be gendered female while "rumor" was masculine in the early modern period (8–14).

84. These instances occur at the induction, lines 50, 67, 83, and 109; act 1, lines 208–9 and 291; act 3, lines 94 and 458–59; interlude 3, lines 3–4; and the epilogue, line 3.

85. See *Knight,* n. 97 in Hattaway.

86. Both the New Mermaids edition cited herein and Sheldon P. Zitner's Revels edition (Manchester: Manchester University Press, 2004) gloss the "twelve companies" thusly.

87. In his edition of *Knight,* Hattaway suggests that this reference might be to a "huge German fencer who lived in London" (69, n.270), which he takes from Edward Sugden's *A Topographical Dictionary to the Works of Shakespeare and His Contemporaries* (Manchester, 1925). If this reference is correct, it corresponds to a line in Dekker and Middleton's *The Roaring Girl,* where Moll says she has "struck up the heels of the high German's size" (2.1.368).

88. David A. Samuelson, "The Order of Beaumont's *The Knight of the Burning Pestle,*" *English Literary Renaissance* 9 (1979), 310.

89. In addition to the three instances previously cited, the other four occur at the induction, lines 83–84 (about Rafe performing *Mucedorus* for the company's wardens); act 1, line 238 (about the current state of knighthood in England); interlude 1, lines 3–4 (about a xenophobic myth regarding the Turk's treatment of his musicians); and act 3, lines 425–28 (about a tale of a witch and her son).

90. Stern, *Documents of Performance,* 36–37. Stern notes that this custom may have been used only outside of London at the beginning of the seventeenth century.

91. *The Norton Shakespeare;* and "The New Inn" in *Ben Jonson: The Devil is an Ass and Other Plays,* ed. Margaret Jane Kidnie (Oxford: Oxford University Press, 2000), 424.

92. F. L. Lucas, ed., *The Complete Works of John Webster,* vol. 1. (New York: Oxford University Press [American Branch], 1937).

93. See Leeds Barroll, *Politics, Plague and Shakespeare's Theater: The Stuart Years* (Ithaca, NY: Cornell University Press, 1991); Tanya Pollard, " 'No Faith in Physic': Masquerades of Medicine Onstage and Off," in *Disease, Diagnosis and Cure on the Early Modern Stage,* ed. Stephanie Moss and Kaara L. Peterson (Aldershot, U.K.: Ashgate, 2004), 29–41; Jonathan Gil-Harris, *Sick Economies: Drama, Mercantilism and Disease in Shakespeare's England* (Philadelphia: University of Pennsylvania Press, 2004); and Mackay, *Persecution.*

94. Mackay, for example, has a nuanced and compelling reading of the contagion metaphor and yet still works solely with this one-way model. More recently, Jennie Votava called for a better understanding of the link between contagion and spectatorship via a transhistorical exploration of dramatic convention—a query that begins to get at a more complex model of spectatorial dynamics. See Mackay, *Persecution,* and Votava, "Dangerous Sensations: Contagion and Spectatorship in Gosson and Shakespeare," presented at the Shakespeare Association of America Conference, St. Louis, MO, April 2014.

95. Alison Hobgood, *Passionate Playgoing in Early Modern England* (Cambridge: Cambridge University Press, 2014), 10; and Matthew Steggle, *Laughing and Weeping in Early Modern Theaters* (Aldershot, U.K.: Ashgate, 2007), 5–7.

96. Anthony Munday, *A Second and Third Blast of Retreat from Plaies and Theaters* (London: Henrie Denham, 1580), 54.

97. Stephen Gosson, *The School of Abuse* (London, 1579).

98. Fletcher, *Faithful Shepherdess,* 7.

99. Mt 27:35, *The New Oxford Annotated Bible* 3rd ed., ed. Michael D. Coogan (Oxford: Oxford University Press, 2001).

100. George Bernard Shaw, *Man and Superman: A Comedy and a Philosophy* (London: Penguin, 1946), 31. See also J. O. Campbell, *Shakespeare's Satire* (London: Oxford University Press, 1943), 198; Edward Honig, "Sejanus and Coriolanus: A Study in Alienation," *Modern Language Quarterly* 12 (1951), 407–21; and Katherine Stockholder, "The Other Coriolanus," *PMLA* 85.2 (1970), 228–36.

101. Cynthia Marshall, "Wound-man: *Coriolanus,* Gender, and the Theatrical Construction of Interiority," in *Feminist Readings of Early Modern Culture: Emerging Subjects,* ed. Valerie Traub, M. Lindsay Kaplan, and Dympna Callaghan (Cambridge: Cambridge University Press, 1996), 95.

102. Ibid., 104.

103. *The Norton Shakespeare.*

104. See Ian Munro's perceptive study of the ways in which the theater appropriated various cultural discourses about the dangers of crowds in *The Figure of the Crowd in Early Modern London: The City and Its Double* (Basingstoke, U.K.: Palgrave, 2005). Munro is primarily interested in how such appropriations signal the theater industries "ambivalence about both its place in the symbolic space of London and its commercial service to the crowded city" (106) rather than on how such discourses played a role in formulating ideas about the theatrical spectator.

105. John Marston, *What You Will,* induction, line 35; and Dekker, *The Gull's Hornbook*, 49.

106. Andrew Gurr and Karoline Szatek, "Women and Crowds at the Theater," *Medieval and Renaissance Drama in England* 21 (2008), 157.

CHAPTER 3

1. Lukas Erne, *Shakespeare as Literary Dramatist,* 2nd ed. (Cambridge: Cambridge University Press, 2013), 1, 2.

2. For example, Julie Stone Peters, *Theatre of the Book, 1480–1880* (Oxford: Oxford University Press, 2000); Douglas A. Brooks, *From Playhouse to Printing House* (Cambridge: Cambridge University Press, 2000); and David Scott Kastan, *Shakespeare and the Book* (Cambridge: Cambridge University Press, 2001).

3. I take this phrase from the title of the World Shakespeare Congress, which took place at Stratford-on-Avon, U.K., in August 1981.

4. See Erne, *Shakespeare as Literary Dramatist*, who cites W. W. Greg, Stanley Wells, Katherine Duncan-Jones, and Ernst Honigmann as sharing this view (10).

5. This wonderfully apt phrase is Barbara Mowat's, which she uses in "The Theater and Literary Culture." See Mowat, in *A New History of Early English Drama,* ed. John D. Cox and David Scott Kastan (New York: Columbia University Press, 1997), 213–30. Mowat also crafts a broad definition of *literary,* as "that which was designed to be read, whether in print or in manuscript, whether fiction or nonfiction, high culture or low culture" (214). My own definition of *literary* for the purposes of this chapter, tends to be material written for popular consumption and commercial profit.

6. Peters, *Theatre of the Book*, 108. See also Kastan, "Plays into Print," in *Books and Readers in Early Modern England,* ed. Jennifer Andersen and Elizabeth Sauer (Philadelphia: University of Pennsylvania Press, 2002), 23–41.

7. Stern, *Documents of Performance in Early Modern England* (Cambridge: Cambridge University Press, 2009), 56.

8. John Pitcher, "Editing Daniel," in *New Ways of Looking at Old Texts: Papers of the Renaissance English Text Society, 1985–1991*, ed. W. Speed Hill (Binghamton, NY: Renaissance English Text Society, 1993), 59.

9. See, for example, Peter Blayney, "The Publication of Playbooks," in *A New History of Early English Drama*, ed. John D. Cox and David Scott Kastan (New York: Columbia University Press, 1997); Zachary Lesser, *Renaissance Drama and the Politics of Publication* (Cambridge: Cambridge University Press, 2004); and Marta Straznicky, ed., *The Book of the Play: Playwrights, Stationers, and Readers in Early Modern England* (Amherst: University of Massachusetts Press, 2006).

10. Even Julie Stone Peters's nuanced study *Theater of the Book* imagines readers and spectators as distinct entities rather than a hybrid one, calling them "double audiences" (108) and stating that "distinctions between the stage and page were increasingly central to the Renaissance understanding of theatre" (105).

11. See Peters, *Theater of the Book*, introduction, 1–2, and chap. 1, 38–49, for examples of this tendency.

12. Heidi Brayman-Hackel, *Reading Material in Early Modern England* (Cambridge: Cambridge University Press, 2005), 45. Brayman-Hackel cites both Roger Chartier and Paul Saenger as proponents of this argument.

13. Ibid., 52.

14. The "one," of course, is the philosopher or theorist.

15. Gurr, *Playgoing in Shakespeare's London*, 3rd ed. (Cambridge: Cambridge University Press, 2004), 1. Gurr is not alone in embracing this binary; Russian formalist Boris Eikhenbaum makes a similar claim: "Sitting in the cinema, we do not essentially feel that we are members of a crowd participating in a mass viewing; on the contrary, the conditions of a film presentation tend to make the viewer feel as if he were in complete isolation" (12). See Eikhenbaum's "Problems of Film Stylistics," *Screen* 15:3 (Autumn 1984), 7–32.

16. Anthony Dawson and Paul Yachnin note that the experience of going to the theater is one that demands a kind of identificatory mobility between individual and collective experiential modes; discourses about theatergoing and other sorts of collective viewing experiences— sporting events, seeing a film at a movie theater with other people, concerts, etc.—similarly fluctuate between articulating individual and collective models of engagement and influence. See *The Culture of Playgoing in Shakespeare's England: A Collaborative Debate* (Cambridge: Cambridge University Press, 2001), 5.

17. In *Playhouse to Printing House* (Cambridge: Cambridge University Press, 2000), Douglas A. Brooks provides a succinct summary of the problems with relying too heavily on Shakespeare as exemplar of early modern playwriting practice and the emergent figure of the author. However, I use Shakespeare's late plays here as an example (rather than the paradigm) of how the idea of the reader shaped playwrights' ideas about and conventions of address for the spectator.

18. Kastan states unequivocally that "Shakespeare had no interest in the printed book or its potential readers." See "Plays into Print," 23.

19. Ibid., 26.

20. Sarah Wall-Randell, "Reading the Book of the Self in Shakespeare's *Cymbeline* and Wroth's *Urania*," in *Staging Early Modern Romance: Prose Fiction, Dramatic Romance and Shakespeare*, ed. Mary Ellen Lamb and Valerie Wayne (New York: Routledge, 2009), 108.

21. See Lori Humphrey Newcomb, *Reading Popular Romance in Early Modern England* (New York: Columbia University Press, 2002); Steve Mentz, *Romance for Sale in Early Modern England* (Aldershot, U.K.: Ashgate, 2006); and the introduction by Mary Ellen Lamb and Valerie Wayne, in *Staging Early Modern Romance*, 1–2. In terms of the complex ways in which intertextuality functioned within early modern culture and its various modes of imprinting texts, see Wayne's essay "Romancing the Wager: *Cymbeline's* Intertexts," in Lamb and Wayne, *Staging Early Modern Romance*, 163–87.

22. Brian Gibbons, "Romance and the Heroic Play," in *The Cambridge Companion to English Renaissance Drama*, 2nd ed., ed. A. R. Braunmuller and Michael Hattaway (Cambridge: Cambridge University Press, 1990), 225.

23. Fredric Jameson, "Magical Narratives: Romance as Genre," *New Literary History* 7.1 (Autumn 1975), 158.

24. The most famous "author-centric" theories of Shakespeare's romances come from the Victorians, most famously Dowden and Strachey. Variations on historicist readings of the romances reflecting the socioeconomic and cultural currents of the seventeenth century include Norman Sanders, "An Overview of Critical Approaches to the Romances," in *Shakespeare's Romances Reconsidered*, ed. Carol McGinnis Kay and Henry E. Jacobs (Lincoln: University of Nebraska Press, 1978), 4; Andrew Gurr, "The Bear, The Statue, and Hysteria in *The Winter's Tale*," *Shakespeare Quarterly* 34 (1983), 420–25; David M. Bergeron, *Shakespeare's Romances and the Royal Family* (Lawrence: University Press of Kansas, 1985); John Gillies, "Shakespeare's Virginian Masque," *English Literary History* 53 (1986), 673–708; William Proctor Williams, "Not Hornpipes and Funerals: Fletcherian Tragicomedy," in *Renaissance Tragicomedy: Explorations in Genre and Politics*, ed. Nancy Klein Maguire (New York: AMS Press, 1987), 20–37; Leah Marcus, *Puzzling Shakespeare: Local Reading and Its Discontents* (Berkeley: University of California Press, 1988); Steven Mullaney, *The Place of the Stage: License, Play and Power in Renaissance England* (Chicago: Chicago University Press, 1988), 137–42; J. Leeds Barroll, *Politics, Plague and Shakespeare's Theater: The Stuart Years* (Ithaca, NY: Cornell University Press, 1991); and Velma Bourgeois Richmond, *Shakespeare, Catholicism and Romance* (New York: Continuum, 2000).

25. See, for example, Allardyce Nicoll, *Shakespeare* (London: Methuen, 1952); Howard Felperin, "Shakespeare's Miracle Play," *Shakespeare Quarterly* 18.4 (1967), 363–74; Barbara Mowat, *The Dramaturgy of Shakespeare's Romances* (Athens: University of Georgia Press, 1976); Walter F. Eggers, Jr., " 'Bring Forth a Wonder': Presentation in Shakespeare's Romances," *Texas Studies in Literature and Language* 18 (1979), 455–77; Miriam Gilbert, " 'This Wide Gap of Time': Storytelling and Audience Response in the Romances," *Iowa State Journal of Research* 53 (1979), 235–41; Kenneth Muir, *Shakespeare's Comic Sequence* (Liverpool: Liverpool University Press, 1979), 151–56; R. S. White, *Shakespeare and the Romance Ending* (Newcastle upon Tyne: Tyneside Free Press, 1981); Richard Paul Knowles, " 'Wishes Fall Out as They're Will'd': Artist, Audience, and *Pericles'* Gower," *English Studies in Canada* 9.1 (1983), 14–24; Richard Hillman, "Shakespeare's Gower and Gower's Shakespeare: The Larger Debt of *Pericles*," *Shakespeare Quarterly* 36.4 (1985), 427–37; Maurice Hunt, "Romance and Tragicomedy," in *A Companion to Renaissance Drama*, ed. Arthur F. Kinney (Oxford: Blackwell, 2002), 384–98; and Christopher J. Cobb, *The Staging of Romance in Late Shakespeare* (Newark: University of Delaware Press, 2007).

26. In *The Winter's Tale*, Mamillius's "sad tale's best for winter" inaugurates the play's tragic spiral with Hermione's arrest, and in *The Tempest*, Prospero's abdication of his "rough magic" calls for drowning his books.

27. For a detailed analysis of the bedroom scene's indebtedness to *The Decameron*, see J. M. Nosworthy's introduction to *Cymbeline*, in *The Arden Shakespeare*, Second Series (London: Routledge, 1994), xx–xxv.

28. Phyllis Gorfain, "Puzzle and Artifice: The Riddle as Metapoetry in *Pericles*," in *Pericles: Critical Essays*, ed. David Skeele (New York: Garland, 2000), 134.

29. Marcus, *Puzzling Shakespeare*, 140.

30. See the prologue to Jonson's 1631 masque *Love's Triumph Through Callipolis* in *The Complete Masques*, ed. Stephen Orgel (New Haven: Yale University Press, 1969).

31. Kevin Sharpe, *Reading Revolutions: The Politics of Reading in Early Modern England* (New Haven: Yale University Press, 2000), 44.

32. Alison Hobgood, *Passionate Playgoing in Early Modern England* (Cambridge: Cambridge University Press, 2014), 168. Critics such as Thomas Cartelli and Jean Howard have similarly noted that Renaissance playwrights' "constant concern with guiding the perceptions and response of those who watched [their] dramas" (Howard, 8); here, I am interested in alterations in the expression of this anxiety. See Jean Howard, *Shakespeare's Art of Orchestration: Stage Technique and Audience Response* (Urbana: University of Illinois Press, 1984); and Thomas Cartelli, *Marlowe, Shakespeare, and the Economy of Theatrical Experience* (Philadelphia: University of Pennsylvania Press, 1991).

33. *Henry V* (0.1.24), in *The Norton Shakespeare*, 3rd ed., ed. Stephen Greenblatt et al. (New York: W. W. Norton, 2016). This is particularly apparent when the prologue asks for "pardon" from the "gentles all" (9) and attempts to yoke together the "imaginary forces" (18) of the audience in order to "piece out our imperfections with your thoughts" (23).

34. The shift I articulate here mirrors one occurring more broadly in early modern English culture during the late sixteenth and early seventeenth centuries, one also trafficking in reading and interpretive practices. In his study of early modern English readers and authors, Stephen B. Dobranski discusses similar changes in devotional hermeneutics, ones largely imputed to the vernacularization of the Bible: "Just the act of translating the Bible into the vernacular and putting it into the hands of more readers transferred the authority of the Word from the pulpit to members of the laity: readers could now experience the Bible outside of the church, in the privacy of their studies." Rather than suggest this practice represents an entirely new way of interacting with the Bible, Dobranski contends it continues a hermeneutic practice that follows Augustine's and Luther's precedent of understanding intellectual and spiritual struggle as part and parcel of Biblical exegesis. The major change, then, is that more people have access to this "personalized" spiritual practice, one that increases with the publication of the King James Bible in 1611. See Dobranski, *Readers and Authorship in Early Modern England* (Cambridge: Cambridge University Press, 2005), 30–31.

35. Mowat, "Theater and Literary Culture," 221.

36. Regarding the long-standing debate about whether Shakespeare wrote *Pericles*, my reading here assumes he was involved in writing portions of it at least, a conclusion now agreed on by most scholars of the play. More significantly, the sort of convention I trace in *Pericles* does not depend on its having been written exclusively by Shakespeare, as these plays are examples rather than originators of this nascent discourse. For a history of the authorship debate, see David Skeele's introduction to *Pericles: Critical Essays*.

37. Ibid., 218. See also Suzanne Gossett's introduction to *Pericles*, The Arden Shakespeare Third Series (London: Thompson Learning, 2004), 18.

38. Mowat, "Theater and Literary Culture," 221.

39. Although other seventeenth-century plays have extradiegetic narrative insertions (such as Time in *The Winter's Tale*), none have as large nor as fully fledged a role as the Gower-narrator.

40. *Pericles, Norton Shakespeare,* 3rd ed.

41. Gossett, *Pericles,* 173, n.8.

42. Cremation was not legalized in England until 1880; more significantly, it was forbidden by the Anglican Church as well as the state. See Sarah Tarlow, *Ritual, Belief, and the Dead in Early Modern Britain and Ireland* (Cambridge: Cambridge University Press, 2011).

43. See David Cressy, "Book Burning in Tudor and Stuart England," *Sixteenth Century Journal* 36.2 (2005), 359–74.

44. Brayman Hackel, *Reading Material,* 46.

45. This phrase is almost inevitably linked to Laura Mulvey's seminal essay on spectatorship and classical Hollywood film, and indeed several critics have used this essay as a means of fleshing out claims or theories about early modern spectatorship and voyeurism (see, for example, Nancy Vickers, "Diana Described: Scattered Women and Scattered Rhyme," *Critical Inquiry* 8.2 (1981), 108; Barbara Freedman, *Staging the Gaze: Postmodernism, Psychoanalysis, and Shakespearean Comedy* (Ithaca, NY: Cornell University Press, 1991), 69, 117, 151; Coppélia Kahn, *Roman Shakespeare: Warriors, Wounds and Women* (New York: Routledge, 1997), 31–32; and Evelyn Gajowski, "Sleeping Beauty, or 'What's the Matter?': Female Sexual Autonomy, Voyeurism, and Misogyny in *Cymbeline,*" in *Re-Visions of Shakespeare: Essays in Honor of Robert Ornstein,* ed. Evelyn Gajowski (Newark: University of Delaware Press, 2004), 97. However, Mulvey's theory of visual pleasure relies heavily on apparatus theory (the premise that film is inherently ideological in that it works to construct a viewer through its technological ability to manipulate point of view and promote identification with particular characters) and Lacanian psychoanalysis; in short, she is interested in a late twentieth-century, Western, heterosexual spectator in this analysis. Because of the historical and technological specificity of Mulvey's theoretical claims in "Visual Pleasure," it is important not to use her paradigms in an overly facile manner: that is, they are not transparencies that can be used to decipher the spectatorial dynamics of any given historical moment. That said, Mulvey's essay does contain certain important (if rather broad) reminders useful for any exploration of *staged* visual pleasure: first, that it is intentionally constructed to obtain a particular response from the viewer; second, that representations of such pleasure are created through a matrix of historical and cultural ideology about what is visually pleasing and an individual's (or group's) particular vision of the same; and third, that while these representations do not guarantee a homogenous response from the audience, if repeated over time within a single work (such as the predominantly subjective camera in *Vertigo*) or in a series of works (such as the subjective camera being always associated with the point of view of the male hero in Hitchcock's works), they can become codified *as* pleasurable for an audience. It is in this sort of "training" of an audience in which I am most interested in my exploration of the romances, but I focus more on the ways in which Shakespeare both attempts to shape his audience and imagines their often necessary, even desirable, resistance. See Mulvey, "Visual Pleasure and Narrative Cinema." *Screen* 16 (1975), 6–18.

46. Although the audience's foreknowledge of the situation at Antioch allows them to share in Gower's omniscience, thereby arguably providing a sense of spectatorial agency, it also commences an attempt to influence how the audience sees various characters and events. While this is similar to William H. Matchett's claim that Shakespeare had learned by this point in his career to "manipulate audience response," I see this disciplinary dynamic of the romances as a by-product of such confidence, one that critiques the concept of the playwright as fully in

control of his own creative processes. See Matchett, "Some Dramatic Techniques in *The Winter's Tale*," *Shakespeare Survey* 22 (1969), 93–107.

47. In the first quarto printing of 1609, this stage direction did not exist: the *Riverside Shakespeare* claims that its first appearance occurred in Round's version in Henry Irving's 1900 edition of the complete works. Most modern editions, however, include a version of this stage direction, with some disparity in where it is placed. The Oxford and Norton editions place it after line 39 of Gower's speech: "So for her many a wight did die," whereas the Riverside and Arden versions place it after line 40: "As yon grim looks do testify." To place it in between the two lines where Gower is actually referencing the dead suitors would make for a more visually dramatic moment; however, its placement after line 40 draws attention to the transition between Gower's narration of past events into the present-day action of the play itself. As I argue, this transition is a significant one, as it marks the first unmediated contact between the audience and the play.

48. Of course, this would depend entirely on the production: any scene contains multiple staging possibilities. However, unlike the opening scene, which contains a stage direction indicating the presence of visual spectacle (the heads on display), the other scenes I mention here seem designed to avert their spectacular possibilities.

49. Whether the knights would be shown parading their devices would again be dependent on the production, but the play's text focuses on the scene of Simonides's and Thaisa's reading of them.

50. Marion Lomax, *Stage Images and Traditions: Shakespeare to Ford* (Cambridge: Cambridge University Press, 1987). Lomax states that "if he had wished, Shakespeare's theater could have presented the deaths of Antiochus and his daughter as a gripping piece of spectacle" (78), noting that a similar stage effect was used for Robert Greene and Thomas Lodge's *A Looking-Glass for London and England* in the early 1590s.

51. John Gower, *Confessio Amantis,* ed. Russell A. Peck (Toronto: University of Toronto Press, 1980), 448; and Laurence Twine, *The Patterne of Painfull Adventures* (London: printed by Valentine Simmes for the Widow Newman, 1594). *Early English Books Online*, http://eebo .chadwyck.com.proxy.mtholyoke.edu:2048/search/full_rec?SOURCE = var_spell.cfg&ACTION = ByID&ID = 99847950&ECCO = param(ECCO)&FILE = ../session/1500164783_6073& SEARCHSCREEN = CITATIONS&DISPLAY = AUTHOR&HIGHLIGHT_KEYWORD = param(HIGHLIGHT_KEYWORD) (accessed February 10, 2007).

52. This scene contains resonances of John 6.1–13, where Christ multiplies the loaves and fishes: "When the people saw the sign he had done, they said, 'This is truly the Prophet, the one who is to come into the world,'" and conversion scenes were prevalent in popular hagiography.

53. For Christian readings of Marina and *Pericles* in general, see G. Wilson Knight, *The Crown of Life: Essays in Interpretation of Shakespeare's Final Plays* (London: Oxford University Press, 1947); Northrop Frye, *The Secular Scripture: A Study of the Structure of Romance* (Cambridge: Harvard University Press, 1976); Robert S. Miola, *Shakespeare and Classical Comedy: The Influence of Plautus and Terence* (Oxford: Oxford University Press, 1994); and Maurice Hunt, "Shakespeare's *Pericles* and the Acts of the Apostles," *Christianity and Literature* 49 (2000), 295–309.

54. The most overt textual example of this sort of privileging in the period is John Foxe's *Actes and Monuments* (1563), or as it was colloquially known, the Book of Martyrs.

55. Twine, *Painefull Adventures*. In both Twine and Gower, Marina is called Tharsia and Lysimachus, Athanagoras.

56. Gower, *Confessio Amantis* (New York: Penguin, 1963), 449.

57. Freedman, in *Staging the Gaze,* describes right spectatorship as a process by which "we identify with the male as the appropriate bearer of the look, the female as the proper object of that look; we identify with reason against sexuality, activity over passivity, and seeing instead of showing" (2), a theory clearly indebted to Laura Mulvey's theory of the cinematic gaze ("Visual Pleasure").

58. Jameson, quoted in Mullaney, *Place of the Stage,* 140.

59. Ibid., 142.

60. Ibid., 144–45.

61. Ibid., 147.

62. Ibid., 145.

63. Stephen Gosson, *The Schoole of Abuse* (London, 1579).

64. See Dobranski, *Readers and Authorship,* 45–46.

65. Roger Fenton, *A Treatise of Usury, Divided into Three Bookes* (London: Printed by Felix Kingston for William Aspley, 1611). *Early English Books Online* (accessed May 27, 2014). http://eebo.chadwyck.com.proxy.mtholyoke.edu:2048/search/full_rec?SOURCE = pgthumbs .cfg&ACTION = ByID&ID = 99837761&FILE = ../session/1508296413_8765&SEARCH SCREEN = CITATIONS&SEARCHCONFIG = var_spell.cfg&DISPLAY = AUTHOR

66. Jakob Böhme, *Aurora, that is, the day-spring, or dawning of the day in the Orient* (London: Printed by John Streater for Giles Calvert, 1656). *Early English Books Online,* (accessed May 27, 2014). http://eebo.chadwyck.com.proxy.mtholyoke.edu:2048/search/full_rec? SOURCE = pgthumbs.cfg&ACTION = ByID&ID = 12394709&FILE = ../session/15082965 76_8965&SEARCHSCREEN = CITATIONS&SEARCHCONFIG = var_spell.cfg&DISPLAY = AUTHOR See also Thomas Shipman's *Carolina, or Loyal Poems* (London, 1683), which uses an altered (and more secular) version of the metaphor: "'Twas ne'r the Sun's right *Looking-Glass* before; Ice is the *Chrystal,* lin'd with *silver Oar.*" *Early English Books Online,* (accessed May 27, 2014). http://eebo.chadwyck.com.proxy.mtholyoke.edu:2048/search/full_rec? SOURCE = pgthumbs.cfg&ACTION = ByID&ID = 11910422&FILE = ../session/1508296720 _9064&SEARCHSCREEN = CITATIONS&SEARCHCONFIG = var_spell.cfg&DISPLAY = AUTHOR

67. The term "destructive spectatorship" is Martin Harries' who describes it as a "twentieth century . . . investment in a formal logic that placed the spectator in a spot where that spectator had to contemplate her own destruction" (9). Whereas Harries's version of destructive spectatorship entails "the threat of, or desire for, an experience of spectatorship so overwhelming that it destroys the spectator" (ibid.), in *Cymbeline,* destructive spectatorship is less about the desire for a spectatorial experience that consumes the viewing subject and more about a viewing subject who is unable to prevent becoming psychically overwhelmed by what she or he witnesses. See Harries, *Forgetting Lot's Wife: On Destructive Spectatorship* (New York: Fordham University Press, 2007).

68. Eve Rachelle Sanders, "Inferiority and the Letter in *Cymbeline,*" *Critical Survey* 12.2 (2000), 57. Sanders also notes that the concatenation of reading and women was as frequently associated with corruption as with edification.

69. Wall-Randell, "Reading the Book of the Self," 109.

70. These include Imogen's reading of two of Posthumus's letters at 1.7 and 3.4 (the first serves as introduction for Iachimo and the second informs Imogen of her husband's command to have her murdered); her reading of Ovid before Iachimo's entrance into her bedroom at 2.2; and Posthumus's receipt of the tablet and its eventual role in the play's resolution (5.4 and 5.5).

71. Nosworthy, introduction, *Cymbeline*, xvii–xxviii.

72. The Ovidian version is "lente currite noctis equi," or "run slowly horses of the night." See *Heroides and Amores*, trans. Grant Showerman, rev. G. P. Goold (Cambridge, MA: Harvard University Press, 1914), 1.13.40.

73. These occur at 1.1.53; 1.7.26; 2.2.3; 3.1.76; 3.2.50; 3.3.56; 3.4.17 and 18; 4.2.316; 5.5.48; and 5.5.435. The "runners-up" are *Julius Caesar* and *Twelfth Night*, each of which have ten instances.

74. *Norton Shakespeare,* 3rd ed.

75. Cynthia Lewis, "'With Simular Proof Enough': Modes of Misperception in *Cymbeline*," *SEL: Studies in English Literature 1500–1900* 31.2 (1991), 344. Other critics have similarly noted the way in which interpretation constitutes one of the play's most significant thematics; for example, see Wilson Knight, *Crown of Life*; Bertrand Evans, *Shakespeare's Comedies* (Oxford: Clarendon, 1960), 245–89; and Brook Thomas, "Cymbeline and the Perils of Interpretation," *New Orleans Review* 10.2–3 (1983), 137–45.

76. The First Lord plays the sycophantic, saccharine yes man to the buffoonish Cloten, while the Second Lord plays the cynical, straight-man role.

77. Gosson uses this term several times with regard to the theater's effect on the spectator—once in *The Schoole of Abuse* (1579), where he discusses how the theater is designed to "ravish the senses," and twice in *Plays Confuted in Five Actions* (London, 1582).

78. In both *Man's Estate: Masculine Identity in Shakespeare* (Berkeley: University of California Press, 1981) and more specifically in *Roman Shakespeare: Warriors, Wounds and Women*, Coppélia Kahn explores the dynamic and function of such male-male competition within Shakespeare's plays and early modern culture. However, although the relationship between Iachimo and Posthumus is definitely a competitive one, I am more interested in the terms through which this particular competition is staged and what that represents in terms of the metatheatrics of the play itself rather than the cultural function of masculine rivalry.

79. In the Arden, Second Series, version of the play, J. M. Nosworthy cites Samuel Johnson's note from *General Observations on the Plays of Shakespeare* (1756), which states that "Shakespeare intended that Iachimo, having gained his purpose, should designedly drop the invidious and offensive part of a wager, and, to flatter Posthumus, dwell long upon the more pleasing part of the representation" (25). The Norton and Riverside versions gloss only the passage's final line, with the Norton providing an uncharacteristically tepid paraphrase: "Provided I have your introduction (to Imogen) to ensure a generous reception (2975), and the Riverside interpreting only the phrase "free entertainment" as "ready reception" (1574). The RSC Shakespeare glosses numerous words and phrases in the speech; interestingly, it unnecessarily glosses "testimony" as "proof," although it is one of the few editions that makes a nod toward the speech's innuendo, glossing "free entertainment" as "informal, friendly reception (both words are capable of a sexual interpretation)" (2254).

80. Jonathan Bate, *Shakespeare and Ovid* (Oxford: Clarendon, 1993), 217.

81. Ibid.

82. Actaeon is not always a part of the Diana bathing scene; however, this particular view of the virgin goddess was a sight that was not supposed to be seen, regardless of who was doing the looking. See, for example, Edmund Spenser's *Faerie Queen*, III.vi.19–21, where Venus surprises Diana while she is bathing. Despite the fact that Venus is a fellow goddess, Diana is clearly displeased.

83. In the Arden, Second Series, edition, Nosworthy makes note of Iachimo's particular choice of the Parthian warrior in this passage as well, explaining that "their [fighting] method

was to discharge darts upon their enemy, then to evade close contact by rapid flight during which they shot their arrows backward"(p. 32, n.20). Nosworthy sees this comparison as relevant only to Iachimo's plan of attack; that is, if Imogen will not respond to his direct assault, he will pursue her through indirect means (or simply give up).

84. Alexander Leggatt makes the following claim: "I have seen four productions of *Cymbeline,* and on each occasion Iachimo's emergence from the trunk was greeted with laughter. For a modern audience, he suggests a jack-in-the-box; for a Jacobean audience, he says Iachimo would probably have suggested a comically old-fashioned devil popping up through the trap door." See "The Island of Miracles: An Approach to *Cymbeline,*" *Shakespeare Studies* 10 (1977), 195.

85. For a historical account of both the humorous "devil" figure in miracle plays and the vice figure of morality plays, see David Bevington's *From Mankind to Marlowe: Growth of Structure in the Popular Drama of Tudor England* (Cambridge, MA: Harvard University Press, 1962).

86. See, for example, J. Payne Collier, *Shakespeare's Library,* 2 vols. (London: Thomas Rodd, 1850); Edward Dowden's Arden 1 edition of *Cymbeline* (London: Methuen, 1903); Horace Howard Furness, ed. *The Tragedie of Cymbeline* (Philadelphia: Lippincott, 1913); Knight, *Crown of Life*; R. G. Hunter, *Shakespeare and the Comedy of Forgiveness* (New York: Columbia University Press, 1965); Leo Salingar, *Shakespeare and the Tradition of Comedy* (Cambridge: Cambridge University Press, 1974); Geoffrey Bullough, *Narrative and Dramatic Sources of Shakespeare,* 8 vols. (New York: Columbia University Press, 1966); R. S. White, *Let Wonder Seem Familiar: Endings in Shakespeare's Romance Vision* (London: Athlone, 1985); Cynthia Marshall, *Last Things and Last Plays: Shakespearean Eschatology* (Carbondale: Southern Illinois University Press, 1991); and Velma Bourgeois, *Shakespeare, Catholicism and Romance* (New York: Continuum, 2000).

87. Melissa Walters, "'Are You a Comedian': The Trunk in *Twelfth Night* and the Intertheatrical Construction of Character," in *Transnational Mobilities in Early Modern Theater*, ed. Robert Henke and Eric Nicholson (Surrey, U.K.: Ashgate, 2014), 59.

88. In James Joyce's posthumously published *Stephen Hero* (Norfolk, CT: New Directions, 1944), the eponymous hero defines epiphany as "the gropings of a spiritual eye which seeks to adjust its vision to an exact focus" (211).

89. Nosworthy, *Cymbeline,* lxxxiii.

90. William Tyndale, *The Obedience of a Christian Man* (Antwerp: 1528). N. Pag. *Early English Books Online,* http://eebo.chadwyck.com/search/fulltext?ACTION = ByID&ID = D10000998406010002&SOURCE = var_spell.cfg&DISPLAY = AUTHOR&WARN = N& FILE = ../session/1426705889_19484 (accessed February 27, 2015).

91. Cheney, *Shakespeare's Literary Authorship* (Cambridge: Cambridge University Press, 2008), 77.

92. While embraced by most of the early sixteenth-century reformers, there was a great deal of contention about whether lay readers should have access to the Bible throughout the early modern period. For a concise account of these tensions in England, see Sharpe, *Reading Revolutions,* 328–30. For an account of how readers' genders affected this anxiety, see Brayman Hackel, *Reading Material,* 206–7, 226–27; Kate Narveson, *Bible Readers and Lay Writers in Early Modern England: Gender and Self-Definition in an Emergent Writing Culture* (Surrey, U.K.: Ashgate, 2012); and Femke Molecamp, *Women and the Bible in Early Modern England: Religious Reading and Writing* (Oxford: Oxford University Press, 2013).

93. Newcomb, *Reading Popular Romance.*

94. Ibid., 14–15, 133–37.

95. Ibid., 135–36.

96. Ibid., 17.

97. Ibid., 123.

98. Ibid., 17.

99. William Shakespeare, *The Winter's Tale,* in The Arden Shakespeare, Second Series, ed. J. H. P. Pafford (New York: Routledge, 1994). See also Mark van Doren, who calls it "the passage no one has been able to read," in *Shakespeare* (New York: H. Holt, 1939), 316.

100. The most familiar examples of this are the Homeric and Virgilian injunctions found at the beginning of *The Iliad* and *The Aeneid,* but for late medieval and early modern examples, cf. the opening of Chaucer's *Troilus and Criseyde* and the opening of Spenser's *The Faerie Queene* and Milton's *Paradise Lost.*

101. Actually, God creates the world in six days, resting on the seventh: the passage seems to follow this idea. The first six "nothings" do the work of dismantling Leontes's world, and on the final anaphora, the passage and the act of destruction rest.

102. Simon Forman, *The autobiography and personal diary of Dr. Simon Forman, the celebrated astrologer, from A. D. 1552, to A. D. 1602,* from the unpublished manuscripts in the Ashmolean Museum, Oxford, ed. James Orchard Halliwell, esq. (London, 1849).

103. Newcomb states that "in particular, critics who have traced the theatricality of Hermione's transformation have concluded that Shakespeare's adaptation relied on audience members' familiarity with *Pandosto*" (*Reading Popular Romance,* 137).

CHAPTER 4

1. *The Norton Shakespeare,* 3rd ed., eds. Stephen Greeblatt, Walter Cohen, Jean E. Howard, Katharine Eisaman Maus, Gordon McMullan, and Suzanne Gossett (New York: W.W. Norton & Company, 2015).

2. In an article on what he terms "interrupted masque," Andrew R. Walkling also notes the hypervisuality of this episode and Prospero's attempt to focus spectatorial attention, but he does not further pursue the play's sensory economies (194). See "The Apotheosis of Absolutism and the Interrupted Masque: Theater, Music and Monarchy in Restoration England," in *Politics, Transgression, and Representation at the Court of Charles II,* ed. Julia Marciari Alexander and Catherine MacLeod (New Haven: Yale University Press, 2007), 193–231.

3. Cf. 1.2.49, 106, 135 and 170.

4. See Chapter 3, 88–90.

5. *The Tempest* likely had its first performance at court around 1611, at which time the Jonson-Jones collaboration was well established. For a brief history of critical readings of *The Tempest*'s masque (particularly its influences), see James Knowles's "Insubstantial Pageants: *The Tempest* and Masquing Culture," in *Shakespeare's Late Plays: New Readings,* ed. Jennifer Richards and James Knowles (Edinburgh: Edinburgh University Press, 1999), 108–25.

6. Among the scholars who have argued for this sort of Jonsonian narrative are Enid Welsford, *The Court Masque: A Study in the Relationship Between Poetry and the Revels* (New York: Russell & Russell, 1962); Steven Orgel, *Ben Jonson: The Complete Masques* (New Haven: Yale University Press, 1969) and *The Illusion of Power: Political Theater in the English Renaissance* (Berkeley: University of California Press, 1975); D. J. Gordon, "Poet and Architect: The Intellectual Setting of the Quarrel Between Ben Jonson and Inigo Jones," in *The Renaissance Imagi-*

nation: Essays and Lectures by D. J. Gordon, ed. Stephen Orgel (Berkeley: University of California Press, 1975), 77–184; Stanley Fish, "Authors-Readers: Jonson's Community of Same," in *Representing the English Renaissance*, ed. Stephen Greenblatt (Berkeley: University of California Press, 1988); and Andrew Gurr, *Playgoing in Shakespeare's London,* 3rd ed. (Cambridge: Cambridge University Press, 2004).

7. Orgel, *The Complete Masques*, 38. All quotes from Jonson's masques taken from this edition.

8. Gurr, *Playgoing,* 103. Gurr is paraphrasing Jonson here, but it is fairly clear that he shares this opinion on some level given his later lament regarding the state of contemporary spectatorship: "The Elizabethan 'company' has gradually become a set of isolated watchers, their minds set in the two dimensions of scenic staging rather than the Elizabethan three" (116).

9. The *machina versatilis* (also called *perikatoi*) was basically a mechanized pivot on which pieces of scenery could turn and hence change without the use of stagehands. The *scena ductilis* consisted of a series of grooves in which painted flats were placed in a series. To change the set from one scene to another, the stagehands had only to pull the foremost flats into the wings, thereby revealing what was behind them. For a detailed explanation of these devices, see Allardyce Nicoll, *Stuart Masques and the Renaissance Stage* (New York: Harcourt, Brace, 1938), 54–63.

10. Tiffany Stern, "Taking Part: Actors and Audience on the Stage at the Blackfriars," in *Inside Shakespeare: Essays on the Blackfriars Stage,* ed. Paul Menzer (Selinsgrove, PA: Susquehanna University Press, 2006), 41.

11. While not written for the King's Men, the dedicatory epistles and commendatory verses to plays such as Beamont's *The Knight of the Burning Pestle* (1607) and Fletcher's *The Faithful Shepherdess* (1608) suggest that pleasing the coterie audiences was a fraught and uncertain enterprise at best and, indeed, one that more than occasionally produced anxiety, even resentment, in those writing for the Blackfriars.

12. Gurr makes a similar case when he says that "long before the proscenium arch's two-dimensional staging and fixed sets the eye was bound to overcome the ear" (*Playgoing,* 107). However, he does not investigate the origins of this idea in the period.

13. By "the spectacular," I mean that part of stagecraft that produces wonder through visual effects. While the seventeenth century was not the only period in English drama to have "special effects" (we need only think of the devil's trapdoor in morality drama or John Dee's "flying machine" from the sixteenth century), it is during this period that they begin to become conventionalized and more widespread.

14. My claim here aligns with Lauren Shohet's, that masque had a much wider influence than most scholarship on early modern English theater has acknowledged. See *Reading Masques: The English Masques and Public Culture* (Oxford: Oxford University Press, 2010).

15. Orgel notes Jonson's dual (and perhaps divided) interests in *The Complete Masques*: "For in writing a masque, Jonson was dealing with two separate problems: the demands of a particular performance . . . and the transmutation of the ephemeral qualities of the moment into a work of literature" (6). More extensive analyses of Jonson's desire to carve out an alternative sphere of *bona fama* in print include Richard Dutton in *Ben Jonson: Authority: Criticism* (New York: St. Martin's, 1996), and Joseph Loewenstein, *Ben Jonson and Possessive Authorship* (Cambridge: Cambridge University Press, 2002).

16. Among these include Bruce Smith's *The Acoustic World of Early Modern England: Attending to the O-Factor* (Chicago: University of Chicago Press, 1999), and *The Key of Green:*

Passion and Perception in Early Modern England (Chicago: University of Chicago Press, 2009); *Sensible Flesh,* Elizabeth D. Harvey, ed., *Sensible Flesh: On Touch in Early Modern Culture* (Philadelphia: University of Pennsylvania Press, 2003); C. M. Woolgar's *The Senses in Late Medieval England* (New Haven: Yale University Press, 2006); and Holly Dugan's *The Ephemeral History of Perfume: Scent and Sense in Early Modern England* (Baltimore: Johns Hopkins University Press, 2011).

17. Allardyce Nicoll assumes that Shakespeare would have witnessed at least one masque firsthand in order to produce the detailed rendition found in *The Tempest*; however, this would not have necessarily been the case. To assume that Shakespeare had to have *seen* a masque in order to reproduce one assumes that the visual imaginary is the dominant one and that by hearing (or reading) accounts of court masques, Shakespeare and other playwrights could not have reproduced them onstage. See Nicoll, *Stuart Masques*, 19.

18. "John Chamberlain (1553–1628)," in *The Oxford Dictionary of National Biography*, doi:10.1093/ref:odnb/5046 (accessed September 16, 2011).

19. John Chamberlain, Letter to Alice Carleton, February 18, 1613, in *The Letters of John Chamberlain,* vol. 1, ed. Norman Egbert McClure (Philadelphia: American Philosophical Society, 1939), 183.

20. James Shirley, *Love's Cruelty, a Critical Edition,* ed. John Frederick Nims (New York: Garland, 1980).

21. *The Tempest* was likely first performed before the king at Whitehall on November 1, 1611, and was subsequently performed sometime during the Princess Elizabeth's betrothal celebrations at Whitehall during the winter of 1612–13. See *The Tempest,* The Arden Shakespeare, Third Series (London: Thompson Learning, 1999), 6.

22. Woolgar, *Senses in Late Medieval England,* 7.

23. *The Complete Works of George Gascoigne,* vol. 2, ed. John W. Cunliffe (Cambridge: Cambridge University Press, 1910), 92.

24. "The Masque of Blackness," lines 67–68. Orgel, *The Complete Masques.*

25. *Complete Works of George Gascoigne,* 101.

26. Ibid., 104.

27. Laneham's identity is somewhat of a cipher in early modern studies. David Scott makes a convincing case that "Robert Laneham" was actually William Patten, teller of the Exchequer. His evidence for this argument includes a "hitherto unnoticed letter" from Patten to his patron, Lord Burghley, in which he confesses to writing the letter under a pseudonym; orthographical symmetries between "Laneham's letter" and other of Patten's writings; and the fact that Patten was indeed present during the queen's visit to Kenilworth. M. C. Bradbrook speculated that the letter was actually written by John Laneham, a member of the Earl of Leicester's Men, who would have likely been involved in the entertainments contrived for the queen's visit. E. K. Chambers takes such musings less far, asking only whether John Laneham "was related to Robert Laneham, Keeper of the Council Chamber door, who described the Kenilworth entertainment?" See Scott, William Patten and the Authorship of 'Robert Laneham's Letter' (1575)," *English Literary Renaissance* 7 (1977), 297–306; Bradbrook, *The Rise of the Common Player* (Cambridge: Harvard University Press, 1962), 143–61; and Chambers, *The Elizabethan Stage,* vol. 2 (Oxford: Clarendon, 1923), 391.

28. Robert Laneham, *A letter whearin part of the entertainment vntoo the Queenz Maiesty at Killingwoorth Castl in Warwik sheer in this soomerz progress is signified* (London, 1575), in

Early English Books Online, https://quod.lib.umich.edu/e/eebo/A05046.0001.001/1:2?cite1
= laneham;cite1restrict = author;g = eebogroup;rgn = div1;view = toc;xc = 1;q1 = dolphin/ (accessed November 2, 2010). Orgel also quotes part of this passage in *The Jonsonian Masque*, as a
means of pointing out how song is one of the ways that masque stages the resolution of discord,
a central concern of the genre. See *The Jonsonian Masque* (Cambridge: Harvard University
Press), 43.

29. Gurr, *Playgoing*, and Smith, *Acoustic World of Early Modern England*.

30. Orgel, following Chambers, cites George Gascoigne's 1572 masque for the double
wedding of the Lord Montague's son and daughter as the earliest surviving example of a masque
in print. See *The Jonsonian Masque*, 37.

31. Cunliffe, ed., *Complete Works of George Gascoigne*, vol. 2, 96.

32. Ibid., 96–97.

33. A similar example of the multisensory can be found in a later episode, where Diana
warns her nymphs about Cupid and his knights:

> In sweetest flowres the subtyll Snakes may lurke:
> The Sugred baite oft hides the harmefull hookes,
> The smoothest words, draw wils to wicked worke,
> And deepe deceipts, do follow fairest looks. (108)

34. Gina Bloom reads the Echo episode as an explication of the tensions of agency that
structured the relationship between Robert Dudley and Elizabeth I. See *Voice in Motion: Shaping Sound in Early Modern England* (Philadelphia: University of Pennsylvania Press, 2007),
187–95.

35. Cunliffe, ed., *Complete Works of George Gascoigne*, vol. 2, 330.

36. Ibid., 338.

37. "The Mask of Proteus" in *Gesta Grayorum*, ed. Desmond Bland (Liverpool: Liverpool
University Press, 1968), 82.

38. Like much of the descriptive apparatus surrounding Elizabeth, the multisensory may
have hardened into convention by this point in the reign. Louis Montrose designates the period
when she was definitively past childbearing age as the point when descriptive conventions begin
to solidify around the multiple images used to signify her chastity (such as Diana, the Spenser-
ian Eliza, and Daphne). See *The Purpose of Playing: Shakespeare and the Cultural Politics of the
Elizabethan Theater* (Chicago: University of Chicago Press, 1996), 155–56.

39. *Proteus* had as its centerpiece a large "rock" that concealed the masquers. As Orgel
points out, it was probably a large painted canvas (*The Jonsonian Masque*, 9).

40. Both Enid Welsford, in *The Court Masque*, and Stephen Orgel have claimed that
Proteus "brings us to a turning point in the history of the masque" (Orgel, *The Jonsonian
Masque*). Whereas Welsford makes this claim based on *Proteus*'s sequencing (how it organizes
dialogue, song, and dance), Orgel sees stagecraft as the axis for this turn: "*The Masque of
Proteus*, with its fixed stage and its unified setting, is the first English masque to conceive, in
however small a way, of the masquing hall as a theater" (ibid.).

41. *The Masque of Blackness*, line 12. Samuel Daniel also writes in the introduction to his
masque *The Vision of Twelve Goddesses* that "these ornaments of delight and peace . . . deserve
to be made memorable." See *The Vision of the Twelve Goddesses: A Royal Masque*, ed. Ernest
Law (London: Bernard Quaritch, 1880), 57.

42. Among the most well known of these commentaries are Orgel's in *The Jonsonian Masque* and, more particularly, in his article "What is a Text?" in *Research Opportunities in Renaissance Drama*, 24 (1981): 3–6; Peter Stallybrass and Allon White's *The Politics and Poetics of Transgression* (Ithaca, NY: Cornell University Press, 1986), 27–79; Stanley Fish's "Authors-Readers: Jonson's Community of the Same," in *Representations* 7 (1984): 26–58; Richard Helgerson's *Self-Crowned Laureates: Spenser, Jonson, Milton and the Literary System* (Berkeley: University of California Press, 1983); Dutton, *Ben Jonson*; and Loewenstein, *Ben Jonson and Possessive Authorship*.

43. Not surprisingly, a number of scholars who work on early modern audiences also work on Jonson and his perception of early modern spectators; however, they focus heavily and almost exclusively on his plays rather than his masques. In large part, this focus follows from their interest in audience response and affective potency; for example, Alison Hobgood claims that "Jonson was far more invested in corporeal feeling and collaboration, not Stoicism and single authorship than we have imagined" (*Passionate Playgoing in Early Modern England* [Cambridge: Cambridge University Press, 2014], 165). Given that masques were intended to be seen only once, and then were usually revised afterward for publication, they provided a unique combination of text written *for* a projected (and more readily known) audience and text written *about* an actual performance event. As such, they are an excellent archive for the language used both to imagine and to describe audiences, language that in turn comes to contribute to both the discursive spectator's form and presence, and, as I argue in this chapter, contribute to "real" spectators' viewing practices.

44. William N. West, "Understanding in the Elizabethan Theaters," in *Renaissance Drama* 35 (2006), 120.

45. Jerzy Limon calls the version that was preserved for posterity the "literary masque," a form he distinguishes from the performed one. Following Orgel (and to some degree Welsford), Limon claims that Jonson's major contribution to the masque form was his development of the literary masque; that is, Jonson leaves his mark on the form by making it as much a literary as a performance entity (Limon, *The Masque of Stuart Culture* [Newark: University of Delaware Press, 1990]). While I agree with this claim in principle, all three critics allocate to Jones a sort of control over the form that I am not convinced he has. Loewenstein's claim that Jonson's authority-authorization was more closely tied to the material realities of printing (rather than "literariness") seems more plausible, as it suggests Jonson's "control" always-already involved compromise: "Though printing exposes [Jonson's] invention to indiscriminate market forces and vulgar misconstruction, it also serves to manifest the superiority of Jonson's 'part' to Jones's, for it enables the spirit of authorial invention to display its transcendence of present occasions" (*Ben Jonson and Possessive Authorship*, 180). My own argument suggests that his attempts to exert a sort of linguistic control over the form results in some arguably less-desirable epiphenomena (at least from Jonson's point of view), such as a more visually oriented spectator.

46. From "Part of King James's Entertainment in Passing to his Coronation," in *Ben Jonson*, vol. 7, ed. C. H. Herford and Percy Simpson (Oxford: Clarendon, 1950), 83–109, lines 265–67. All quotes from Jonson's entertainments other than masque are taken from this edition. In most cases, I have modernized the spelling to go along with Orgel and Robert Strong's othographical emendations of the court masques in *Inigo Jones and the Theater of the Stuart Court* (London: Sotheby Parke Bernet, 1973).

47. As James Knowles notes, the fact that no record has survived of many Jonsonian civic pageants means that any analysis of his works and career is decidedly partial. However, the

1609 civic pageant that Knowles discusses in this same essay (*The Entertainment at Britain's Burse*) still demonstrates some tendency to imagine James and Anna through the multisensory mode:

> In this great King
> And his fairer Queen do strike the harmony
> Which harmony hath power to touch
> the dulleste earthe

See Knowles, "Jonson's *Entertainment at Britain's Burse*," in *Re-Presenting Ben Jonson: Text, History and Performance,* ed. Martin Butler (New York: St. Martin's, 1999), 141–51.

48. Thomas Dekker, *The Dramatic Works of Thomas Dekker,* vol. X (Cambridge: Cambridge University Press, 1961), 16.

49. Limon reads these two personae as a by-product of the way Jonson conceives of the masque form itself, calling the early masques "journalistic" and the later ones "literary." Again, Limon's reading assumes that Jonson *attains* the sort of control he seeks over the form (Limon, *The Masque of Stuart Culture,* 19).

50. John Pory to Sir Robert Cotton, quoted in Orgel and Strong, *Inigo Jones,* 105. Jones's *mikrokosmos* or rotating globe is thought by some critics to have inspired Prospero's "Revels" speech. See, for example, Ernest B. Gilman, "'All Eyes': Prospero's Inverted Masque," in *Renaissance Quarterly* 33.2 (1980): 214–30.

51. Orgel and Strong, in *Inigo Jones,* cite some of the preparations that were recorded by Andrew Kerwyn, paymaster of the Works.

52. See Orgel, *The Jonsonian Masque,* 18.

53. For a specific Jonsonian example, see his "A Panegyre," in Hereford and Simpson, eds., *Ben Jonson,* 113.

54. Except for *Beauty,* this tendency holds true even in those of Jonson's masques that precede his introduction of the antimasque. In *Blackness,* the first (brief) homage to James comes at line 190, with a longer and more explicit one found at lines 230 to 244. In *Hymenai,* there is a brief reference to James and Anna at lines 84 to 88; the major encomium, however, ends the masque (874–86).

55. Like *Blackness,* to which *Beauty* is the sequel, it was commissioned by Anna, so there is no particular thematic exigency for the immediate focus on James.

56. Created at a moment of particular political intricacy—the beginning of Prince Henry's majority—both Martin Butler and Tom Bishop point out that *Oberon* disrupts the masque's absolute focus on the monarch (James), as Henry performs as the masque's title character. While this "split screen" focus may contribute to Jonson's portrayal of James (that is, James's "ineffability" becomes diminished in comparison to Henry's luminous promise) in *Oberon,* I would argue that *all* of the Jonson-Jones collaborations have a split focus, as Anna also had her own faction at court and was, particularly with the early masques, a creative collaborator in addition to a participant. Additionally, the tendency to represent the wonder evoked by James's presence via a parsed version of the multisensory metaphor continues post-*Oberon,* as this analysis shows; it is further developed in *The Gypsies Metamorphosed,* composed nearly ten years after Henry's death. See Butler, "Courtly Negotiations," and Bishop, "The Gingerbread Host: Tradition and Novelty in the Jacobean Masque," in *The Politics of the Stuart*

Court Masque, ed. David Bevington and Peter Holbrook (Cambridge: Cambridge University Press, 1998), 88–120.

57. Orgel, *Complete Masques,* 14.

58. Orgel claims that this unity comes from Jones's extensive use of the *scena ductilis,* which he sees as a device that mirrors (rather than competes with) Jonson's poetic turn toward creating a world of balance and symmetry in form and subject matter (for example, *Oberon* displays a sort of triangulated harmony between masque, antimasque, and revels). Ibid., 17–20.

59. Among these are the inclusion of the semicomic antimasque and the movement from chaos to order within the narrative trajectory. Ibid., 16.

60. Ibid., 18.

61. The specifics of these moments are as follows: the first command to "Look!" precedes the "opening" of a rock that reveals Oberon's palace, accomplished by means of the *scena ductilis.* The second emphasizes the spectacular design and lighting of Oberon's palace: "Look! does not this palace show / Like another sky of lights?" (101–2), and the third precedes Oberon's (played by Prince Henry) entry in a chariot "drawn by two white bears" (230–31).

62. *Gypsies* was performed three times in quick succession: on August 3, 1621, at George Villiers's seat of Burley-on-the-Hill in Rutland; on August 5 at Francis Manners's seat of Belvior Castle in Leicestershire; and finally at Windsor Palace sometime in early September. For a detailed explication of these three versions and the variants between them, see W. W. Greg's *Jonson's Masque of Gipsies in the Burley, Belvoir and Windsor Versions* (London: Oxford University Press, 1952). For further elucidation of how *Gypsies* and other "running masques" differed from the more "standard" court masques (performed only once for a special occasion), see James Knowles, "The 'Running Masque' Recovered: A Masque for the Marquess of Buckingham c. 1619–20," *English Manuscript Studies 1100–1700* 8 (2000), 79–135; and John H. Astington's "Buckingham's Patronage and The Gypsies Metamorphosed," *Theater Survey* 43.2 (2000), 133–47.

63. In the passage, Jonson touches briefly on taste, sound, and scent. At line 138, he mentions "the sweet and fruitful dew"; at 148, he references the sound of the pheasant's call; and at 156, he makes an odd reference to casting "a kind and odoriferous shade." The rest of the passage is filled with elaborate visual references, such as "purple-swelling nectar" (137), the "gaudy peacock" (144), and Minerva's needle that embroiders "th'enamored earth with all her riches" (141).

64. E. K. Chambers, ed. *Aurelian Townshend's Poems and Masks* (Oxford, Oxford University Press, 1912), 83.

65. Francis Bacon, *The Essayes or Counsels, Civill and Morall,* ed. Michael Kiernan (Oxford: Oxford University Press, 2000), 117.

66. Ibid.

67. Ibid., original italics.

68. Ibid., 8.

69. Quoted in Hereford and Simpson, *Ben Jonson,* vol. 10, 410–11.

70. Orgel, *Complete Masques,* 39.

EPILOGUE

1. Ben Jonson, "Bartholomew Fair," in *Ben Jonson: The Alchemist and Other Plays,* ed. Gordon Campbell (Oxford: Oxford University Press, 1995).

2. Jonson's use of "curious" here has several possible connotations. As it is paired with "envious," it likely connotes one of its less flattering (and now obsolete) meanings. The *OED* cites as one of the more frequent usages in the period "anxious, concerned or solicitous." When placed in contrast to "favoring and judicious," "curious" might also denote an audience member who tries to find problems with the play; for example, in the induction, Jonson mentions those who come to the theater to "censure by contagion, or upon trust, from another's voice, or face" (Ind. 88–89).

3. West, "Understanding in the Elizabethan Theaters." *Renaissance Drama* 35 (2006), 123.

4. Ibid., 132.

5. John Webster, *The Complete Works of John Webster,* ed. F. L. Lucas (New York: Gordian, 1966).

6. John Milton, "Comus," in *The Complete Poetry of John Milton*, ed. John T. Shawcross (New York: Doubleday, 1990).

7. These results are based on searches conducted on *EEBO* (*Early English Books Online* database) during the period from June 26 through July 18, 2017. The details of the search results for *audience* are as follows: for 1580 to 1600, 1,204 hits in 325 unique records; for 1601 to 1620, 1,663 hits in 588 records; for 1621 to 1640, 1,598 hits in 658 records; and for 1641 to 1660, 3,751 hits in 1,302 records. The details for *spectator* are as follows: for 1580 to 1600, 87 hits in 40 records; for 1601 to 1620, 566 hits in 305 records; for 1621 to 1640, 1,383 hits in 569 records; and for 1641 to 1660, 2,913 hits in 1,376 records. These results exclude all non-English uses of the terms (Latin for *spectator* and French for *audience*) and any record that is a duplicate copy of the exact same text. However, the results do include hits yielded from different editions of the same text (e.g., Spenser's 1590 and 1596 editions of *The Faerie Queene,* or even John Gilpin's treatise *The Quakers Shaken,* both texts printed in 1653, though one published by S. B. and the other printed for Simon Waterson), and also include texts published under different names or assembled in various different compilations (e.g., Samuel Daniel's 1612 *The First Part of the Historie of England* and his 1618 *The Collection of the Historie of England,* or Ben Jonson's 1612 *The Alchemist* and that play republished in his 1616 *The Workes*). All searches were conducted to include variant spellings (e.g., *spectatour*) and variant forms (e.g., *spectators, audiences*).

It should be noted that given *EEBO's* limitations in scope and searchability, these results are by no means definitive or exhaustive as to the popularity of these terms. Yet despite these limitations, the results are nevertheless suggestive as to the terms' significance and increase in usage. In addition, *audience* has a greater range of uses (for example, it is often used for an interaction we would now more commonly call "a meeting," in, e.g., "He had an audience with the king," whereas *spectator* tends to be tied more closely to acts of witnessing.

8. Peter Heylyn, *Ecclesia Restaurata*. Printed for H. Twyford, T, Dring, J. Place, and W. Palmer (London: 1660), in *Early English Books Online* (accessed June 10, 2011). http://eebo.chadwyck.com.proxy.mtholyoke.edu:2048/search/full_rec?SOURCE = pgimages.cfg&ACTION = ByID&ID = 12706619&FILE = ../session/1511842840_18049&SEARCHSCREEN = CITATIONS&VID = 66032&PAGENO = 1&ZOOM = &VIEWPORT = &SEARCHCONFIG = var_spell.cfg&DISPLAY = DATE_DESC&HIGHLIGHT_KEYWORD =

9. Richard Allestree, *The Gentleman's Calling* (London: Printed for T. Garthwait, 1660). *Early English Books Online* (accessed May 25, 2016). http://eebo.chadwyck.com/search/full_rec?SOURCE = pgthumbs.cfg&ACTION = ByID&ID = 12711828&FILE = ../session/1508443263_1100&SEARCHSCREEN = CITATIONS&SEARCHCONFIG = var_spell.cfg&DISPLAY = AUTHOR

10. Nathaniel Hardy, *The arraignment of licentious liberty, ard oppressing tyranny in a sermon preached before the right honourable House of Peers, in the Abbey-church at Westminster, on the the day of their solemn monethly fast* (London: Printed by T.R. and E.M. for Nat. Webb and Wil, 1647), in *Early English Books Online* (accessed May 25, 2016). http://eebo.chadwyck .com/search/full_rec?SOURCE = pgthumbs.cfg&ACTION = ByID&ID = 99861892&FILE = ../session/1508444423_3080&SEARCHSCREEN = CITATIONS&SEARCHCONFIG = var_ spell.cfg&DISPLAY = AUTHOR.

11. Anthony Burgess, *A Treatise of Original Sin* (London, 1658). Accessed June 11, 2011. http://eebo.chadwyck.com/search/full_rec?SOURCE = pgthumbs.cfg&ACTION = ByID& ID = 12258862&FILE = ../session/1508443814_1893&SEARCHSCREEN = CITATIONS& SEARCHCONFIG = var_spell.cfg&DISPLAY = AUTHOR.

12. Henry Hammond, *Charis kai Eirene, or a pacifick discourse of God's grace and decrees* (London: Printed for R. Royston at the Angel in Ivy-lane, 1660). Accessed April 19. 2014. http://eebo.chadwyck.com/search/full_rec?SOURCE = pgthumbs.cfg&ACTION = ByID& ID = 15585262&FILE = ../session/1508443988_2196&SEARCHSCREEN = CITATIONS& SEARCHCONFIG = var_spell.cfg&DISPLAY = AUTHOR.

13. Robert Burton, *The anatomy of melancholy what it is. With all the kindes, causes, symptomes, prognostickes, and severall cures of it. In three maine partitions with their severall sections, members, and subsections. Philosophically, medicinally, historically, opened and cut up* (London: Printed by John Lichfield and James Short for Henry Cripps, 1621). Accessed April 14, 2014. http://eebo.chadwyck.com/search/full_rec?SOURCE = pgthumbs.cfg&ACTION = ByID& ID = 99857427&FILE = ../session/1508444251_2587&SEARCHSCREEN = CITATIONS& SEARCHCONFIG = var_spell.cfg&DISPLAY = AUTHOR. Other examples of the God-as-spectator metaphor include William Cowper's *A holy alphabet for Sion's scholars* (London: Printed by H .Lownes for John Budge, 1613): "We know, that in afflictions it is some comfort How God is a spectator and partaker with us in all our afflictions"; William Fuller's *The mourning of Mount Libanon: or, The temple's teares* (London: Printed by Thomas Harper for Robert Bostocke, 1628): "Remember, that God is his spectator and angels auditors"; and John Stoughton's *Choice Sermons preached upon selected occasions, in Cambridge* (London: Printed by Richard Hodgkinson for Daniel Frere, 1639): "The Church of God is an honourable stage, God, and Men, and Angels, are judicious spectators." All three texts accessed between April 16, 2016 and April 20, 2016 on *Early English Books Online.*

14. A recent example of this kind of "disruptive" theater is Punchdrunk's 2011 *Sleep No More.* A loose adaptation of *Macbeth,* this site-specific production asked spectators to move through a variety of scenes or theatrical "exhibits," producing an interactive experience.

15. Susan Bennett, *Theater Audiences: A Theory of Production and Reception* (London: Routledge, 1997), 3.

16. Pierre Bourdieu, *Language and Symbolic Power,* ed. John B. Thompson, trans. Gino Raymond and Matthew Adamson (Cambridge: Polity, 1991), 211.

17. At the time this manuscript was being completed, the *OED* did not yet have a definition for the term *trigger warning. Merriam Webster* online defines it as "a statement cautioning that content (as in a text, video, or class) may be disturbing or upsetting." See "trigger warning," Merriam-Webster.com, https://www.merriam-webster.com/dictionary/triggerwarning (accessed June 21, 2017).

18. Jack Halberstam, "Trigger Happy: From Content Warning to Censorship," *Signs: Journal of Women and Culture in Society* 42.2 (2017): 535–42.

19. Greg Lukianoff and Jonathan Haidt, "Is Political Correctness Back on Campus?" in *The Atlantic*, August 17, 2015. Accessed May 11, 2016. http://www.theatlantic.com/politics/archive/2015/08/is-political-correctness-back-on-campus/432570/.

20. In addition to journalistic pieces on trigger warnings (a number of which I reference subsequently), there have been a number of professional articles: see Rob Goodman, "Ovid Had No Trigger Warning," *Chronicle of Higher Education*, September 4, 2015; Rani Neutill, "My Trigger-Warnings Disaster: *9 ½ Weeks, The Wire* and How Coddled Young Radicals Got Discomfort All Wrong," *Salon*, October 28, 2015, http://www.salon.com/2015/10/28/i_wanted_to_be_a_supporter_of_survivors_on_campus_and_a_good_teacher_i_didnt_realize_just_how_impossible_this_would_be/; and Sarah Brown, "A Brief Guide to the Battle over Trigger Warnings," *Chronicle of Higher Education*, August 26, 2016. Scholarly articles have also proliferated on the topic, albeit at a slower pace. For example, a recent volume of *First Amendment Studies* (50.2, 2016) was devoted to the topic of trigger warnings. Other examples include Angela M. Carter's "Teaching with Trauma: Trigger Warnings, Feminism and Disability Pedagogy," *Disability Studies Quarterly* 35.2 (2015), n. p., http://dsq-sds.org/article/view/4652/3935; and Halberstam's "Trigger Happy." With the exception of Carter's article, which demonstrates the greatest nuance regarding pedagogy, all these articles take a declarative stance on whether trigger warnings are a viable, even vital, part of contemporary pedagogy or an attack on free speech and the role of "discomfort" in developing critical thinking skills.

21. Alexa Lothian, "Choose Not to Warn: Trigger Warnings and Content Notes from Fan Culture to Feminist Pedagogy," *Feminist Studies* 42.3 (2016), 744.

22. Ibid. Lothian's study traces trigger warnings to the 1980s, when warnings were published on slash zines.

23. Halberstam, "Trigger Happy," 537.

24. Ibid., 538.

25. William Reville, "A Dangerous Censorship Takes Hold on Campus," *Irish Times*, May, 5, 2016. Reville is a retired professor of biochemistry.

26. John Fletcher, "The Faithful Shepherdess," in *The Works of Francis Beaumont and John Fletcher*, ed. Arnold Glover (New York: Octagon, 1969).

27. Reville ("Dangerous Censorship") also exhibits a tendency in this article to conflate the experience of students who are actually triggered by certain texts or films and those who are made uncomfortable by them. Angela M. Carter convincingly argues that the majority of scholars and scholarly organizations conflate these experiences. See Carter, "Teaching with Trauma."

28. Reville, "Dangerous Censorship."

29. Ibid.

30. Halberstam, for example, queries whether "the trigger warning developed and took on meaning through a series of intergenerational miscommunications and misunderstandings" ("Trigger Happy," 536). Another version of the intergenerational explanation is the "special snowflake" narrative, one that has become a favorite of the American right. It describes a prevalent type of contemporary American college student who exhibits a profound narcissism in which they consider their particular idiosyncrasies and worldview as a privileged form of ontology and epistemology. Regarding the technology explanation, law professor Eric Posner has hypothesized that "perhaps overprogrammed children engineered to the specifications of college admissions offices no longer experience the risks and challenges that breed maturity. Or maybe in our ever-more technologically advanced society, the responsibilities of adulthood

must be delayed until the completion of a more extended period of education." Posner, "Universities Are Right—and Within Their Rights—to Crack Down on Speech and Behavior," *Slate,* February 12, 2015, http://www.slate.com/articles/news_and_politics/view_from_chicago/2015/02/university_speech_codes_students_are_children_who_must_be_protected.html (accessed June 2, 2016).

31. Dennis Kennedy in *The Spectator and the Spectacle: Audiences in Modernity and Postmodernity* (Cambridge: Cambridge University Press, 2009), 8–9.

BIBLIOGRAPHY

Aaron, Michelle. *Spectatorship: The Power of Looking On.* London: Wallflower, 2007.

Agnew, Jean-Christophe. *Worlds Apart: The Market and the Theater in Anglo-American Thought, 1550–1750.* Cambridge: Cambridge University Press, 1986.

Allestree, Richard. *The Gentleman's Calling.* London, 1660.

Altman, Rick. *The American Film Musical.* Bloomington: Indiana University Press, 1987.

———. *Silent Film Sound.* New York: Columbia University Press, 2004.

———, ed. *Sound Theory/Sound Practice.* New York: Routledge, 1992.

Anderson, Benedict. *Imagined Communities.* Rev. ed. London: Verson, 1991.

Astington, John H. "Buckingham's Patronage and the Gypsies Metamorphosed." *Theater Survey* 43:2 (2000): 133–47.

Bacon, Francis. *The Essayes or Counsels, Civill and Morall.* Edited by Michael Kiernan. Oxford: Oxford University Press, 2000.

Barber, C. L. *Creating Elizabethan Tragedy.* Edited by Richard Wheeler. Chicago: University of Chicago Press, 1988.

Barish, Jonas. *The Antitheatrical Prejudice.* Berkeley: University of California Press, 1981.

Barroll, Leeds. *Politics, Plague and Shakespeare's Theater: The Stuart Years.* Ithaca, NY: Cornell University Press, 1991.

Bate, Jonathan. *Shakespeare and Ovid.* Oxford: Clarendon, 1993.

———, and Eric Rasmussen, eds. *William Shakespeare Complete Works* (RSC). New York: Modern Library, 2007.

Beare, John I. *Greek Theories of Elemental Cognition from Alcmaeon to Aristotle.* Oxford: Clarendon, 1906.

Beaumont, Francis. *The Knight of the Burning Pestle.* Edited by Sheldon P. Zitner. Manchester: Manchester University Press, 2004.

Beck, Jay, and Tony Grajeda, eds. *Lowering the Boom: Critical Studies in Film Sound.* Urbana: University of Illinois Press, 2008.

Benjamin, Walter. *Illuminations: Essays and Reflections.* Edited by Hannah Arendt. Translated by Harry Zohn. New York: Schocken Books, 2007.

Bennett, Susan. *Theater Audiences: A Theory of Production and Reception.* London: Routledge, 1997.

Bergeron, David M. "Paratexts in Francis Beaumont's *The Knight of the Burning Pestle.*" *Studies in Philology* 106.4 (2009): 456–67.

———. *Shakespeare's Romances and the Royal Family.* Lawrence: University Press of Kansas, 1985.

Berry Ralph. *Shakespeare and the Awareness of the Audience.* London: Macmillan, 1985.

Bersani, Leo. *The Freudian Body: Psychoanalysis and Art*. New York: Columbia University Press, 1996.

Bevington, David. *From Mankind to Marlowe: Growth of Structure in the Popular Drama of Tudor England*. Cambridge, MA: Harvard University Press, 1962.

———, ed. *Medieval Drama*. Boston: Houghton Mifflin, 1975.

Bevington, David, and Milla Riggio. " 'What Revels Are in Hand?' Marriage Celebrations and Patronage of the Arts in Renaissance England." In *Shakespeare and Theatrical Patronage in Early Modern England*. Edited by Paul Whitfield White and Suzanne R. Westfall, 125–49. Cambridge: Cambridge University Press, 2002.

Billings, Valerie. "Female Spectators and the Erotics of the Diminutive in *Epicoene* and *The Knight of the Burning Pestle*." *Renaissance Drama* 42.1 (2014): 1–28.

Bishop, Tom. "The Gingerbread Host: Tradition and Novelty in the Jacobean Masque." In *The Politics of the Stuart Court Masque*. Edited by David Bevington and Peter Holbrook, 88–120. Cambridge: Cambridge University Press, 1998.

Blackstone, Mary A., and Louis Cameron. "Towards 'A Full and Understanding Auditory': New Evidence of Playgoers at the First Globe Theater." *Modern Language Review* 90 (1995): 556–71.

Blau, Herbert. *The Audience*. Baltimore: Johns Hopkins University Press, 1990.

Blayney, Peter. "The Publication of Playbooks." In *A New History of Early English Drama*. Edited by John D. Cox and David Scott Kastan, 383–422. New York: Columbia University Press, 1997.

Bliss, Lee. "Don Quixote in England: The Case for 'The Knight of the Burning Pestle.'" *Viator* 18 (1987): 361–80.

———. *Francis Beaumont*. Boston: Twayne, 1987.

Bloom, Gina. *Voice in Motion: Shaping Sound in Early Modern England*. Philadelphia: University of Pennsylvania Press, 2007.

Böhme, Jakob. *Aurora, that is, the day-spring, or dawning of the day in the Orient*. London, 1656.

Botelho, Keith. *Renaissance Earwitnesses: Rumor and Early Modern Masculinity*. Basingstoke, U.K.: Palgrave Macmillan, 2009.

Bourdieu, Pierre. *Language and Symbolic Power*. Edited by John B. Thompson. Translated by Gino Raymond and Matthew Adamson. Cambridge: Polity, 1991.

Bourgeois, Velma. *Shakespeare, Catholicism, and Romance*. New York: Continuum, 2000.

Bowers, Fredson, ed. *The Dramatic Works of Thomas Dekker*. 4 vols. Cambridge: Cambridge University Press, 1961.

Bradbrook, M. C. *The Rise of the Common Player*. Cambridge, MA: Harvard University Press, 1962.

———. *Themes and Conventions of Elizabethan Tragedy*. Cambridge: Cambridge University Press, 1960.

Braunmuller, A. R., and Michael Hattaway, eds. *The Cambridge Companion to English Renaissance Drama*. Cambridge: Cambridge University Press, 1990.

Brayman Hackel, Heidi. *Reading Material in Early Modern England*. Cambridge: Cambridge University Press, 2005.

Breton, Nicholas. *Pasquils fooles-cap sent to such (to keepe their weake braines warme) as are not able to conceiue aright of his mad-cap*. London, 1600.

Brooker, Will, and Deborah Jermyn, eds. *The Audience Studies Reader*. London: Routledge, 2003.

Brooks, Douglas A. *From Playhouse to Printing House*. Cambridge: Cambridge University Press, 2000.

Brown, Pamela Allen. *Better a Shrew Than a Sheep*. Ithaca, NY: Cornell University Press, 2003.

Brown, Sarah. "A Brief Guide to the Battle over Trigger Warnings." *Chronicle of Higher Education* (2016): 8.

Buhler, James, David Neumeyer, and Rob Deemer, eds. *Hearing the Movie: Music and Sound in Film History*. New York: Oxford University Press, 2001.

Bullough, Geoffrey. *Narrative and Dramatic Sources*. 8 vols. New York: Columbia University Press, 1966.

Burgess, Anthony. *A Treatise of Original Sin*. London, 1647.

Burton, Robert. *The anatomy of melancholy what it is. With all the kindes, causes, symptomes, prognostickes, and severall cures of it. In three maine partitions with their severall sections, members, and subsections. Philosophically, medicinally, historically, opened and cut up*. London: Printed by John Lichfield and James Short for Henry Cripps, 1621.

Burton, William. *The Rowsing of the Sluggard, in 7. Sermons Published at the request of divers godly and well affected*. London: Printed by the Widow Orwin for Thomas Man, 1589.

———. *A sermon preached in the Cathedrall Church in Norwich, the xxi. day of December, 1589. By W. Burton, minister of the word of God there. And published for the satisfying of some which took offence thereat*. London, 1589.

Butler, Judith. *Bodies That Matter: On the Discursive Limits of "Sex."* New York: Routledge, 1993.

Butler, Martin. "Courtly Negotiations." In *The Politics of the Stuart Court Masque*. Edited by David Bevington and Peter Holbrook, 20–40. Cambridge: Cambridge University Press, 1998.

Bynum, Caroline Walker. *Holy Feast and Holy Fast: The Religious Significance of Food to Medieval Women*. Berkeley: University of California Press, 1987.

Campbell, Gordon. *Ben Jonson: The Alchemist and Other Plays*. Oxford: Oxford University Press, 1995.

Campbell, J. O. *Shakespeare's Satire*. London: Oxford University Press, 1943.

Canetti, Elias. *Crowds and Power*. Translated by Carol Stewart. New York: Viking, 1962.

Cartelli, Thomas. *Marlowe, Shakespeare, and the Economy of Theatrical Experience*. Philadelphia: University of Pennsylvania Press, 1991.

Carter, Angela M. "Teaching with Trauma: Trigger Warnings, Feminism and Disability Pedagogy." *Disability Studies Quarterly* 35.2 (2015): n.p.

Caruth, Cathy. *Unclaimed Experience: Trauma, Narrative, and History*. Baltimore: Johns Hopkins University Press, 1996.

Cervantes, Miguel de. *Don Quixote*. Translated by Walter Starkie. New York: New American Library, 1957.

Chambers, E. K. *Aurelian Townshend's Poems and Masks*. Oxford: Oxford University Press, 1912.

———. *The Elizabethan Stage*. 4 vols. Oxford: Clarendon, 1974.

Chartier, Roger. *Cardenio Between Cervantes and Shakespeare*. Cambridge: Polity, 2013.

Cheney, Patrick. *Shakespeare's Literary Authorship*. Cambridge: Cambridge University Press, 2008.

Clewell, Tammy. "Mourning Beyond Melancholia: Freud's Psychoanalysis of Loss." *Journal of the American Psychoanalytic Association* 52.1 (2004): 43–67.

Cobb, Christopher, J. *The Staging of Romance in Late Shakespeare.* Newark: University of Delaware Press, 2007.

Collier, J. Payne. *Shakespeare's Library.* 2 vols. London: Thomas Rodd, 1850.

Coogan, Michael D., ed. *The New Oxford Annotated Bible.* Oxford: Oxford University Press, 2001.

Cook, Ann Jennalie. *The Privileged Playgoers of Shakespeare's London, 1576–1642.* Princeton: Princeton University Press, 1981.

Cowper, William. *A holy alphabet for Sion's scholars.* London: Printed by H. Lownes for John Budge, 1613.

Craik, Katherine, and Tanya Pollard, eds. *Shakespearean Sensations: Experiencing Literature in Early Modern England.* Cambridge: Cambridge University Press, 2013.

Cressy, David. "Book Burning in Tudor and Stuart England." *Sixteenth Century Journal* 36.2 (2005): 359–74.

Cunliffe, John W. *The Complete Works of George Gascoigne.* 2 vols. Cambridge: Cambridge University Press, 1910.

Daniel, Samuel. *The Vision of the Twelve Goddesses: A Royal Masque.* Edited by Ernest Law. London: Bernard Quaritch, 1880.

Davidson, Donald. "What Metaphors Mean." *Critical Inquiry* 5 (1978): 31–47.

Davison, Francis. "The Masque of Proteus." In *Gesta Grayorum.* Edited by Desmond Bland. Liverpool: Liverpool University Press, 1968.

Dawson, Anthony B., and Paul Yachnin. *The Culture of Playgoing in Shakespeare's England: A Collaborative Debate.* Cambridge: Cambridge University Press, 2001.

Day, John. *The Isle of Gulls.* London: Printed for William Sheares, 1633.

Dekker, Thomas. *The Gull's Hornbook.* Edited by R. B. McKerrow. New York: AMS Press, 1971.

Dent, Arthur. *A sermon of repentaunce a very godly and profitable sermon preached at Lee in Essex by Arthur Dent, Minister of God's word.* London, 1582.

Dessen, Alan C. *Elizabethan Drama and the Viewer's Eye.* Chapel Hill: University of North Carolina Press, 1977.

———. *Elizabethan Stage Conventions and Modern Interpreters.* Cambridge: Cambridge University Press, 1984.

Doane, Mary Ann. *The Desire to Desire: The Woman's Film of the 1940s.* Bloomington: Indiana University Press, 1987.

Dobranski, Stephen B. *Readers and Authorship in Early Modern England.* Cambridge: Cambridge University Press, 2005.

Dolan, Francis E. *Marriage and Violence: The Early Modern Legacy.* Philadelphia: University of Pennsylvania Press, 2008.

Dollimore, Jonathan. *Radical Tragedy, Religion, Ideology and Power in the Drama of Shakespeare and His Contemporaries.* Brighton: Harvester, 1984.

Dowden, Edward, ed. *Cymbeline.* In *The Arden Shakespeare*, First Series. London: Methuen, 1903.

Dugan, Holly. *The Ephemeral History of Perfume: Scent and Sense in Early Modern England.* Baltimore: Johns Hopkins University Press, 2011.

Dutton, Richard. *Ben Jonson: Authority: Criticism.* New York: St. Martin's, 1996.

Edgeworth, Robert. *Sermons very fruitfull, godly, and learned, preached and sette foorth by Maister Roger Edgeworth.* London: Printed by Robert Cali, 1557.

Eggers, Jr., Walter F. " 'Bring Forth a Wonder': Presentation in Shakespeare's Romances." *Texas Studies in Literature and Language* 18 (1979): 455–77.

Eikhenbaum, Boris. "Problems of Film Stylistics." *Screen* 15.3 (1984): 7–32.

Erne, Lukas. *Shakespeare as Literary Dramatist.* 2nd ed. Cambridge: Cambridge University Press, 2013.

Evans, Bertrand. *Shakespeare's Comedies.* Oxford: Clarendon, 1960.

Evans, G. Blakemore. *The Riverside Shakespeare.* Boston: Houghton Mifflin, 1997.

Felperin, Howard. "Shakespeare's Miracle Play." *Shakespeare Quarterly* 18.4 (1967): 363–74.

Fenton, Roger. *A Treatise of Usury, Divided Into Three Bookes.* London: Printed by Felix Kingston for William Aspley. 1611.

Fish, Stanley. "Authors-Readers: Jonson's Community of Same." *Representations* 7 (1984): 26–58.

Fletcher, John. *The Faithful Shepherdess.* Edited by Florence Ada Kirk. New York: Garland, 1980.

Forman, Simon. *The autobiography and personal diary of Dr. Simon Forman, the celebrated astrologer, from A. D. 1552, to A. D. 1602.* Edited by James Orchard Halliwell, esq. London, 1849.

Freedman, Barbara. *Staging the Gaze: Postmodernism, Psychoanalysis, and Shakespearean Comedy.* Ithaca, NY: Cornell University Press, 1991.

Freud, Sigmund. *Group Psychology and the Analysis of the Ego.* Edited and translated by James Strachey. New York: W. W. Norton, 1959.

———. *The Language of Psychoanalysis.* Translated by Donald Nicholson-Smith. New York: W. W. Norton, 1973.

———. *The Standard Edition of the Complete Psychological Works of Sigmund Freud.* Edited and translated by James Strachey and Anna Freud. London: Hogarth Press, 1971.

Frye, Northrop. *The Secular Scripture: A Study of the Structure of Romance.* Cambridge, MA: Harvard University Press, 1976.

Fuller, William. *The mourning of Mount Libanon: or, The temple's teares.* London: Printed by Thomas Harper for Robert Bostocke, 1628.

Furness, Howard, ed. *The Tragedie of Cymbeline.* Philadelphia: Lippincott, 1913.

Fuss, Diana. *Identification Papers.* New York: Routledge, 1995.

Gajowski, Evelyn. "Sleeping Beauty, or 'What's the Matter?': Female Sexual Autonomy, Voyeurism, and Misogyny in *Cymbeline.*" In *Re-Visions of Shakespeare: Essays in Honor of Robert Ornstein.* Edited by Evelyn Gajowski, 89–107. Newark: University of Delaware Press, 2004

Gascoigne, George. "Supposes." In *Drama of the English Renaissance I: The Tudor Period.* Edited by Russell A. Fraser and Norman Rabkin. New York: Macmillan, 1976.

Gibbons, Brian. "Romance and the Heroic Play." In *The Cambridge Companion to English Renaissance Drama,* 2nd ed. Edited by A. R. Braunmuller and Michael Hattaway, 197–227. Cambridge: Cambridge University Press, 1990.

Gilbert, Miriam. " 'This Wide Gap of Time': Storytelling and Audience Response in the Romances." *Iowa State Journal of Research* 53 (1979): 235–41.

Gil-Harris, Jonathan. *Sick Economies: Drama, Mercantilism and Disease in Shakespeare's England.* Philadelphia: University of Pennsylvania Press, 2004.

Gil-Harris, Jonathan, and Natasha Korda, eds. *Staged Properties in Early Modern English Drama.* Cambridge: Cambridge University Press, 2002.

Gillies, John. "Shakespeare's Virginian Masque." *English Literary History* 53 (1986): 673–708.

Gilman, Ernest B. " 'All Eyes': Prospero's Inverted Masque." *Renaissance Quarterly* 33.2 (1980): 214–30.

Glover, Arnold, ed. *The Works of Francis Beaumont and John Fletcher.* New York: Octagon, 1969.

Golding, Arthur, trans. *The Joyful and royal entertainment of the ryght high and mightie Prince, Frauncis the Frenche Kings only brother.* London: Imprinted by Thomas Dawson for William Ponosby, 1582.

Goodman, Rob. "Ovid Had No Trigger Warning." *Chronicle of Higher Education,* 62 (1): B4–B5, September 4, 2015.

Gordon, D. J. "Poet and Architect: The Intellectual Setting of the Quarrel Between Ben Jonson and Inigo Jones." In *The Renaissance Imagination: Essays and Lectures by D. J. Gordon.* Edited by Stephen Orgel, 77–184. Berkeley: University of California Press, 1975.

Gorfain, Phyllis. "Puzzle and Artifice: The Riddle as Metapoetry in *Pericles.*" In *Pericles: Critical Essays.* Edited by David Skeele, 133–46. New York: Garland, 2000.

Gorky, Maxim. *Nizhegorodoski listok.* In *In the Kingdom of the Shadows: A Companion to the Early Cinema.* Edited by Colin Harding and Simon Popple. Madison, NJ: Fairleigh Dickinson University Press, 1996.

Gossett, Suzanne, ed. *Pericles.* In *The Arden Shakespeare,* Third Series. London: Thompson Learning, 2004.

Gosson, Stephen. *Plays Confuted in Five Actions.* London, 1582.

———. *The Schoole of Abuse.* London, 1579.

Gourlay, Patricia S. "Guilty Creatures Sitting at a Play: A Note on Hamlet, Act II, Scene 2." *Renaissance Quarterly* 24.2 (1971): 221–25.

Gower, John. *Confessio Amantis.* New York: Penguin, 1963.

Greenblatt, Stephen. *Renaissance Self-Fashioning from More to Shakespeare.* Chicago: University of Chicago Press, 1980.

Greenblatt, Stephen, Walter Cohen, Suzanne Gossett, Jean E. Howard, Katharine Eisaman Maus, and Gordon McMullen, eds. *The Norton Shakespeare,* 3rd ed. New York: W. W. Norton, 2016.

Greg, W. W. *Jonson's Masque of Gipsies in the Burley, Belvoir and Windsor Versions.* London: Oxford University Press, 1952.

———, and E. Boswell, eds. *Records of the Court of the Stationers' Company, 1576 to 1602.* London: Bibliographic Society, 1930.

Gunning, Tom. "The Cinema of Attractions: Early Film, Its Spectator and the Avant-Garde." In *Early Cinema: Space, Frame, Narrative.* Edited by Thomas Elsaesser, 63–70. London: British Film Institute, 1990.

Gurr, Andrew. "The Bear, the Statue, and Hysteria in *The Winter's Tale.*" *Shakespeare Quarterly* 34 (1983): 420–25.

———. *Playgoing in Shakespeare's London.* 3rd ed. Cambridge: Cambridge University Press, 2004.

Gurr, Andrew, and Karoline Szatek. "Women and Crowds at the Theater." *Medieval and Renaissance Drama in England* 21 (2008): 157–69.

Halberstam, Jack. "Trigger Happy: From Content Warning to Censorship." *Signs: Journal of Women and Culture in Society* 42.2 (2017): 535–42.

Halperin, David. *One Hundred Years of Homosexuality and Other Essays on Greek Love.* New York: Routledge, 1990.

Halpern, Richard. *Shakespeare's Perfume: Sodomy and Sublimity in the Sonnets, Wilde, Freud and Lacan.* Philadelphia: University of Pennsylvania Press, 2002.

Hammond, Henry. *Charis kai Eirene, or a pacifick discourse of God's grace and decrees.* London, 1660.

Harbage, Alfred. *Shakespeare and the Rival Traditions.* New York: Macmillan, 1952.

———. *Shakespeare's Audience.* New York: Columbia University Press, 1941.

Hardy, Nathaniel. *The arraignment of licentious liberty, and oppressing tyranny in a sermon preached before the right honourable House of Peers, in the Abbey-church at Westminster, on the the day of their solemn monethly fast.* London: Printed by T.R. and E.M. for Nat. Webb and Wil, 1647.

Harries, Martin. *Forgetting Lot's Wife: On Destructive Spectatorship.* New York: Fordham University Press, 2007.

Harvey, Elizabeth D., ed. *Sensible Flesh: On Touch in Early Modern Culture.* Philadelphia: University of Pennsylvania Press, 2003.

Hattaway, Michael. *Elizabethan Popular Theater.* London: Routledge, 1982.

———, ed. *The Knight of the Burning Pestle.* 2nd ed. London: Methuen, 2002.

Helgerson, Richard. *Self-Crowned Laureates: Spenser, Jonson, Milton and the Literary System.* Berkeley: University of California Press, 1983.

Heller-Roazen, Daniel. *The Inner Touch: Archaeology of a Sensation.* New York: Zone Books, 2007.

Henderson, Diana. "The Theater and Domestic Culture." In *A New History of Early English Drama.* Edited by John D. Cox and David Scott Kastan, 173–94. New York: Columbia University Press, 1997.

Hereford, C. H., and Percy Simpson, eds. *Ben Jonson.* 11 vols. Oxford: Clarendon, 1950.

Heylyn, Peter. *Ecclesia Restaurata, or, The history of the Reformation of the Church of England.* London: Printed for H. Twyford, T. Dring, J. Place, and W. Palmer, 1660.

Heywood, Thomas. *An Apology for Actors.* London: Printed by Nicholas Okes, 1612.

Higgins, John. *Huloets dictionarie newelye corrected, amended, set in order and enlarged, vvith many names of men, tovvnes, beastes, foules, fishes, trees, shrubbes, herbes, fruites, places, instrumentes &c.* London, 1572.

Hillman, Richard. "Shakespeare's Gower and Gower's Shakespeare: The Larger Debt of *Pericles.*" *Shakespeare Quarterly* 36.4 (1985): 427–37.

Hobgood, Alison. *Passionate Playgoing in Early Modern England.* Cambridge: Cambridge University Press, 2014.

Hoeniger, F. David., ed. *Pericles.* In *The Arden Shakespeare,* Second Series. London: Methuen, 1963.

Honig, Edward. "Sejanus and Coriolanus: A Study in Alienation." *Modern Language Quarterly* 12 (1951): 407–21.

Howard, Jean E., *Shakespeare's Art of Orchestration: Stage Technique and Audience Response.* Urbana: University of Illinois Press, 1984.

———. *The Stage and Social Struggle in Early Modern England.* London: Routledge, 1994.

———. "Women as Spectators, Spectacles and Paying Customers." In *Readings in Renaissance Women's Drama: Criticism, History, and Performance, 1594–1998.* Edited by S. P. Cerasano and Marion Wynne-Davies, 1–86. London: Routledge, 1998.

Hunt, Maurice. "Romance and Tragicomedy." In *A Companion to Renaissance Drama.* Edited by Arthur F. Kinney, 384–98. Oxford: Blackwell, 2002.

———. "Shakespeare's *Pericles* and the Acts of the Apostles." *Christianity and Literature* 49 (2000): 295–309.

Hunter, R. G. *Shakespeare and the Comedy of Forgiveness.* New York: Columbia University Press, 1965.

Ingram, William. *The Business of Playing: The Beginnings of the Adult Professional Theater in Elizabethan London.* Ithaca, NY: Cornell University Press, 1992.

Irving, Henry. *The Complete Works of William Shakespeare.* London: Clear-Type Press, 1900.

Jagose, Annamarie. "Feminism's Queer Theory." *Feminism and Psychology* 19.2 (2009): 157–74.

Jameson, Fredric. "Magical Narratives: Romance as Genre." *New Literary History* 7.1 (1975): 135–63.

Jonson, Ben. *Epicoene or the Silent Woman.* Edited by Richard Dutton. Manchester: Manchester University Press, 2008.

———. "The Devil is An Ass." In *The Devil is An Ass: And Other Plays.* Edited by Margaret Jane Kidnie. Oxford: Oxford University Press, 2000.

Joyce, James. *Stephen Hero.* Norfolk, CT: New Directions, 1944.

Kahn, Coppélia. *Man's Estate: Masculine Identity in Shakespeare.* Berkeley: University of California Press, 1981.

———. *Roman Shakespeare: Warriors, Wounds and Women.* New York: Routledge, 1997.

Kastan, David Scott. "Plays into Print." In *Books and Readers in Early Modern England.* Edited by Jennifer Andersen and Elizabeth Sauer, 23–41. Philadelphia: University of Pennsylvania Press, 2002.

———. *Shakespeare and the Book.* Cambridge: Cambridge University Press, 2001.

———. "Workshop and/as Playhouse: Comedy and Commerce in *The Shoemaker's Holiday.*" *Studies in Philology* 84 (1987): 324–37.

Kennedy, Dennis. *The Spectator and the Spectacle: Audiences in Modernity and Postmodernity.* Cambridge: Cambridge University Press, 2009.

Knight, G. Wilson. *The Crown of Life: Essays in Interpretation of Shakespeare's Final Plays.* London: Oxford University Press, 1947.

Knowles, James. "Insubstantial Pageants: *The Tempest* and Masquing Culture." In *Shakespeare's Late Plays: New Readings.* Edited by Jennifer Richards and James Knowles, 108–25. Edinburgh: Edinburgh University Press, 1999.

———. "Jonson's *Entertainment at Britain's Burse.*" In *Re-Presenting Ben Jonson: Text, History and Performance.* Edited by Martin Butler, 114–51. New York: St. Martin's, 1999.

———. "The 'Running Masque' Recovered: A Masque for the Marquess of Buckingham c. 1619–20." *English Manuscript Studies 1100–1700* 8 (2000): 79–135.

Knowles, Richard Paul. "'Wishes Fall Out as They're Will'd': Artist, Audience, and *Pericles'* Gower." *English Studies in Canada* 9.1 (1983): 14–24.

Knutson, Roslyn. "Falconer to the Little Eyases: A New Date and Agenda for the 'Little Eyases' Passage in Hamlet." *Shakespeare Quarterly* 46.1 (1995): 1–31.

Korda, Natasha. *Labors Lost: Women's Work and the Early Modern English Stage.* Philadelphia: University of Pennsylvania Press, 2011.

Kozloff, Sara. *Invisible Storytellers: Voice-Over Narration in American Fiction Film.* Berkeley: University of California Press, 1988.

Kyd, Thomas. *The Spanish Tragedy.* Edited by J. R. Mulryne. London: Methuen, 2007.

Lacan, Jacques. *Ecrits.* Translated by Bruce Fink. New York: W. W. Norton, 2006.

Laneham, Robert. *A letter whearin part of the entertainment vntoo the Queenz Maiesty at Killingwoorth Castl in Warwik sheer in this soomerz progress is signified.* London, 1575.

Laplanche, J., and J.-B. Pontalis. *The Language of Psychoanalysis.* Translated by Donald Nicholson-Smith. New York: W. W. Norton, 1973.

Leggatt, Alexander. "The Audience as Patron: *The Knight of the Burning Pestle.*" In *Shakespeare and Theatrical Patronage.* Edited by Paul Whitfield White and Suzanne Westfall, 296–314. Cambridge: Cambridge University Press, 2002.

———. "The Island of Miracles: An Approach to *Cymbeline.*" *Shakespeare Studies* 10 (1977): 191–209.

Lesser, Zachary. *Renaissance Drama and the Politics of Publication.* Cambridge: Cambridge University Press, 2004.

Levin, Richard. "Women in the Renaissance Theater Audience." *Shakespeare Quarterly* 40 (1989): 165–74.

Lewis, Cynthia. " 'With Simular Proof Enough': Modes of Misperception in *Cymbeline.*" *Studies in English Literature 1500–1900* 31.2 (1991): 343–64.

Limon, Jerzy. *The Masque of Stuart Culture.* Newark: University of Delaware Press, 1990.

Lodge, Thomas. *Protogenes can know Apelles by his line though he se him not and wise men can consider by the penn the aucthoritie of the writer thoughe they know him not.* London, 1579.

Loewenstein, Joseph. *Ben Jonson and Possessive Authorship.* Cambridge: Cambridge University Press, 2002.

Lomax, Marion. *Stage Images and Traditions: Shakespeare to Ford.* Cambridge: Cambridge University Press, 1987.

Lopez, Jeremy. *Theatrical Convention and Audience Response in Early Modern Drama.* Cambridge: Cambridge University Press, 2003.

Lothian, Alexa. "Choose Not to Warn: Trigger Warnings and Content Notes from Fan Culture to Feminist Pedagogy." *Feminist Studies* 42.3 (2016): 743–56.

Low, Jennifer, and Nova Myhill, eds. *Imagining the Audience in Early Modern Drama.* New York: Palgrave Macmillan, 2011.

Lucas, F. L. *The Complete Works of John Webster.* 4 vols. New York: Gordian, 1966.

Lukianoff, Greg, and Jonathan Haidt. "Is Political Correctness Back on Campus?" *Atlantic*, August 17, 2015, n.p.

Lunney, Ruth. *Marlowe and the Popular Tradition: Innovation in the English Drama Before 1595.* Manchester: Manchester University Press, 2002.

Mackay, Ellen. *Persecution, Plague, and Fire: Fugitive Histories of the Stage in Early Modern England.* Chicago: Chicago University Press, 2011.

Maravall, José Antonio. *The Culture of the Baroque.* Translated by Terry Cochran. Minneapolis: University of Minnesota Press, 1986.

Marcus, Leah. *Puzzling Shakespeare: Local Reading and Its Discontents.* Berkeley: University of California Press, 1988.

Marshall, Cynthia. *Last Things and Last Plays: Shakespearean Eschatology.* Carbondale: Southern Illinois University Press, 1991.

———. *The Shattering of the Self: Violence, Subjectivity, and Early Modern Texts.* Baltimore: Johns Hopkins University Press, 2002.

———. "Wound-man: *Coriolanus,* Gender, and the Theatrical Construction of Interiority." In *Feminist Readings of Early Modern Culture: Emerging Subjects.* Edited by Valerie Traub, M. Lindsay Kaplan, and Dympna Callaghan, 93–118. Cambridge: Cambridge University Press, 1996.

Massey, Irving. "A Note on the History of Synaesthesia." *Modern Language Notes* 71.3 (1956): 203–6.

Masten, Jeffrey. "Beaumont and/or Fletcher: Collaboration and the Interpretation of Renaissance Drama." *English Literary History* 59 (1992): 346–47.

———. "My Two Dads: Collaboration and the Reproduction of Beaumont and Fletcher." In
Queering the Renaissance. Edited by Jonathan Goldberg, 280–309. Durham: Duke University Press, 1997.

———. *Textual Intercourse: Collaboration, Authorship, and Sexualities in Renaissance Drama.*
Cambridge: Cambridge University Press, 1997.

Matchett, William H. "Some Dramatic Techniques in *The Winter's Tale.*" *Shakespeare Survey,*
22 (1969): 93–107.

Matthew, H. G. C., and Brian Harrison, eds. *The Oxford Dictionary of National Biography.*
Oxford: Oxford University Press, 2004.

Maus, Katharine. "A Womb of His Own: Male Renaissance Poets in the Female Body." In
Sexuality and Gender in Early Modern Europe: Institutions, Texts, Images. Edited by James
Grantham Turner, 89–108. Cambridge: Cambridge University Press, 1993.

Mazzio, Carla. "Acting with Tact: Touch and Theater in the Renaissance." In *Sensible Flesh:
On Touch in Early Modern Culture.* Edited by Elizabeth Harvey, 159–86. Philadelphia:
University of Pennsylvania Press, 2003.

———. "Dreams of History: An Introduction." In *Historicism, Psychoanalysis and Early Modern Culture.* Edited by Carla Mazzio and Douglas Trevor, 1–18. New York: Routledge,
2000.

———. *The Inarticulate Renaissance: Language Troubles in an Age of Eloquence.* Philadelphia,
University of Pennsylvania Press, 2009.

McClure, Norman Egbert. *The Letters of John Chamberlain.* 2 vols. Philadelphia: American
Philosophical Society, 1939.

McLuskie, Kathleen. "Figuring the Consumer for Early Modern Drama." In *Rematerializing
Shakespeare: Authority and Representation on the Early Modern Stage.* Edited by Bryan
Reynolds and William N. West, 186–206. Basingstoke, U.K.: Palgrave Macmillan, 2005.

Mentz, Steve. *Romance for Sale in Early Modern England.* Aldershot, U.K.: Ashgate, 2006.

Menzer, Paul. "The Actor's Inhibition: Early Modern Acting and the Rhetoric of Restraint."
Renaissance Drama 35 (2006): 83–112.

Metz, Christian. *The Imaginary Signifier: Psychoanalysis and Cinema.* Translated by Celia Britton, Annwyl Williams, Ben Brewster, and Alfred Guzzetti. Bloomington: Indiana University Press, 1982.

Middleton, Thomas. *The Family of Love.* London, 1608.

Miola, Robert S. *Shakespeare and Classical Comedy: The Influence of Plautus and Terence.*
Oxford: Oxford University Press, 1994.

Molecamp, Femke. *Women and the Bible in Early Modern England: Religious Reading and Writing.* Oxford: Oxford University Press, 2013.

Montrose, Louis. *The Purpose of Playing: Shakespeare and the Cultural Politics of the Elizabethan
Theater.* Chicago: University of Chicago Press, 1996.

Mowat, Barbara. *The Dramaturgy of Shakespeare's Romances.* Athens: University of Georgia
Press, 1976.

———. "The Theater and Literary Culture." In *A New History of Early English Drama.* Edited
by John D. Cox and David Scott Kastan, 213–30. New York: Columbia University Press,
1997.

Muir, Kenneth. *Shakespeare's Comic Sequence.* Liverpool: Liverpool University Press, 1979.

Mullaney, Steven. "Affective Technologies: Towards an Emotional Logic of the Early Modern Stage." In *Embodiment and Environment in Early Modern England*. Edited by Mary Floyd-Wilson and Garrett A. Sullivan, Jr., 71–89. Basingstoke, U.K.: Palgrave Macmillan, 2007.

———. *The Place of the Stage: License, Play and Power in Renaissance England* Chicago: Chicago University Press, 1988.

———. *The Reformation of Emotion in the Age of Shakespeare*. Chicago: University of Chicago Press, 2015.

Mulvey, Laura. "Visual Pleasure and Narrative Cinema." *Screen* 16 (1975): 6–18.

Munday, Anthony. *A Second and Third Blast of Retreat from Plaies and Theaters*. London: Henrie Denham, 1580.

Muñoz, José Esteban. *Disidentification: Queers of Color and the Performance of Politics*. Minneapolis: University of Minnesota Press, 1999.

Munro, Ian. *The Figure of the Crowd in Early Modern England: The City and Its Double*. Basingstoke, U.K.: Palgrave, 2005.

Nabokov, Vladimir. *Lectures on Don Quixote*. Edited by Fredson Bowers. Preface by Guy Davenport. New York: Harcourt Brace, 1983.

Narveson, Kate. *Bible Readers and Lay Writers in Early Modern England: Gender and Self-Definition in an Emergent Writing Culture*. Surrey, U.K.: Ashgate, 2012.

Nashe, Thomas. "Piers Penniless His Supplication to the Devil." In *Thomas Nashe: The Unfortunate Traveler and Other Works*. Edited by J. B. Steane. London: Penguin, 1972.

Neill, Michael. "'Wit's Most Accomplished Senate': The Audience of the Caroline Private Theaters." *Studies in English Language* 18 (1978): 341–60.

Neutill, Rani. "My Trigger-Warnings Disaster: *9½ Weeks*, *The Wire* and How Coddled Young Radicals Got Discomfort All Wrong." *Salon*, October 28, 2015.

Newcomb, Lori Humphrey. *Reading Popular Romance in Early Modern England*. New York: Columbia University Press, 2002.

Newman, Karen. "City Talk: Women and Commodification." In *Staging the Renaissance: Reinterpretations of Elizabethan and Jacobean Drama*. Edited by David Scott Kastan and Peter Stallybrass, 181–95. New York and London: Routledge, 1991.

Newton, Thomas, ed. *Seneca, His Tenne Tragedies*. New York: Knopf, 1927.

Nicoll, Allardyce. *Shakespeare*. London: Methuen, 1952.

———. *Stuart Masques and the Renaissance Stage*. New York: Harcourt, Brace and Company, 1938.

Northbrooke, John. *Spiritus est vicarius Christi in terra. A treatise wherein dicing, dauncing, vaine playes or enterluds with other idle pastimes [et]c. commonly vsed on the Sabboth day, are reproued by the authoritie of the word of God and auntient writers*. London, 1577.

Nosworthy, J. M., ed. *Pericles*. In *The Arden Shakespeare*, Second Series. London: Routledge, 1955.

O'Connell, Michael. *The Idolatrous Eye: Iconoclasm and Theater in Early-Modern England*. Oxford: Oxford University Press, 2000.

Oran, William, Einar Bjorvand, and Ronald Bond, eds. *The Yale Edition of the Shorter Poems of Edmund Spenser*. New Haven: Yale University Press, 1989.

Orgel, Stephen, ed. *Ben Jonson, The Complete Masques*. New Haven: Yale University Press, 1969.

———. *The Illusion of Power: Political Theater in the English Renaissance*. Berkeley: University of California Press, 1975.

———. *The Jonsonian Masque*. Cambridge: Harvard University Press, 1965.

————. "Nobody's Perfect: Or Why Did the English Stage Take Boys for Women." *South Atlantic Quarterly* 88 (1989): 7–29.

————. "What is a Text?" *Research Opportunities in Renaissance Drama* 24 (1981): 3–6.

Orgel, Stephen, and Roy Strong. *Inigo Jones and the Theater of the Stuart Court*. London: Sotheby Parke Bernet, 1973.

Osborne, Laurie E. "Female Audiences and Female Authority in *The Knight of the Burning Pestle*." *Exemplaria* 3.2 (1991): 491–517.

Ovid. *Heroides and Amores*. Translated by Grant Showerman. Revised by G. P. Goold. Cambridge, MA: Harvard University Press, 1914.

Pafford, J. H. P. *The Winter's Tale*. In *The Arden Shakespeare*, Second Series. London: Routledge, 1963.

Pearson, Roberta E., and William Uricchio. "'The Formative and Impressionable Stage': Discursive Constructions of the Nickelodeon's Child Audience." In *American Movie Audiences: From the Turn of the Century to the Early Sound Era*. Edited by Melvyn Stokes and Richard Maltby, 64–77. London: British Film Institute, 1999.

Peters, Julie Stone. *Theatre of the Book, 1480–1880*. Oxford: Oxford University Press, 2000.

Pitcher, John. "Editing Daniel." In *New Ways of Looking at Old Texts: Papers of the Renaissance English Text Society, 1985–1991*. Edited by W. Speed Hill, 57–73. Binghamton, NY: Renaissance English Text Society, 1993.

Plato. *The Symposium*. Translated by Alexander Nehamas and Paul Woodruff. Indianapolis: Hackett, 1989.

Pollard, Tanya. *Drugs and Theater in Early Modern England*. Oxford: Oxford University Press, 2005.

————. "'No Faith in Physic': Masquerades of Medicine Onstage and Off." In *Disease, Diagnosis and Cure on the Early Modern Stage*. Edited by Stephanie Moss and Kaara L. Peterson, 29–41. Aldershot, U.K.: Ashgate, 2004.

Posner, Eric. "Universities Are Right—and Within Their Rights—to Crack Down on Speech and Behavior." *Slate*, February 12, 2015.

Prynne, William. *Histrio-mastix: The Players Scourge*. London: Printed by E. A. and W. I. for Michael Sparke, 1633.

Purcell, Stephen. *Shakespeare and Audience in Practice*. Basingstoke, U.K.: Palgrave Macmillan, 2013.

Reville, William. "A Dangerous Censorship Takes Hold on Campus." *Irish Times*, May, 5, 2016.

Richmond, Velma Bourgeois. *Shakespeare, Catholicism and Romance*. New York: Continuum, 2000.

Rossi, Doc. "Brecht on Shakespeare: A Revaluation." *Comparative Drama* 30.2 (1996): 158–87.

Rotenstreich, Nathan. *Alienation: The Concept and Its Reception*. Leiden: E. J. Brill, 1989.

Rous, Francis. *Thule, or Vertue's History: To the honorable and vertuous Mistris Amy Audely. By F.R. The first booke*. London, 1598.

Rutter, Carol Chillington. *Enter the Body: Women and Representation on Shakespeare's Stage*. London: Routledge, 2001.

Salingar, Leo. *Shakespeare and the Tradition of Comedy*. Cambridge: Cambridge University Press, 1974.

Samuelson, David A. "The Order of Beaumont's *The Knight of the Burning Pestle*." *English Literary Renaissance* 9 (1979): 302–18.

Sanders, Eve Rachelle. "Inferiority and the Letter in *Cymbeline*." *Critical Survey* 12.2 (2000): 49–70.

Sanders, Norman. "An Overview of Critical Approaches to the Romances." In *Shakespeare's Romances Reconsidered*. Edited by Carol McGinnis Kay and Henry E. Jacobs, 1–10. Lincoln: University of Nebraska Press, 1978.

Scott, David. "William Patten and the Authorship of 'Robert Laneham's Letter' (1575)." *English Literary Renaissance* 7 (1977): 297–306

Sedgwick, Eve. *The Epistemology of the Closet*. Berkeley: University of California Press, 1990.

Shapiro, Michael. *Children of the Revels: The Boy Companies of Shakespeare's Time and Their Plays*. New York: Columbia University Press, 1977.

Sharpe, Kevin. *Reading Revolutions: The Politics of Reading in Early Modern England*. New Haven: Yale University Press, 2000.

Sharpham, Edward. *Cupid's Whirligig*. London, 1607.

Shaw, George Bernard. *Man and Superman: A Comedy and a Philosophy*. London: Penguin, 1946.

Shawcross, John T, ed. *The Complete Poetry of John Milton*. New York: Doubleday, 1990.

Shipman, Thomas. *Carolina, or Loyal Poems*. London, 1683.

Shirley, James. *Love's Cruelty, a Critical Edition*. Edited by John Frederick Nims. New York: Garland, 1980.

Shohet, Lauren. *Reading Masques: The English Masques and Public Culture*. Oxford: Oxford University Press, 2010.

Sidney, Philip. *An Apologie for Poetrie*. London: Printed for Henry Olney, 1595.

Silverman, Kaja. *The Acoustic Mirror: The Female Voice in Psychoanalysis and Cinema*. Bloomington: Indiana University Press, 1988.

Sjogren, Britta. *Into the Vortex: Female Voice and Paradox in Film*. Urbana: University of Illinois Press, 2006.

Skeele, David. "*Pericles* in Criticism and Production: A Brief History." In *Pericles: Critical Essays*. Edited by David Skeele. New York: Garland, 2000.

Smith, Bruce. *The Acoustic World of Early Modern England: Attending to the O-Factor*. Chicago: University of Chicago Press, 1999.

———. *The Key of Green: Passion and Perception in Early Modern England*. Chicago: University of Chicago Press, 2009.

———. *Phenomenal Shakespeare*. Malden, MA: Wiley-Blackwell, 2010.

Smith, Henry. *The sermons of Maister Henrie Smith gathered into one volume*. London: Printed by Richard Field for Thomas Man, 1593.

Spenser, Edmund. *The Faerie Queene*. Edited by Thomas P. Roche, Jr. London: Penguin, 1987.

Steggle, Matthew. *Laughing and Weeping in Early Modern Theaters*. Aldershot, U.K.: Ashgate, 2007.

Stern, Tiffany. *Documents of Performance in Early Modern England*. Cambridge: Cambridge University Press, 2009.

———. "Taking Part: Actors and Audience on the Stage at the Blackfriars." In *Inside Shakespeare: Essays on the Blackfriars Stage*. Edited by Paul Menzer, 35–53. Selinsgrove, PA: Susquehanna University Press, 2006.

Stockholder, Katherine. "The Other Coriolanus." *PMLA* 85.2 (1970): 228–36.

Stoughton, John. *Choice Sermons preached upon selected occasions, in Cambridge*. London: Printed by Richard Hodgkinson for Daniel Frere, 1639.

Straznicky, Marta. ed. *The Book of the Play: Playwrights, Stationers, and Readers in Early Modern England.* Amherst: University of Massachusetts Press, 2006.

Strong, Roy. *Henry, Prince of Wales and England's Lost Renaissance.* London: Thames and Hudson, 1986.

Summers, David. *The Judgment of Sense: Renaissance Naturalism and the Rise of Aesthetics.* Cambridge: Cambridge University Press, 1990.

Tarlow, Sarah. *Ritual, Belief, and the Dead in Early Modern Britain and Ireland.* Cambridge: Cambridge University Press, 2011.

Taylor, Gary, and John Lavagnino, eds. *Thomas Middleton: The Collected Works.* Oxford: Clarendon, 2007.

Taylor, Marion A. "Lady Arabella Stuart and Beaumont and Fletcher." *Papers in Language and Literature* 8 (1972): 252–60.

Thomas, Brook. "Cymbeline and the Perils of Interpretation." *New Orleans Review* 10.2–3 (1983): 137–45.

Thompson, Leslie. "Who's In, Who's Out? *The Knight of the Burning Pestle* on the Blackfriars Stage." In *Inside Shakespeare: Essays on the Blackfriars Stage.* Edited by Paul Menzer, 61–71. Selinsgrove, PA: Susquehanna University Press, 2006,

Traub, Valerie. "The New Unhistoricism in Queer Studies." *PMLA* 128.1 (2013): 21–39.

Twine, Laurence. *The Patterne of Painefull Adventures.* London, 1594.

Tylus, Jane. "'Par Accident': The Public Work of Early Modern Theater." In *Reading the Early Modern Passions: Essays in the Cultural History of Emotion.* Edited by Gail Kern Paster, Katherine Rowe, and Mary Floyd-Wilson, 253–71. Philadelphia: University of Pennsylvania Press, 2004.

Tyndale, William. *The Obedience of a Christian Man.* Antwerp: 1528.

van Doren, Mark. *Shakespeare.* New York: H. Holt, 1939.

Vaughan, Virginia, and Alden T. Vaughan, eds. *The Tempest.* In *The Arden Shakespeare,* Third Series. London: Thompson Learning, 1999.

Vickers, Nancy. "Diana Described: Scattered Women and Scattered Rhyme." *Critical Inquiry* 8.2 (1981): 265–79.

Votava, Jennie. "Dangerous Sensations: Contagion and Spectatorship in Gosson and Shakespeare," presented at the Shakespeare Association of America Conference, St. Louis, MO, April 2014.

Waldron, Jennifer. "'The Eye of Man Hath Not Heard': Shakespeare, Synaesthesia, and Post-Reformation Phenomenology." *Criticism* 54.3 (2012): 403–17.

Walkling, Andrew R. "The Apotheosis of Absolutism and the Interrupted Masque: Theater, Music and Monarchy in Restoration England." In *Politics, Transgression, and Representation at the Court of Charles II.* Edited by Julia Marciari Alexander and Catherine MacLeod, 233–51. New Haven: Yale University Press, 2007.

Wall-Randell, Sarah. "Reading the Book of the Self in Shakespeare's *Cymbeline* and Wroth's *Urania.*" In *Staging Early Modern Romance: Prose Fiction, Dramatic Romance and Shakespeare.* Edited by Mary-Ellen Lamb and Valerie Wayne, 107–21. New York: Routledge, 2009.

Walters, Melissa. "'Are You a Comedian': The Trunk in *Twelfth Night* and the Intertheatrical Construction of Character." In *Transnational Mobilities in Early Modern Theater.* Edited by Robert Henke and Eric Nicholson, 53–68. Surrey, U.K.: Ashgate, 2014.

Wayne, Valerie. "*Don Quixote* and Shakespeare's Collaborative Turn to Romance." In *The Quest for Cardenio: Shakespeare, Fletcher, Cervantes and the Lost Play.* Edited by David Carnegie and Gary Taylor, 217–38. Oxford: Oxford University Press, 2012.

Webster, John. *The White Devil*. Edited by Elizabeth M. Brennan. New York: W.W. Norton, 1966.

Weimann, Robert. *Shakespeare and the Popular Tradition in the Theater*. Baltimore: Johns Hopkins University Press, 1978.

Weis, Elizabeth, and John Belton, eds. *Film Sound: Theory and Practice*. New York: Columbia University Press, 1985.

Welsford, Enid. *The Court Masque: A Study in the Relationship Between Poetry and the Revels*. New York: Russell & Russell, 1962.

West, William N. "Understanding in the Elizabethan Theaters." *Renaissance Drama* 35 (2006): 113–43.

Westfall, Suzanne. "The Useless Dearness of the Diamond: Theories of Patronage Theater." In *Shakespeare and Theatrical Patronage in Early Modern England*. Edited by Paul Whitfield White and Suzanne R. Westfall, 13–42. Cambridge: Cambridge University Press, 2002.

White, R. S. *Let Wonder Seem Familiar: Endings in Shakespeare's Romance Vision*. London: Athlone Press, 1985.

———. *Shakespeare and the Romance Ending*. Newcastle upon Tyne, U.K.: Tyneside Free Press, 1981.

White, Thomas. *A sermon preached at Pawles Crosse on Sunday the thirde of Nouember 1577*. London: Printed by Henry Bynneman for Francis Coldock, 1578.

Whitney Charles. *Early Responses to Renaissance Drama*. Cambridge: Cambridge University Press, 2006.

Whitted, Brent E. "Staging Exchange: Why *The Knight of the Burning Pestle* Flopped at Blackfriars in 1607." *Early Theatre: A Journal Associated with the Records of Early English Drama* 15.2 (2012): 111–30.

Wickham, Glynne, Herbert Berry, and William Ingram, eds. *English Professional Theater, 1530–1660*. Cambridge: Cambridge University Press, 2000.

Willett, John, ed. and trans. *Brecht on Theatre*. New York: Hill and Wang, 1964.

Williams, William Proctor. "Not Hornpipes and Funerals: Fletcherian Tragicomedy." In *Renaissance Tragicomedy: Explorations in Genre and Politics*. Edited by Nancy Klein Maguire, 139–54. New York: AMS Press, 1987.

Woolgar, C. M. *The Senses in Late Medieval England*. New Haven: Yale University Press, 2006.

Yachnin, Paul. "Performing Publicity." *Shakespeare Bulletin* 28.2 (2010): 201–19.

Zitner, Sheldon P., ed. *The Knight of the Burning Pestle*. Manchester: Manchester University Press, 2004.

Zwierlein, Anne-Julia. "Male Pregnancies, Virgin Births, Monsters of the Mind: Early Modern Melancholia and (Cross-)Gendered Constructions of Creativity." In *The Literature of Melancholia: Early Modern to Postmodern*. Edited by Martin Middeke and Christina Wald, 35–49. Basingstoke, U.K.: Palgrave Macmillan, 2005.

INDEX

Page numbers in italics refer to figures

Jonson, Ben (*continued*)
from sound, 139–40, 145; separating spectators from hearers, 145–46;
"understanders," 20, 86, 129, 147–48, 164n65; use of synaesthetic mode, 129–32, 136, 138–39, 144–47; *The Vision of Delight*, 140, 195n63. See also *The Gypsies Metamorphosed*; *Hymenai*; masque; *The Masque of Beauty*; *The Masque of Blackness*; *Oberon*, *The Fairy Prince*
Joyce, James, 109; *Stephen Hero*, 188n88

Kahn, Coppélia, 187n78
Kastan, David Scott, 176n55, 181n18
Kenilworth Castle, 124–25, 128, 191–92n27
Kennedy, Dennis, 3, 156–57, 166n19
Kerwyn, Andrew, 194n51
Keysar, Robert, 72
The King's Men, 17, 56, 119, 173n20, 190n11
The Knight of the Burning Pestle (Beaumont), 18–19, 53–82, 84, 150, 170n80, 172n7, 172n10, 174n29, 175n40, 175n46, 175n47, 177n65, 179n87, 190n11; and alienation, 61, 63, 67, 70; anxiety over female word of mouth, 73–77; and audience resistance, 56, 62–65, 67; Citizen as melancholic, 69; class issues in, 57, 62, 67–68; as a commercial failure, 18, 50–51, 54, 56, 63, 70–73, 80, 84, 170n80, 173n12, 173n13, 177n63; contagion metaphor in, 77–78; dedicatory epistle, 54, 71–74, 80, 82; and disidentification, 61–63, 67–68; and the female spectator, 72–79, 178n77, 178n79; fragmented structure of, 69–70; generating spectatorial violence, 60; and identification, 61–64, 67–69; influenced by *Don Quixote*, 54, 172n7; and *The London Merchant*, 63, 66, 69, 72–73, 76, 78; matrilineal inheritance model, 177n68; mother-son relationships in, 72; playgoing as a commercial exchange, 64–66, 69; in print, 54, 71, 82, 177n67; silencing the audience, 70; and stage sitting, 65; subject to consumer desire, 56–58, 63; and tainted spectator, 77; use of *The Four Prentices of London*, 66–68; violence against the spectator, 58, 60, 66, 69–70, 73–74, 78, 80–81; violence of artistic-commercial tension, 58; violence on the vehicle of representation, 19, 55–56; and the violent spectator, 18–19, 63, 65–69, 73–76, 79–80, 176n54, 176n56

Knowles, James, 190–91n5, 194n47
Knutson, Roslyn, 171–72n4, 172n5
Korda, Natasha, 178n76
Kyd, Thomas: *The Spanish Tragedy*, 39–40, 168n50

Lacan, Jacques, 9, 184n45; and the mirror stage, 62–63, 162n30, 175n40
Laneham, John, 191–92n27
Laneham, Robert, 125–27, 142, 192n28; identity of, 191–92n27
legal documents, 16, 18
Leggatt, Alexander, 56–57, 63, 70, 108–9, 188n84
Laplanche, J., 175n46
Lesser, Zachary, 177n63
letters. *See* correspondence, personal
Lewis, Cynthia, 99
Limon, Jerzy, 193n45, 194n49
listening/hearing, 45–46, 117; aligned with "readerly," 85, 89; to music, 127; place in sensory hierarchy, 41–43; relation to looking, 20, 30–31, 93, 118, 120, 125, 130, 139, 145–46, 147, 191n17; and "understanding," 147. *See also* ear; multisensory metaphor; music; senses; sound; synaesthesia
literary: definition of, 180n5
liturgical drama, 38–39, 168n42, 168n43
Lodge, Thomas, 48; *A Looking-Glass for London and England*, 185n50
Loewenstein, Joseph, 191n15
Lomax, Marion, 185n50
looking/seeing, 34, 92, 108, 117, 126–27, 134, 162n27, 186n57; dangers of, 3; the language of, 130–44; in masques, 137–40; passive, 148; place in sensory hierarchy, 41–43, 121; potential to mislead, 88; as ravishment, 122, 142; relation to acting, 32; relation to listening, 20, 30–31, 46, 93, 118, 120, 125, 130, 139, 145, 147, 191n17; "right," 61, 88, 96–98, 100, 111–12; spectatorial, 4, 27, 29, 34, 122, 181n16; voyeuristic, 28. *See also* eye; gaze; multisensory metaphor; senses; sight; synaesthesia
looking-glass, 34, 97
Lopez, Jeremey, 8, 11–13, 41, 162n37, 162n40, 163n53, 165–66n16, 169n53
Lothian, Alexa, 153, 198n22
Low, Jennifer, 173n18, 173–74n22
Lukianoff, Greg, 151–52

ACKNOWLEDGMENTS

Like any endeavor that takes shape over multiple years and locations, this book bears the imprint of myriad influences. Those most immediately legible come from three extraordinary women who have transformed my thinking and way of approaching the world. Jean Howard, who ignited by fascination with the early modern world, continues to provide me with a model of intellectual, social, and pedagogical engagement. I have yet to sound the depths of Valerie Traub's generosity of time, intellect, and humanity; these have paid multiple dividends in my scholarship and life. Besides the bountiful harvests reaped from close contact with Barbara Hodgdon's prescient insights into performance and fearless scholarly career, she and Richard Abel have become a surrogate family to me and mine.

A number of other people have played significant roles in the development of *Monster*. Its earliest incarnations were nurtured by friends and colleagues at the University of Michigan: to Laura Williamson Ambrose, Kentston Bauman, LaMont Egle, Ari Friedlander, Caroline Giordano, Gavin Hollis, David Lavinsky, Marjorie Rubright, and Chad Thomas, I offer my sincere thanks. Many faculty members at Michigan also lent their support and insight to this project in its early form—in particular, Richard Abel, Giorgio Bertellini, Linda Gregerson, Daniel Herwitz, Steven Mullaney, Lucia Saks, Michael Schoenfeldt, Gaylyn Studlar, and Theresa Tinkle.

In its later stages, *Monster* found a number of generous interlocutors, individuals who have also played significant roles in the development of the first phase of my faculty career. Gregory Semenza and Will West have been some of the earliest advocates and mentors of my scholarly endeavors, and their faith in my work has played a significant role in this project's completion. Shreena Gandhi, Gail Griffin, Marin Heinritz, Bruce Mills, Andrew Mozina, Tom Rice, and Di Seuss were terrific mentors in approaching the ever-elusive balance of scholarship and teaching. I am extraordinarily grateful for the camaraderie and encouragement provided by the English department at Rhode Island College; in particular, I thank Pamela Benson, Vincent Bohlinger, Jennifer Cook, Joan Dagle, Emily Danforth, Anita Duneer, Spencer Hall, Maureen Reddy, Barbara Shapiro, and Alison Shonkwiler. My department at Mount Holyoke College encouraged patience and fortitude during a particularly challenging moment in the book's genesis. I thank Amy Martin, Nigel Alderman, Elizabeth Young, and Donald Weber for their good advice and Chris Benfey, Suparna Roychoudhury, Kate Singer, and Wesley Yu for their friendship. Coppélia Kahn warmly welcomed me into the Mahindra Center's Shakespeare Studies seminar community; her interest and advocacy helped keep the project's fires burning during the crucial and lengthy revision phase. Diana Henderson and Marina Leslie were similarly welcoming as co-chairs of the Women and Early Modern Culture seminar, and I am grateful not only for their support but for their creation of a place for emerging scholars to present their work in a supportive-yet-rigorous environment. In addition, Diana Henderson read and provided feedback on a draft of the manuscript: her trenchant observations were more transformative than I imagine she knows. Several others, including Jane Hwang Degenhardt, Jeff Doty, Linda McJannet, Meg Pearson, Kelly Stage, Travis Williams, Emily Winerock, and Adam Zucker have many times provided encouragement, intellectual sustenance, and friendship for which I am deeply thankful.

My readers provided thoughtful and detailed commentary on the manuscript; their advice has proven invaluable in further honing its contents, and I hope to have the opportunity to thank them personally for their time, enthusiasm, and deep engagement with *Monster*. Allison Hobgood read an earlier version of the manuscript; her exacting commentary pushed me to clarify the book's claims and methodology.

This project has had no greater advocate than Jerome Singerman, and I am acutely aware of my inability to find the perfect words with which thank him here for his faith, patience, high standards, and overall savvy. Simply stated, this project would not be what it is without him. To those junior scholars who have heard (as I had) that there is no generosity, risk taking, or advocacy left in academic publishing, particularly for first-time authors, I assure you that these ethics are alive and well in at least one member of that profession. In addition I thank Lily Palladino at the University of Pennsylvania Press for her time, rigor, and patience.

Finally, thanks are due to those at my life's center. My mother, Agnes Rodgers, no matter what endeavors I have pursued, has provided the love and encouragement I needed to follow my instincts. My sons, Owen, Calvin, and Gabriel, remind me daily that one's life and self is far more than the sum of one's work. And, to my partner, Kentston Bauman, who has been there every step of the way and stopped short of nothing (including putting his own career on hold) in order to stand with me in seeing it through to completion, I dedicate this book.